Beware Raiders!

Beware Raiders!

German Surface Raiders in the Second World War

BERNARD EDWARDS

Pen & Sword
MARITIME

First published in Great Britain in 2001 by Leo Cooper
and reprinted in this format in 2014 by
PEN & SWORD MARITIME
An imprint of
Pen & Sword Books Ltd
47 Church Street
Barnsley, South Yorkshire
S70 2AS

ISBN 978 1 47382 283 2

A CIP catalogue record for this book is
available from the British Library

Pen & Sword Books Ltd incorporates the Imprints of Aviation, Atlas,
Family History, Fiction, Maritime, Military, Discovery, Politics, History,
Archaeology, Select, Wharncliffe Local History, Wharncliffe True Crime,
Military Classics, Wharncliffe Transport, Leo Cooper, The Praetorian Press,
Remember When, Seaforth Publishing and Frontline Publishing

For a complete list of Pen & Sword titles please contact
PEN & SWORD BOOKS LIMITED
47 Church Street, Barnsley, South Yorkshire, S70 2AS, England
E-mail: enquiries@pen-and-sword.co.uk
Website: www.pen-and-sword.co.uk

Chapter One

The raider came over the horizon like a questing hawk, her clipper bows thrusting through the lumpy South Atlantic chop, a thin haze of blue smoke streaming astern from her squat funnel. She was closing rapidly on the British tramp, which seemed oblivious to her presence.

Her quarry was the Liverpool-registered *Domingo de Larrinaga*, bound from Bahia Blanca to Belfast and Hull and down to her marks with 7,500 tons of grain. It was five minutes before nine on the morning of 31 July 1940, and the 5358-ton British ship was then some 300 miles north-west of Ascension Island and making a respectable 9½ knots for Freetown. On reaching that port she was to join a convoy which, it was hoped, would take her safely home through the U-boat-infested waters of the North Atlantic.

The morning was fine and warm, with the last of the South-East Trades chasing fluffy cotton-wool clouds across an otherwise flawless blue sky. On the bridge of the *Domingo de Larrinaga* Captain William Chalmers drew contentedly on his first pipe of the day, giving little thought to the enemy. His ship was full, homeward bound and in relatively safe waters – so far as any ocean could be called safe in these troubled times.

When his attention was drawn to the other ship coming up on the port quarter, Chalmers examined her through his binoculars and, seeing the large blue and white flag and the name *Kassos* painted on her side, he had no reason to believe she was other than another homeward-bound Greek tramp. Then, as she began to overhaul the British ship, Chalmers' suspicions were aroused.

1

This was no ordinary Greek tramp. She was too smartly turned out, too well-painted, and possessed a turn of speed no self-respecting Greek shipowner with his eye on the fuel bills would ever contemplate. Chalmers lowered his binoculars, alarm bells beginning to ring in his head.

The *Domingo de Larrinaga* heeled under full starboard helm as Chalmers brought her round to present her stern to the stranger. Below decks, her sweating firemen hurled coal into the roaring furnaces of her three elderly Scotch boilers, and she lurched forward, great clouds of black smoke rolling back from her funnel. More as a matter of form than intent, Chalmers sent his gun's crew aft to man the 4-inch gun on the stern. The gun was ancient, a left-over from another war, its crew, drawn mainly from the fo'c'sle, had little training in its use.

As the British ship worked up speed, her radio officer, Neil Morrison, switched on his long-silent transmitter and began sending the 'QQQQ' signal, code for 'I am being attacked by an unidentified enemy ship'. Morrison, a Scot from the Outer Hebrides with fifteen years' sea service, was well aware of the futility of his call for help. Freetown was nearly 900 miles away and British warships were very thin on the water in the South Atlantic. But the orders from the bridge were clear. Morrison was to continue sending until an answer came or he was told to stop – and the radio officer knew what that might mean.

On deck, 22-year-old Fireman Robert Deus, cooling off after a long, hot watch in the stokehold, gripped the ship's side rail and stared astern at the pursuing ship and felt the sweat chill on his naked back. Only moments before he had been deep in a day-dream of home and his bride of three months – in her last letter she had told him they were to have a child. Now Deus, a Liverpool Basque like the formidable Captain Ramon de Larrinaga, who founded the Larrinaga Steamship Company in 1864, for the first time began to have serious doubts about his safe homecoming.

The grim chase went on for another two hours, with the *Domingo de Larrinaga*'s sturdy Clyde-built engine hammering out a desperate tattoo as her engineers pushed it to its uttermost limits. And all the time Neil Morrison's morse key matched the staccato beat of the engine as he continued to call for help. On

2

the bridge Captain William Chalmers clenched his teeth on his empty pipe, feeling his gallant ship's agony through the vibrating teak-wood deck beneath his feet. His silent pursuer had not yet declared herself, but her menace was obvious. Aft, on the *Domingo de Larrinaga*'s poop deck, her scratch gun's crew crouched over their open sights and waited for the order to fire.

At 1055, when she was within 2½ miles of the British tramp, the raider at last dropped her disguise. Down came the Greek ensign, the German swastika was run up in its place, a canvas screen was lowered over the neutral hull markings and the screens rolled back from her guns. Having thus advertised her nationality and intent, the raider broke out the two-letter flag signal 'SN' at her yardarm. The message, in International Code, was unambiguous: 'You should stop immediately. Do not scuttle. Do not lower boats. Do not use the wireless. If you disobey I shall open fire on you.'

William Chalmers' worst fears were now confirmed – he had fallen in with a German raider. For a moment, knowing how heavily the odds must be stacked against him, he considered surrender. But then surprise gave way to anger and a determination not to give up his command easily. Passing word to the wireless room to continue sending, and to the engine-room to pile on more speed, he turned his back on the enemy.

At 4000 yards, the raider opened fire with her forward gun, pitching a 75-mm shell across the *Domingo de Larrinaga*'s bows. Four more warning shots followed, each throwing up a spout of water close ahead of the British ship. And yet she still continued to run away, her defiant calls for help filling the ether, sometimes drowned by the high-pitched jamming of the raider's transmitter.

Then, with brutal suddenness, it was all over. The German ship fired a full salvo with her heavy guns, all aimed with deadly accuracy. The *Domingo de Larrinaga* staggered under a hammer blow and the whole of her midships section disappeared in a cloud of smoke and flame. She sheered to port and then drifted slowly to a halt. The German raider *Pinguin* had joined the war at sea with a savage attack that was to set the tone for the rest of her piratical career, a career begun in the Baltic some six weeks earlier.

In June 1940 Britain lay quiet and untroubled under the pale blue skies of early summer. A gentle breeze rustled the fields of new corn, and in towns and cities across the land the pace of life appeared purposeful but unhurried. An outside observer might have been forgiven for thinking this was a nation at peace and unthreatened.

But this was only the calm before the storm. Barely a month had passed since the 'phoney' war across the Channel, in which for eight long months the opposing armies faced each other with passive belligerence, had come to an abrupt end. At dawn on 10 May 124 divisions of crack German troops had spilled out over the plains of Holland and Belgium, carrying all before them. Caught completely unawares, the Allied armies retreated in confusion.

British ingenuity in the face of defeat produced Operation 'Dynamo', snatching 340,000 British and Allied soldiers from the beaches of Dunkirk, but these men were exhausted and humiliated, their heavy arms and equipment abandoned on what was now enemy soil. They landed in Britain carrying only rifles and bayonets – and in many cases even the rifles had gone. This was an army ill-fitted to meet a German invasion then in preparation. And the long nightmare was only beginning.

Norway had already fallen, and on 10 June Italy, eager to join the wolves at the kill, declared war on Britain and France. Then, on the 14th of that month, Paris surrendered to the Germans and the French had no more fight left in them. Britain stood alone.

As an island nation, Britain's first priority was to keep open her sea lanes. Along these flowed, from the Americas and her dominions and colonies overseas, the vital food and war materials without which no credible defence could be mounted. This was an undertaking now made infinitely more difficult by the fact that German U-boats had gained access to new bases from the North Cape to Biscay, thereby vastly increasing their operational range in the Atlantic. Furthermore, their ranks had been swelled by a considerable fleet of Italian boats, which, although they would never match the expertise and daring of the U-boats, constituted an increased threat of attack from beneath the water. The Royal Navy, seriously depleted by the disastrous Norwegian campaign and Dunkirk, was hard-pressed to guarantee safe conduct to the merchantmen. As in the previous war, the echoes of which had still not died after twenty-two years, the Admiralty found itself having to make do with second best. His Majesty's armed merchant cruiser *Andania* might be said to fall within that category.

On 15 June 1940 the *Andania* was ploughing a lonely furrow in the grey wastes of the North Atlantic, her mission to guard the 240-mile-wide passage between Iceland and the Faeroes. In more affluent times, this patrol would have been carried out by destroyers backed up by armed trawlers, but Dunkirk had taken a heavy toll of the destroyers, while the trawlers had been withdrawn to help protect the Channel coast against the impending invasion. HMS *Andania* was filling the gap to the best of her limited ability.

Built on the River Tyne in 1922 for the Cunard White Star Line, the 13,950-ton *Andania*, with accommodation for 500 first-class and 1,200 third-class passengers, gave good service on the North Atlantic run between the wars, carrying mainly emigrants from Europe to the United States of America. With ample space for cargo and a service speed of 15 knots, she was ideally suited for her role. In 1940, pressed into service as a warship, she was a sad misfit.

In the First World War the Admiralty showed great enthusiasm for requisitioning passenger liners into service as armed merchant cruisers. It was a move the Admirals lived to regret, for these ships were totally unsuited to this role. They were too big, too slow, lacked manoeuvrability and had thin-skinned hulls. Armed with guns surplus to the Navy's requirements, they were no match for the big ships of the German fleet and presented unmissable targets for the torpedoes of the fast-growing U-boat Arm. These converted passenger liners soon became a liability the Royal Navy could not afford, no fewer than seventeen of them being lost in hopelessly one-sided actions in the course of the war.

It is a sad but inescapable fact of British politics that whenever peace prevails savage cut-backs are made in the defence of the realm, partly to save money, but also to quieten the strident voices of those who would yield to the sword without a fight. The years following 1918 were no exception and when war broke out again in 1939 the Admiralty was once more forced to look around for substitute warships. It would seem the Admirals had learned no lessons from the armed merchant cruiser fiasco of the First World War. The British merchant fleet had by this time acquired a number of fast, modern cargo ships, mainly in the liner trades, which would have been ideal for conversion to auxiliary cruisers, but these were ignored, deemed by some nonsensical logic to be unsuitable. Once again, possibly due to the intrenched snobbishness of the Royal Navy, preference was given to the large passenger liners. It may well be that these were elegant ships, immaculately maintained and manned by professionals, but their high profile and sheer awkwardness should have ruled them out of any more active role in the war than trooping or as depot ships lying deep in well-defended lochs. Perversely, forty-six such ships had been commissioned by the spring of 1940.

As before, the armament of the new armed merchant cruisers (AMCs) was a war behind. Many of the 6-inch guns fitted had seen action as secondary armament of battleships and heavy cruisers at Jutland, and before. In some cases, the bores of these guns were worn almost smooth by long usage, seriously impeding their accuracy. They had no shields to protect their crews and, mounted high on the open decks of an AMC, they suffered cruelly at the hands of the weather. Misfires and jammed mechanisms were common, and there were times when the only means of bringing a gun to bear was by physically heaving the barrel around.

HMS *Andania* was no exception to the rule. A high-sided ship with tall masts and funnel that protruded above the horizon, like all British AMCs, she carried no spotter aircraft and was visible to her enemies long before she saw them. Her guns, eight 6-inch and two 3-inch high-angle of First World War vintage, looked impressive enough, but, due to the clutter of the ex-merchantman's decks, some guns had a very restricted arc of fire and her gunnery control was so basic as to be almost primitive. In her holds were stowed 15,000 empty oil drums, which it was hoped would keep her afloat in the event of her hull being laid open by torpedo, mine or gunfire.

In all probability it was such an eventuality that was on Captain D.K. Bain's mind when, at a little before 2230 on 15 June

6

1940, he paid a late visit to the *Andania*'s bridge. Already that month, two of the *Andania*'s sisters, HMS *Carinthia*, 20,277 tons and HMS *Scotstoun*, 17,046 tons, had been lost in these waters, sunk by U-boats.

In the half-light of this brief Arctic summer's night, the *Andania* was 75 miles south-west of Iceland and steering a course of 240° at 15 knots. It would soon be time to reverse course and steam back through the Faeroes Channel on yet another leg of what Bain was becoming to regard as a fruitless patrol. His orders were to seek, find and intercept the Finnish steamer *Brita Thorden*, believed to be on passage from Petsamo to New York via Reykjavik. This ship was known to have on board the Icelandic Director of Posts and Telegraphs, a pro-German agitator the British government was anxious to keep away from Iceland, only recently occupied by British troops. Bain was authorized to remove this man from the *Brita Thorden* and place him out of harm's way.

The weather at the time was not conducive to a successful search for one smallish ship in the 240-mile-wide Faeroes-Iceland passage, with a succession of unseasonal gales accompanied by fog or drizzle having prevailed for the past week. Visibility was poor and, not having seen the sun or stars for some days, Bain was not even sure of his own position, let alone that of a small neutral ship that might already have passed him unseen at any time. It was some consolation to Bain that his highly vulnerable ship, wrapped in this damp North Atlantic murk, would be all but invisible to marauding U-boats.

Wedged in the conning tower of *U-A*, wet and chilled to the bone, Korvettenkapitän Hans Cohausz experienced a similar sense of security, but his was more justified. *U-A*, an early Type VII U-boat secretly built in Spain in 1929, when Germany was anxious to hide her preparations for war, was trimmed right down with her hull, almost submerged. She was invisible to the *Andania*'s lookouts, but from her conning tower the vast bulk of the ex-passenger liner was unmistakable as it suddenly emerged from the gloom. Cohausz immediately cleared the conning tower and went to periscope depth.

Having satisfied himself that all was well on the bridge, Captain Bain was about to go below to catch an hour or two of much-needed sleep when there was a muffled explosion beneath his feet and *Andania* staggered as a torpedo slammed into her starboard side.

Bain hit the alarm bells and, as their shrill clamour sounded throughout the ship, the rain cleared away and the visibility improved dramatically. The sudden clearance revealed a periscope 1,500 yards to starboard, momentarily catching the guns' crews unawares. The starboard side guns opened fire as soon as they could be brought to bear, but by this time they were shooting at an empty sea.

The *Andania* was now listing heavily to starboard, damage control parties reporting to the bridge that the ship had been hit between her Nos 5 and 6 holds and the sea was pouring into the hull. Her rudder, damaged beyond repair, was jammed hard over, and very soon water entering the engine-room knocked out the main generators, plunging the ship into darkness. She began to lose headway and settle by the stern.

Bain took control of the situation, ordering the engine-room to transfer oil to correct the list, and, with the ship once more upright with her emergency generators operating, it seemed that it might be possible to save her. Radio silence was then broken to call for help.

But Hans Cohausz had not yet gone away. At 2345 the track of another torpedo was seen racing in from starboard. With his rudder jammed, Bain was powerless to take avoiding action. He felt the chill fingers of death run down his spine as he gripped the bridge rail, his knuckles whitening, waiting for the *coup de grace* which surely must follow. The seconds ticked away with agonizing slowness as the avenging furrow of white water sped towards the helpless liner. When the torpedo missed the *Andania*'s stern by a mere 100 yards Bain breathed again.

Half an hour passed, with the crippled AMC drifting aimlessly before the wind, an enormous slab-sided target 520 feet long and towering 70 feet out of the water. And yet, when he fired his third torpedo, Cohausz missed again. The torpedo passed 50 feet astern of the *Andania*.

The *Andania* was now well down by the stern, her three after holds completely flooded and water rising in the engine-room. All available pumps were working, but they could not check the relentless ingress of the sea. Only the empty oil drums in her holds were keeping the liner afloat.

At a few minutes before one o'clock on the morning of 16 June Hans Cohausz lined up his sights on the waterlogged AMC and fired his fourth torpedo. It may have been that he was a poor marksman, or perhaps the fault lay with the torpedo – German torpedoes were notoriously unreliable at this stage of the war – but he missed this sitting duck of a target yet again. The *Andania*'s gunners, however, despite the predicament of their ship, were not finished, and the German now found himself under attack. They had marked the track of his last torpedo and opened fire along its bearing. With shells falling uncomfortably close, *U-A* was forced to retire into the darkness.

At 0115, his ship now clearly doomed, Captain Bain ordered all non-essential crew to abandon ship. Fortunately, the wind and sea had dropped and, although there was still a heavy swell, the boats were lowered without mishap, pulling away to lie off and await events. Another hour passed, with the torpedoed ship rolling sluggishly in the swell, but by 0230, in the grey light of a new day, the relentlessly rising water in the engine-room shut off the pumps and the fight was over. At 0240 Bain called his boats together and the *Andania* was left to her fate.

Luckily for the men of the *Andania*, they were not left adrift for long in these bleak, inhospitable waters. Within a few hours their SOS was answered by the Icelandic trawler *Skallagrinur*, which took them aboard and later transferred them to a British naval ship. This, in turn, took them to Scapa Flow. The *Andania* sank at 0655 on 16 June.

The chance meeting between HMS *Andania* and Hans Cohausz's *U-A* was to have serious repercussions on the war at sea. The loss of the patrolling AMC left a wide gap in the defences of the North-Western Approaches to the British Isles, a gap which the Germans were to take full advantage of a few days later.

Chapter Two

The sinking of HMS *Andania* by the patrolling submarine *U-A* was assumed by the Admiralty to be a deliberate diversionary action to cover the breakout of another German auxiliary cruiser. Three of these, *Atlantis*, *Widder* and *Thor*, all converted merchantmen, had already escaped into the Atlantic. While the Admirals may have been wrong in the interpretation they put on *U-A*'s actions, they were right in assuming another raider was about to emerge.

As the *Andania* slipped beneath the waves off Iceland at dawn on 16 June 1940, a thousand miles to the south-east, in the Gulf of Danzig, the sun was well above the horizon and giving the promise of a fine, warm day to come. Swinging to an anchor in a quiet reach of the gulf close to the South Middle Bank, the German cargo liner *Kandelfels* was in the final stages of her metamorphosis from harmless merchantman to ship of war. Her company livery was last to go, the smart black hull and gleaming white upperworks disappearing under a coat of sombre wartime grey.

The 7766-ton *Kandelfels*, built at Bremen in 1936 for Deutsche Dampschiffarts Gesellschaft, better known as the Hansa Line, had arrived in Hamburg from India on 1 September 1939, just as German troops crossed the border into Poland, signalling the start of the second European bloodbath in the space of twenty-five years. As soon as the last sling of cargo from the East was winched up from the *Kandelfels'* holds, she was requisitioned by the German Navy.

A modern, twin-screw ship with a service speed of 17 knots and a low silhouette, the *Kandelfels* was ideally suited for recruitment to the Kriegsmarine's elite squadron of *Hilfskreuzers* (auxiliary cruisers) soon to be unleashed on Allied merchant shipping in the distant oceans beyond the reach of the U-boats. Unlike the highly vulnerable British AMCs, stop-gap ships used for patrol and convoy escort work, the role of the *Hilfskreuzers* – there would be nine in all – was predatory. Fast and heavily armed, they would emulate the buccaneers of old, hiding in the shadows out of reach of the enemy's warships and aircraft, picking off victims wherever and whenever the opportunity arose.

Unfortunately, the German grand plan for the conquest of Europe was initially so successful that an adjustment of priorities was necessary. The Kriegsmarine's 'grey wolves' went to the back of the queue. Conversion of the *Kandelfels* from merchant ship to auxiliary cruiser was originally scheduled to take three months, but, owing to more urgent demands on dockyard space and workers, it was 6 February 1940 before she emerged from the Bremen yard of Weser AG. as *Hilfskreuzer 33*. Outwardly, she was still a merchant ship, but behind counterweighted steel shutters, capable of being raised in two seconds, were six 5.9-inch guns. Concealed by false ventilators, watertanks or packing cases were one 75-mm, one twin 37-mm and four 20-mm guns. Similarly hidden were two twin 21-inch torpedo tubes, two 3-metre range finders, two 60-cm searchlights, and in her holds two spotter aircraft. A quick change of identity could be effected by telescoping the foremast, raising collapsible bulwarks to heighten the forecastle and raising or lowering collapsible sampson posts.

In theory HK 33 was a formidable warship, but in reality her 5.9s were 40-year-old guns taken from the obsolete pre-dreadnought battleship *Schlesien*, her smaller guns of similar vintage. Her scout planes, too, were obsolescent; single-engined, open-cockpit Heinkel HE 59 floatplanes, known to be notoriously unstable on the water. To ensure her future success, she was in need of a dedicated and experienced crew, men willing to take the calculated risk without too much thought for their own self-preservation. In this respect, at least, she was well blessed.

In command of HK 33 was 43-year-old Kapitän-zur-See Ernst-Felix Krüder, a slim, taciturn man, who had risen to command from the ranks – rare achievement in anyone's navy at the time. Krüder, with twenty-five years service in the German Imperial Navy, was an expert in mine warfare and had seen action at Jutland and in the Black Sea in the First World War. Between the wars he had served in the Inspectorate of Officers' Training and Education, where he had gained a great deal of experience in handling men. With a clear, analytical mind and the ability to improvise, Ernst-Felix Krüder was an excellent choice to take an auxiliary cruiser with a crew of 345 into the unknown. Many of that crew were naval reservists from the merchant ships; Krüder's first lieutenant, Leutnant Erich Warning, had been Staff Captain of the North German Lloyd liner *Bremen*, while his navigator, Leutnant Wilhelm Michaelson, was lately in command of the 14,700-ton liner *Steuben*. Expertise in the way of the sea and ships Krüder's men had in abundance, but whether they had the aggression and determination to make war remained to be seen.

It was the custom for commanders of German auxiliary cruisers to name their own ships, and when HK 33 was commissioned on 6 February 1940, in a brief ceremony on board Krüder christened her *Pinguin (Penguin)*. It was a choice which puzzled his crew, but then, unlike their captain, they were not yet fully aware of their ship's ultimate destiny.

Over the seven weeks that followed, the *Pinguin* carried out trials on the River Weser, testing her engines, exercising her guns and initiating her as yet untried crew into the strange world of a ship that was half merchantman and half warship. Any faults found in the ship and her equipment were rectified and, having taken on ammunition, coal and provisions, the *Pinguin* passed through the Kiel Canal into the Baltic. There, in sheltered waters away from prying eyes, Krüder drilled his gun and torpedo crews relentlessly, until they reached the peak he judged would give them a fighting chance against the best guns of the Royal Navy. At the same time mine-laying exercises were carried out and boats' crews were sent away at every possible opportunity, so as to perfect the launching, handling and retrieval of their craft. These men would play a vital role in the *Pinguin*'s coming adventure.

The raider, her skills honed to perfection, returned to Kiel on

26 May for a few persistent faults in her gear to be corrected and to top up her oil, water and stores. She also took on board five live pigs, which would be fattened up on scraps from the galley during the voyage. As many crew members as possible were given shore leave, their last on German soil for many months, perhaps years, to come. She sailed on 10 June and again headed east into the Baltic, arriving in the Gulf of Danzig on the following day. She was given a berth in the naval base of Gotenhaven – as the Polish port of Gdynia had been renamed by Hitler – and worked under the cover of darkness taking on mines and torpedoes. On 17 June, anonymous in her new grey livery, the *Pinguin* left the Gulf of Danzig with 380 mines and 25 torpedoes in her holds. She was on her way to war.

In the early summer of 1940, although Britain stood alone and under threat of invasion, she had not lost control of the North Sea. Cruisers and destroyers of the Home Fleet constantly patrolled these waters, while the RAF kept watch overhead and submarines cruised below the surface. The primary object of these forces was to keep a lookout for an enemy invasion fleet, but any German ships venturing out into the North Sea, particularly lone merchantmen, did so at extreme peril. They could expect no help from their own navy; Germany's capital ships remained firmly tied up in port, and her light naval forces had taken such a severe mauling at the hands of the Royal Navy in the Norwegian campaign that they could offer little protection.

The *Pinguin*, with all her potential to wreak havoc on the high seas, was a special case, and on the morning of the 18th she rendezvoused off Gedser, southern point of the Danish island of Lolland, with the minesweeper *Sperrbrecker IV* and the torpedo boats *Jaguar* and *Falke*. The latter were powerful, well-armed ships of over 900 tons. The *Wolf*-class *Jaguar* carried three 5-inch and four 37-mm guns, and the *Falke*, a Möwe-class boat, mounted three 4.1-inch and four 37-mm. Both carried six 21-inch torpedo tubes and had a top speed of 34 knots.

The small convoy passed through the Great Belt, the main channel between the Danish islands, in tight formation, entering the Kattegat at around 2100. At midnight, off the island of Anholt, *Sperrbrecker IV* left, and the *Pinguin* continued north at 15 knots with *Jaguar* and *Falke* keeping close company. British submarines were reported to be very active in this area and there could be no relaxing of vigilance.

The sun had already risen again when, at 0400 on the 19th, the three ships rounded the northern tip of Jutland and moved into the Skagerrak. It was a perfect early summer's day, with a clear blue sky and a fresh easterly breeze kicking up white horses on the water. The air was clean and salt-laden, and, after the long months of preparation, the unrelenting pressures of the rigorous training programme, the crew of the raider faced the open sea eagerly, masters of their own destiny at last.

Air cover in the form of a Dornier 18 flying boat and two fighters materialized at the seaward end of the Skagerrak and remained overhead until darkness closed in again. At midnight *Pinguin*'s escort was reinforced by two M-class minesweepers, who brought with them a Norwegian pilot. The enlarged convoy then entered the deep-water channel behind the maze of islands that fringe the Atlantic coast of Norway. Protected by the islands, *Pinguin* was safe from Allied warships, but the channels, although deep, were narrow and tortuous, requiring careful navigation.

The port of Bergen was abeam to starboard at 0800 on the 20th and here *Jaguar* and *Falke* parted company, their escort duties over. The *Pinguin* and the two M-boats continued north, entering Sörgulen Fjord, some 50 miles north of Bergen, at 1630 that afternoon. The raider went deep into the fjord to an anchorage, while her escort remained on guard off the entrance.

Hidden from the prying eyes of enemy aircraft by the densely-wooded, steep-sided slopes of the fjord, the *Pinguin* took on the disguise it was hoped would see her clear of the coast and into the Atlantic. Over the next thirty-six hours, with the help of shore labour, the raider was transformed into the Russian cargo ship *Petschura*, port of registry Odessa, her hull black with the Soviet hammer and sickle prominent on her sides. When the work was finished, the disguise was convincing, but, should suspicions be aroused, German intelligence had established there was a real *Petschura*, conveniently laid up in Murmansk and unlikely to put to sea for some time.

The *Pinguin* left Sörgulen Fjord at 0100 on 22 June. She was now under the control of the Operations Division of the

Seekriegsleitung (SKL), the German Naval Staff in Berlin. Her orders were to break out into the Atlantic through the Denmark Strait and from there to proceed south to a position off Cape Verde, where she would rendezvous with and refuel and provision Hans Cohausz's *U-A*. Fresh from his success in sinking the *Andania*, Cohausz had already moved south to cover the approaches to Freetown, now being used as an assembly point for Allied convoys.

Having serviced *U-A*, Krüder's orders were to round the Cape of Good Hope into the Indian Ocean, and there begin his campaign against Allied merchant shipping. It was anticipated that his harvest would be a rich one, for, in the absence of U-boats, the British considered the Indian Ocean to be a safe area and most merchantmen were sailing unescorted. Additionally, Krüder hoped to create further mayhem by mining the approaches to ports on the south and east coasts of Australia, and, later, the west coasts of India and Ceylon. And, as if this programme was not ambitious enough, at the end of the year the *Pinguin* was to sail south into the chill waters of Antarctica to attack the British and Norwegian whaling fleets. It was with this most southerly operation in mind that Krüder had named his ship.

The night was very black when the *Pinguin* weighed anchor and was escorted out of Sörgulen Fjord by her minesweepers. Under a heavily overcast sky with rain squalls sweeping in from the sea, the darkened raider made her way carefully down the fjord following the dimmed blue stern lights of the M-boats. Within the hour she was face to face with her first enemy of the war, the open sea. Clearing the mouth of the fjord at about 0200, she found herself heading into the teeth of a strong SW'ly wind, which rapidly increased to a full gale. Rain squalls severely restricted the visibility and, in a rising sea and swell, the ship took on an awkward corkscrewing movement. For many of her crew, having spent too long ashore or in sheltered waters, the curse of seasickness was an unwelcome visitor.

As for the ship herself, although she rolled and pitched heavily, the weather held no real dangers. The same could not be said for her escorts. M-17 and M-18 were both under 700 tons and narrow in the beam, and, while they may have been at home in the comparatively quiet waters of the Baltic, out here in the open

Atlantic their seaworthiness was tested to the extreme. Plunging from crest to trough, rolling violently and shipping green water overall, the minesweepers took a severe pounding as they struggled to keep up with the bigger ship. Some 16 miles out of Sörgulen, after consultation with Krüder, they turned back and ran for shelter.

There is little complete darkness in these high latitudes in summer and by 0230 the sun was again climbing to the horizon, bringing a grey half-light to the overcast and revealing row upon row of white-topped waves marching in from the south-west. *Pinguin*, steering due west, had the wind and sea on the port bow, a distinct advantage, but Krüder, anxious to clear the coast before full daylight, was pushing his ship hard. With her twin 900 horsepower diesels thrusting her through the water at full revolutions, she had worked up to 15 knots, but was pounding heavily as she met the oncoming waves. Krüder feared he might soon be forced to slow down to avoid damage to his forward guns.

The decision was made for him when, just before 0300, a sharp-eyed lookout on the bridge spotted a periscope breaking the surface half a mile on *Pinguin*'s port bow. It was followed seconds later by the submarine's conning tower. This looked like an accidental surfacing, for almost immediately both conning tower and periscope disappeared again in a welter of foam. Krüder sent his men to their action stations.

Prior to sailing from Sörgulen Fjord, Krüder had been assured by SKL that all German U-boats in the area had been warned to keep well clear of the *Pinguin*'s track. In which case, this could only be a British boat lying in wait for German blockade runners. Mindful that the *Pinguin* was currently disguised as the Russian *Petschura*, Krüder hauled around to the north, hoping to give the impression he was heading for the North Cape and Russian waters. Ignoring the weather, he rang for emergency full speed and the *Pinguin*, now beam-on to the seas, surged forward, rolling heavily.

Almost immediately the submarine came to the surface again and gave chase, black smoke pouring from her exhausts. She was about 2 miles astern of the *Pinguin*, wallowing in the heavy seas, which broke clean over her, so that from time to time she almost disappeared from view. An Aldis lamp winked from her conning

16

tower. 'What ship?' *Pinguin*'s yeoman read from the impatient flashes. Krüder, acting out his role as a non-English speaking Russian merchant captain, ignored the signal. A few minutes later the lamp flashed again. 'Heave to, or we open fire!'

Krüder chose to ignore the order. He had the submarine dead astern, thereby presenting the smallest possible target. Moreover, the enemy's movements in the sea were so violent as to make her a very poor platform from which to take aim. *Pinguin* pressed on at full speed and the submarine began to drop astern.

The German captain's assessment of the situation proved correct when, a few minutes later, three underwater explosions were heard. No torpedo tracks had been seen, but it was certain that the enemy sub had fired a salvo, three torpedoes either hitting the bottom or missing the *Pinguin* and exploding at the end of their run. And that was that. The submarine held on doggedly for another hour, but she could not match the *Pinguin*'s speed. She fell further and further astern until she gave up and turned away.

Assuming that the British submarine would have reported sighting a suspect enemy ship, Krüder held a north-easterly course throughout the day, running parallel to the Norwegian coast at a distance of about 70 miles. At 0843 a Heinkel 115 float plane passed low overhead, the same aircraft, or another of the same type, appearing at 2100. *Pinguin* was being watched over from the air, otherwise she had the sea to herself.

Krüder now had a choice of two routes in his attempt to break out into the North Atlantic. He could either take the shortest way out, passing between the Faeroes and Iceland or continue north to round Jan Mayen Island, and thence south-west through the Denmark Strait. The latter route would add something like 700 miles to the passage, but Krüder, unaware that the Faeroes Channel was temporarily unguarded following the sinking of the *Andania* by *U-A*, opted for the longer northerly route. He was also not aware that, as a direct result of the loss of the AMC, the Admiralty had ordered the cruisers *Newcastle* and *Sussex* to reinforce patrols in the Denmark Strait.

At 2300, when on the latitude of Trondheim, Krüder altered course to 320° to head for Jan Mayen. It was Midsummer's Night, with no real darkness, and, perversely, the foul weather that had provided invaluable cover for the *Pinguin* since sailing now took a turn for the better. The wind dropped to a mere fresh breeze, the sea went down and the rain cleared away. The heavy overcast remained, but visibility improved dramatically. Then, early on the 23rd, the wind veered to the north-east and the sun broke through.

With no darkness to hide his ship Krüder felt dangerously exposed to his potential enemies, but he had little choice. The only course of action open to him was to make all possible speed for Jan Mayen and take cover in the fog banks normally found shrouding the island at this time of the year. Once hidden in the fog, he could then bide his time, waiting for suitable murky weather to cloak his breakout through the Denmark Strait.

Krüder was to be disappointed, for the weather beyond the Arctic Circle is as unpredictable as in any other part of the globe. As the day progressed and the *Pinguin* pushed north-westwards, although the wind was light and the sea a flat calm, the hoped-for fog did not materialize. The air was in fact crystal clear, so clear that at 0400 on the 24th, when it was fully light, the tip of the 7,500-ft Beerenberg, Jan Mayen's volcanic peak, was visible at a distance of almost 100 miles.

Although Jan Mayen was said to be uninhabited, except for a Norwegian weather station, Krüder was reluctant to close the land, but he had no other alternative. *Pinguin* rounded the northern side of Jan Mayen at noon with all her guns' crews stood-to and the ship in a state immediate readiness. The weather remained stubbornly fine and clear, but if the raider was seen from the shore she provoked no reaction. Once clear of the island, Krüder set course due west, running for the ice edge off the east coast of Greenland, where the warm summer air flowing over the frozen sea was guaranteed to bring dense fog.

To the great relief of all on board, not least her commander, the *Pinguin* ran into falling visibility when she was within 100 miles of the Greenland coast. By 1925 she was in thick fog and feeling her way towards the ice edge at slow speed. The ice was sighted just after 2100 and Krüder altered to run south-westwards, parallel to the coast and keeping just to seaward of the ice. Visibility in the fog had improved to around 500 yards, just sufficient for careful navigation, but it was a nerve-wracking business. There were icebergs about and, although the ship was down to a crawl, the danger of collision with one of these drifting monsters was very real, but this was a risk Krüder was prepared to take in the interests of a quick breakout into the Atlantic. For the moment he was grateful for the sanctuary of the fog.

Pinguin's luck ran out on the morning of the 25th after she had steamed only 75 miles to the south-west. The fog suddenly thinned, then lifted altogether, giving way to the unseasonal clear weather experienced earlier. Krüder was now sorely tempted to make a dash for the Denmark Strait at full speed, but, with British cruisers in the offing, this could be suicidal. The weather forecasts he was receiving from SKL, based on reports sent in by German weather ships which lurked in these waters disguised as trawlers, indicated that conditions were likely to worsen over the next few days as a warm front moved up from the south. Krüder reversed course and steamed back into the fog to await the promised deterioration in the weather. Once hidden in this silent world of swirling mist, he informed SKL of his decision, using a special shorthand code devised for auxiliary cruisers. A ten-second burst of morse was sufficient to pass his message, a signal so brief that it had faded before any of the network of British W/T direction finding stations constantly monitoring the airwaves could home in on it.

The waiting was long and tedious, with the *Pinguin*, her engines idling, patrolling up and down off the ice edge, her crew largely unoccupied but unable to relax, for the hidden dangers in this fog-shrouded wilderness were many. It was a morale-sapping situation that Krüder had hoped not to meet this early in the voyage. He was very much relieved when, on the morning of the 28th, the barometer began to fall steeply and the wind picked up, sweeping away the fog. In its place came low, overhanging clouds laden with heavy rain. The warm front had arrived.

Running on one engine and making 9 knots, the *Pinguin* moved south again. The wind settled down in the east, rising to force 6 and building up an ugly beam sea that soon began to send freezing spray flying over the raider's bridge. The skies came even lower, so that morning became night again, and it seemed that the *Pinguin* had drifted from one bad dream into another, this one far more malevolent. The sea was short and she rolled jerkily, adding to the misery of those on board. And then the ice came back. It began with isolated floes, which posed no danger to the ship, but soon growlers, and then full-sized bergs, came looming out of the murk. It was a nerve-jangling experience that lasted an agonising twenty-four hours. When the wind eased and visibility improved on the afternoon of the 29th Krüder was exhausted and greeted the clearance with immense relief, even though it did leave his ship exposed to detection by British ships, who might now be patrolling this area in strength.

Krüder need not have concerned himself, for the Royal Navy was elsewhere engaged. When France signed an armistice with the German invaders on 16 June, it immediately became clear that something must be done to avoid her substantial navy falling into enemy hands. The French ships, which included six battle-ships and two battlecruisers, were tied up in Oran, Dakar and Martinique, and were given the choice of surrendering to the Royal Navy or being sunk where they were. In order to provide the show of force necessary to back up this ultimatum, units of the Home Fleet were called in, leaving much of the North Atlantic, including the Denmark Strait, without adequate cover.

Pinguin emerged from the Denmark Strait on the morning of 1 July, having sighted nothing more threatening than a few isolated icebergs. She was now relatively safe, free to lose herself in the broad reaches of the North Atlantic. Her rendezvous with *U-A* off Dakar was planned for 18 July, which gave her time to spare. Krüder decided to put this to good use, steaming south along the meridian of 35° West at reduced speed, thereby conserving fuel, and at the same time being on the lookout for any unescorted Allied merchantmen taking the northern route between Canada and Britain. His luck was not good, for in five days he sighted only one ship, and this turned out to be the British armed merchant cruiser HMS *Carmania*. Believing the *Carmania* to be faster and more heavily armed than the *Pinguin*, Krüder turned away and ran. There was no reaction from the other ship, which seemed not to have sighted the raider.

By midday on the 7th the *Pinguin* was approaching the USA–UK convoy route and it was necessary to proceed with extreme caution. Over the next two days clusters of masts and funnels were seen on the horizon from time to time and evasive action was taken. The weather was fine, with excellent visibility, and, in spite of the *Pinguin*'s low silhouette, there was always the risk that an inquisitive convoy escort might sight her and come racing over the horizon. The appearance of a Russian ship in these waters would certainly arouse suspicion and could easily result in a gun fight *Pinguin* might lose. Another disguise was needed, and on the 10th, in fine warm weather, all hands turned to with paint brushes and the *Petschura*'s bogus voyage ended as it had begun. By nightfall *Pinguin* had taken on the identity of the Greek cargo vessel *Kassos*.

As the *Pinguin* sailed on southwards to her rendezvous with the U-boat, 5000 miles away in the Indian Ocean an encounter took place which would have a profound effect on the war at sea.

On the morning of 11 July the 7506-ton British ship *City of Bagdad*, outward bound from the UK with a full cargo for Penang, was approaching Sumatra and nearing the end of her long voyage. At 0730 she sighted what appeared to be another British cargo vessel on her starboard beam. There was nothing unusual about this; she was near one of the crossroads of the Indian Ocean frequented by British merchantmen. Then, suddenly, the other ship went hard over and headed straight for the *City of Bagdad*. She passed close astern and then came round to run on a parallel course, keeping about 1½ miles off. A flag signal fluttered from her yards, but this was unreadable from the British ship, despite the close proximity. However, the suspicions of Captain Armstrong White, master of the *City of Bagdad*, were already aroused. He ordered his wireless operator to transmit the 'QQQQ' signal, indicating that they were being attacked by a disguised enemy merchant ship.

The 'enemy merchant ship' was in fact the *Atlantis*, ex-*Goldenfels*, sister-ship to the *Pinguin*, which had sailed from Germany in March under the command of Kapitän-zur-See Bernhard Rogge and had already caused considerable disruption to Allied shipping in the South Atlantic and Indian Ocean.

The *Atlantis* ran up her shutters and opened fire as soon as the first urgent notes of the *City of Bagdad*'s transmission were heard. The raider's guns pounded the British ship with salvo after salvo of 6-inch shells, until she was stopped and on fire with three of her crew lying dead and two others injured. A boarding party from the *Atlantis* then sank her with explosive charges.

21

The *City of Bagdad* might have been just another victim for the *Atlantis* to add to her mounting score but for one important omission by the British ship's crew. In the confusion of the attack they failed to dump overboard the vital BAMS (Broadcasting for Allied Merchant Ships) code books. These were seized by the boarding party and sent back to Germany via Japan at the first possible opportunity. Within weeks Berlin was reading all coded signals to and from Allied merchant ships. It was some months before the Admiralty became aware that their ciphers had been compromised.

On 12 July, at the request of SKL, the *Pinguin* broke radio silence to report her position. She was then 700 miles north-west of the Cape Verde Islands, having been continuously at sea for almost three months. SKL's reply contained the latitude and longitude of the proposed meeting with *U-A* on the 18th.

The rendezvous position was reached at noon on the 17th. It was a lonely spot midway between Africa and the West Indies and well away from the shipping lanes. Krüder stopped his ship and waited, growing increasingly anxious as the hours dragged by, for, although the *Pinguin* was in an empty ocean, there was always the risk that a British warship might appear on the horizon. He heaved a sigh of relief when, at first light on the 18th, a long, low grey shape materialized out of the morning mist. *U-A* was on time.

Unfortunately, the U-boat brought with her an unwelcome change in the weather. A fresh NE'ly wind blew up, raising a choppy sea that made it impossible for the transfer of supplies to take place. Krüder decided to head south in search of calmer waters, on the way passing 70 tons of diesel oil to the submarine, so that she would have sufficient fuel to reach Biscay should it not be possible to store her.

On the 20th the two ships reached a position 720 miles south-west of the Cape Verde Islands, where the sea was calm enough to bring *U-A* alongside the *Pinguin*. This was the first time ever that a U-boat had been stored at sea by a raider and the inevitable problems arose. It was soon discovered that the submarine's hydroplanes prevented her from coming close alongside and most of one day was lost in rigging sheer legs to bridge the gap. The torpedoes, eleven in all, were ferried across using flotation bags.

It was a slow operation, and it was not until the afternoon of the 25th that the transfer was completed.

The *Pinguin* then took *U-A* in tow and set course to the south-east to meet up with the track followed by Allied ships between South American ports and Freetown. Once on this line, *U-A* had orders to make for the approaches to Freetown and there lie in wait for ships entering and leaving the harbour. Freetown was the assembly point for UK convoys, so Cohausz anticipated he would find more than sufficient targets for his newly-acquired torpedoes.

The opportunity for action presented itself sooner than expected. At 2300 on the 25th the lights of a ship were sighted to port and on a converging course, and *U-A* at once cast off to investigate. Krüder, being only an interested spectator at this stage, held the *Pinguin* back in the dark to await developments.

After about an hour had passed, Cohausz returned to report failure. He had identified the ship as an Allied tanker, an easy enough target, but his first torpedo had been a 'rogue'. It ran in circles before turning back to home in on the U-boat that fired it and Cohausz was forced to take violent evasive action to avoid being sunk by his own torpedo. By the time he regained control, the tanker had disappeared into the night, probably not even aware of its brush with disaster.

U-A was taken in tow again, but a heavy swell developed the next day and the towrope snapped. From then on the U-boat proceeded under her own power with the *Pinguin* keeping company. Cohausz took his leave at noon on the 28th when they were 850 miles to the west of Freetown. The raider, her supply and escort duties at an end, was now free to begin her own war.

Chapter Three

Forced to abandon the burning bridge of the *Domingo de Larrinaga*, Captain Chalmers retreated to the after end of the deck and looked down with dismay at the chaos reigning below. His ship was ablaze from stem to stern, her multi-national crew running before the flames in blind panic. Being a ship of the old school, built on the Clyde in 1929, long before the preservation of the rain forests became an issue, the *Domingo de Larrinaga* had been turned into a self-fuelling bonfire by the *Pinguin*'s shells. After more than a month under the hot tropic sun, her wood-sheathed upper decks and varnished teakwood fittings were tinder dry. They burned enthusiastically.

Chalmers cursed himself for a fool. Since the pocket battleship *Graf Spee*'s reign of terror had been ended off the River Plate by the Royal Navy in December 1939, he had believed the South Atlantic, at least, was safe for Allied shipping. How wrong he had been proved – and how wrong he had been to underestimate his pursuer. Now eight of his crew lay dead, four others were injured and his ship was rapidly turning into a funeral pyre threatening to consume them all, living and dead. With a hopeless shrug, he gave the order to abandon ship.

Fireman Robert Deus had already left the ship, unceremoniously blown overboard when one of the *Pinguin*'s first shells exploded close to him as he stood on deck. When he regained consciousness, he was deep under water, totally disoriented and with his lungs about to burst. Instinctively, he kicked out and shot to the surface, where he lay gasping for breath. He caught sight

24

of the burning ship and was overwhelmed by despair. For a brief moment he contemplated slipping back into the cool depths, then he thought of the unborn child back in Liverpool and struck out determinedly for the ship. He had not gone far when he came across his watchmate, fellow Basque John Martinez, who had also ended up in the sea. Martinez, a poor swimmer, was already foundering when Deus came to his aid. Both men were in a state of complete exhaustion when the *Pinguin*'s cutter found them and fished them out of the water.

The cutter, under the command of Leutnant Erich Warning, carried an armed boarding party and the *Pinguin*'s surgeon, Doctor Wenzel, accompanied by two sick berth attendants. Although ruthless in dealing with the British ship, Krüder was a seaman first, and therefore a humanitarian. He was aware that men must be dying aboard the *Domingo de Larrinaga*: Wenzel would do what he could for them. As for the ship herself, the scuttling charges Warning carried in the bottom of the cutter would seal her fate. Krüder could not afford to take prizes at this early stage of the voyage.

As Chalmers and his men were struggling to get the boats away, the German cutter bumped against the *Domingo de Larrinaga*'s side, grappling irons were thrown, and Leutnant Warning, pistol in hand, led the way aboard. While the armed sailors took over the ship, Wenzel and his team attended to the wounded, who had been laid out on the hatches. By this time the fire was completely out of control. Stopping only to signal the *Pinguin* by lamp, advising Krüder of the situation, Warning sent his men below to set the charges, urging them to waste no time.

With the explosive charges set and ticking away, the British and Germans climbed into their respective boats. With them went the injured, among them Radio Officer Neil Morrison, who had continued to transmit until a shell hit the wireless room, breaking both his legs and knocking him unconscious. The dead were left to go down with their ship.

Warning had set the scuttling charges to explode after nine minutes, calculating that this would allow ample time for the boats to pull clear of the ship. In the case of the British lifeboats, all propelled by oars, this sufficed; with slow, measured strokes, they pulled clear of the doomed ship. The German cutter, on the other hand, her engine refusing to start, remained firmly stuck alongside.

The seconds ticked by relentlessly as Bootsmann Rauch, the *Pinguin*'s brawny boatswain, struggled with the reluctant diesel, priming and cranking vigorously while the others in the boat fidgeted nervously. The charges planted in the *Domingo de Larrinaga*'s engine-room, designed to blow her hull apart, were directly under the cutter.

And still, no matter how hard Rauch cranked and how loudly he cursed, the engine refused to fire. With less than two minutes to go by his watch, Leutnant Warning resorted to boathooks and oars in a desperate attempt to shove the boat off. But the cutter was a heavy wooden boat, once a lifeboat aboard the 50,000-ton transatlantic liner *Europa*. Without its engine, it was dead in the water, and despite the efforts of everyone on board able to push or pull, it refused to part company with the ship it had come to destroy.

Nine minutes came and went, then ten, then twelve, then fourteen, and still the anticipated explosion did not come. Gradually, the electric tension that had built up in the cutter was relaxed and the crew looked to Warning for orders. Suspecting that the fuses had not been properly lit in the rush to clear the burning ship and had subsequently gone out, the prize officer was tempted to reboard, but he resisted taking what could have been a very grave risk. His dilemma was solved when the cutter's engine finally burst into life. An audible sigh of relief went up when he backed the boat off and headed for the *Pinguin*.

Appraised of the situation by Warning, Krüder agreed with the Leutnant's decision to abandon the crippled ship, but he was not pleased. The *Pinguin* was dangerously close to the British naval base of Freetown and already her wireless office was reporting the air waves alive with ominous messages. The pressing need now was to sink the *Domingo de Larrinaga* and get away before the Royal Navy came hunting. Krüder considered using his heavy guns, thereby giving the *Pinguin*'s guns' crews some much-needed practice, but this might take too long. Reluctantly, he decided he must sacrifice one of his precious torpedoes.

The torpedo ran true, striking the *Domingo de Larrinaga*

squarely amidships. A muffled thud came over the water, then a tall column of dirty water, debris and steam shot high in the air from the burning ship. Slowly, almost gracefully, she heeled over, righted herself again, then slid beneath the waves, leaving only a cloud of steam and smoke to mark her grave.

It had taken Krüder four hours to dispose of his first victim – not an encouraging start for a commerce raider whose continued existence would depend on a quick kill and an even quicker getaway. But, as the *Pinguin* headed south at full speed her wireless office intercepted and decoded a message from the Admiralty to all ships warning of a German raider sighted in the South Atlantic. The position given was 1,300 miles south of the *Pinguin*, which when the news of the sinking of the *Domingo de Larrinaga* came through, must cause a great deal of confusion in London, where it was not yet known that the *Pinguin* was at large.

The Admiralty's message, no doubt with good cause, had been more than economical in its content. The 'sighting' mentioned had in fact been a brutal engagement between two armed merchant cruisers, the German *Thor* and the British *Alcantara*.

At 0900 on Sunday 28 July, the *Alcantara*, a 22,000-ton ex-Royal Mail liner, was patrolling near the island of Trinidade, off the coast of Brazil, with orders to intercept German blockade runners, when she sighted smoke on the horizon. The *Alcantara* immediately gave chase, working up to 22 knots. Her quarry, the 3,862-ton *Thor*, ex-*Santa Cruz* of the Hamburg South America Line, likewise increased to full speed.

The *Thor*, a 1938-built fruit carrier had a top speed of 20 knots, and the chase was obviously going to be prolonged. When this became clear to Captain J.G.P. Ingham, commanding the *Alcantara*, he decided, with typical British aplomb, to carry on with his usual Sunday morning routine. Divine Service was held on deck, followed by Captain's Inspection, which Ingham carried out with meticulous attention to detail. It was not until 1300, when the *Thor*'s masts and funnel were clearly visible from the bridge, that the *Alcantara*'s men were sent to their action stations.

When the German ship was hull up she suddenly presented her port side to the *Alcantara*, hoisted her battle ensign and opened fire. Her first broadside fell over the British ship, but the second straddled her. The *Alcantara*'s bridge received a direct hit, her wireless aerials were brought down, communication between the bridge and her guns was cut, and two men were killed and eight injured. This was a devastating blow to the British ship and she was powerless to answer back. The range, at 16,000 yards, was well beyond the reach of her Boer War vintage 6-inch guns.

Despite being hit repeatedly, the *Alcantara* continued the chase and finally closed the range to 10,000 yards, at which she was able to open fire with good effect, scoring several hits on the *Thor*. But that was as far as the British AMC's luck went. As she continued to close the gap, one of *Thor*'s 5.9-inch shells ploughed into her engine-room. By great good fortune the shell failed to explode, but the hole it made in the hull below the waterline was big enough to cause serious flooding in the engine space. The *Alcantara*'s generators were damaged and some of her vital pumps put out of action. Reluctantly, Ingham stopped his ship to allow a patch to be rigged over the hole, a slow and difficult operation. Meanwhile, the *Thor*, on fire and trailing black smoke, disappeared into the oncoming darkness.

The *Alcantara/Thor* engagement ended inconclusively for both sides, but it did signal to the Admiralty that the South Atlantic was no longer an exclusively British ocean. News of the attack on the *Domingo de Larrinaga* by a surface raider, coming three days later, served to confirm this unwelcome truth. By the time the Royal Navy had strengthened its forces in the area, both the *Thor* and *Pinguin* had moved on to other pastures.

Aboard the *Pinguin*, Krüder's intention was to steer due south until he reached the River Plate-Cape of Good Hope trade route. From there he planned to steer east in the hope of falling in with unescorted Allied merchantmen as they made their way to and from the Indian Ocean. This they were doing in increasing numbers following the closure of the Mediterranean to shipping.

It would seem that the news of German raiders at large in the South Atlantic had emptied the ocean of shipping, for, as she steamed south at 16 knots, bucking a boisterous trade wind that sent sheets of spray flying over her bows, the horizon was bare. Only one lone ship was sighted and this turned out to be the Japanese cargo ship *Hawaii Maru*, bound for Buenos Aires. With

Japan being neutral, but friendly to Germany, Krüder was obliged to leave her well alone.

Latitude 36 degrees south was reached on 5 August, the *Pinguin* having by then put nearly 2000 miles between her and her first and only victim. Krüder, hoping for better times to come, now turned east for the Cape, shaping course to pass north of Tristan da Cunha. As he did so, the weather began to deteriorate, the playful south-east trades giving way to a succession of westerly gales with a steadily falling thermometer. The southern winter was near at hand.

In the meantime, the *Pinguin*'s erstwhile companion, *U-A*, had also seen action. She had failed to intercept any convoys out of Freetown, but, moving further north, had chanced upon a lone Jugoslav steamer, the 4200-ton *Rad*. Bound from Philadelphia to Durban with a cargo of fertiliser, the 30-year-old Jugoslav, heading for the Cape at 8 knots, made an easy target for Hans Cohausz. One torpedo was sufficient to send her to the bottom.

U-A's subsequent career was anything but distinguished and she was never again to be within striking distance of a target comparable to her first, the 14,000-ton *Andania*. Moving further north, she sank three more small tramps during August, the Greek *Aspasia* on the 15th, the Hungarian *Kelet* on the 19th and the Panama-flag *Tuira* on the 20th. One of these was in ballast, the other two carrying low-grade bulk cargoes. It was March 1941 before *U-A* saw action again, slightly damaging the British steamer *Dunaff Head* south of Ireland. Thereafter, she retired to the Baltic to join Admiral Dönitz's training squadron. Her contribution to Germany's war at sea had not been significant, and had Ernst Krüder been aware of this he might well have wondered if all the trouble he had taken to play shepherd to the U-boat had been worth it.

Steaming east for the Cape of Good Hope in increasingly squally weather, the *Pinguin* once more apparently had the ocean to herself, much to Krüder's delight. The future success of his mission was heavily dependent on the element of surprise. Then, late on 10 August, a fine but dark night, the light of the stars showed a large merchant ship passing to port, bound north. This was a fat-looking prize and *Pinguin*'s officers were anxious to go to battle stations, but Krüder stayed his hand. The stranger might just be a British armed merchant cruiser on patrol. She was in the right place and was the right size. And so the two darkened ships slid past each other in the night without a challenge from either side.

Krüder's caution was well founded, for although the north-bound ship was not a British cruiser, any attack on her would have been a major blunder. She was, in fact, the Norwegian-flag *Tirranna*, one of Wilhelmsen's crack Far East cargo liners taken as a prize by the *Pinguin*'s sister-raider *Atlantis*, and then on her way back to France carrying a large number of Allied prisoners of war.

The *Tirranna*, blissfully ignorant of her narrow escape in the South Atlantic, crossed the Equator and steamed north unseen, only to be sunk by a British submarine in the Bay of Biscay when just a few hours from port. Fortunately, her crew and the majority of the prisoners were saved.

Reaching well down into the Roaring Forties, the *Pinguin* passed Cape Agulhas, the southernmost point of Africa, on 19 August and so entered the Indian Ocean, where it was hoped she would realize her full potential. In these waters the Royal Navy was stretched beyond all conceivable limits and had few escorts to spare for convoys, so most merchantmen were said to be sailing alone. Now the voyage promised to become an adventure. However, with entry into the Indian Ocean came the news that, having become aware of the capture of the BAMS code books from the *City of Bagdad* by the *Atlantis*, the British had changed their merchant shipping codes. Krüder had lost the advantage of being able to read wireless traffic between Allied ships.

As the *Pinguin*, maintaining a prudent distance off the South African coast, passed from one ocean into another, the Norwegian tanker *Filefjell*, southbound from Abadan to the UK, was crossing the Equator some 3000 miles to the north-east. Unlike the German raider, which was fighting its way through rough seas backed by a bitter wind blowing straight off the Antarctic ice, the 7616-ton motor tanker was bowling along in 'flying fish' weather. It was the Indian Ocean at its best; flawless blue sky, light balmy winds and the azure blue sea glassy calm. Only a low, undulating swell, generated by the South-West

Monsoon still raging to the north, pushed gently at the ship's deep-laden hull, giving her a slow, easy roll.

But, as she moved from the northern hemisphere into the south, there was no 'Crossing the Line' ceremony on board the *Filefjell*. Owned by Olsen & Ugelstad of Oslo, and commanded by Captain Josef Nordby, the tanker was operating under British Admiralty control, and had on board 10,000 tons of high-octane aviation spirit. Before sailing from Abadan, Nordby had been warned that a German surface raider – in this case the *Atlantis* – was at work near the Equator, having sunk Henderson Line's 7,769-ton *Kemmendine* only two days after her encounter with the *City of Bagdad* on 11 July. Wisely, Nordby had not passed on this knowledge to his crew, who were already nervous at living on top of a floating bomb in a war zone. The twin-screw *Filefjell* had a good turn of speed and, the Indian Ocean being very wide, Nordby hoped to slip through to the Cape unseen.

Another sharp reminder of the danger the Norwegian ship faced came on the morning of the 24th when she was near the French island of Reunion. Her wireless operator, Thorleif Hendriksen, picked up an SOS from the British cargo ship *King City*, who reported she was being attacked by a surface raider. The *King City*, bound from Cardiff to Singapore with a cargo of coal for the naval base, was then 180 miles north of Rodriguez Island, some 600 miles north-east of the *Filefjell*. Her brief call for help was followed by an ominous silence. This was obviously the *Atlantis* at work again, in which case the *Filefjell* had escaped her net. For the time being, at least, the Norwegian tanker was safe.

Later that day, with the noontime ritual of fixing the ship's position by the sun over, Josef Nordby remained on the bridge savouring the warm afternoon sunshine. As so often happened in these quiet moments, his thoughts turned to his native Oslo, now under German occupation. For more than four months now he had been a man without a country, his only home the *Filefjell* – and with the Allies so obviously losing the war, he could antici- pate no change in his status in the foreseeable future.

Nordby's reverie was interrupted a few minutes before one o'clock by the unmistakable drone of an aircraft engine. Snatching up his binoculars, he swept the horizon. The plane was just a small black dot low in the sky to port, but growing rapidly bigger as it flew directly towards the ship. He spoke quietly to the officer of the watch, instructing him to hoist the Norwegian flag and send the crew to action stations, not that the latter action would be of any avail. Although she was under British control, the *Filefjell* carried no guns with which to defend herself.

Nordby relaxed again when the aircraft roared overhead at about 500 feet, its British markings clearly visible. It was a two-seater, single-engined seaplane of the type any British cruiser might carry. A welcome visitor. The plane circled the *Filefjell* briefly, inspecting her. Nordby waved and pointed to his flag, and the pilot appeared to acknowledge his wave before flying off to the south, apparently satisfied.

Contrary to expectations, no British warship came over the horizon, but the seaplane was back again within the hour. It approached very low over the water, climbing as it reached the tanker. Nordby was puzzled by its behaviour; his crew gathered nervously on the deck below. Then the plane fired a Very light, which burst over the ship in a cascade of glowing red balls. The men on the deck dived for cover and then sheepishly re-appeared when they realized the display of pyrotechnics was harmless. Nordby, now more than a little worried, ordered a large Norwegian flag to be spread out on the deck, so that the circling aircraft should have no doubts as to the nationality of his ship.

After her second circuit the plane turned towards the *Filefjell* and then swept in so low that it seemed that her wings must touch the masts. As she zoomed across the tanker, a small black object fell away from her underside and hurtled towards the deck. Again the Norwegians scattered.

The bomb-like missile failed to explode and, on close exami-nation, proved to be nothing more lethal than a weighted bag containing a message. The bag was carried to the bridge and handed to Nordby. He extracted the crumpled sheet of paper, smoothed it out and read: 'ON ACCOUNT VICINITY OF ENEMY RAIDER ALTER COURSE TO 180 DEGREES DISTANCE 140 MILES. FROM THAT POINT TAKE UP COURSE DIRECT TO 31 DEGREES NORTH 37 DEGREES EAST. THENCE YOU GET FURTHER INFOR-MATIONS. DO NOT USE WIRELESS. SIGNED HOPKINS, COMMANDER HMS CUMBERLAND.'

32

At first sight the note seemed genuine to Nordby, confirming his supposition that a British warship was in the vicinity. Accordingly, he altered course as directed, following in the wake of the seaplane as it flew off to the south. But with the aircraft out of sight over the horizon, the Norwegian captain began to have second thoughts. There was something about the note that did not ring true. He was aware of the existence of the *Cumberland*, a heavy cruiser, but, if she was really in the area, what possible reason could she have for making a rendezvous with his ship? And somehow the note did not read right; the English was too stilted. Wary that he might be running into a trap, Nordby decided to resume his original course and called on the engine-room to make all possible speed.

Forty-six-year-old Josef Nordby had spent a lifetime at sea, during which by necessity he had developed a shrewd awareness of the approach of danger. And on this occasion his perception was correct. The seaplane that had twice visited the *Filefjell* and dropped the message was not British, but none other than the *Pinguin*'s Heinkel with crude British roundels painted on the underside of its wings. Launched by Krüder early on the morning of the 26th, the seaplane had sighted the Norwegian tanker by chance when some 150 miles north of the *Pinguin*. As there was little hope of the raider intercepting the tanker before nightfall, the Heinkel's pilot, Leutnant Werner, returned to the parent ship to report and refuel. The note dropped on the second visit was Krüder's attempt to make the enemy come to him, and the deception had almost worked.

At 1720, with the sun low on the horizon and darkness little more than an hour away, there was still no sign of any other ship, and Nordby assumed it was safe to send out an SOS. This was an unfortunate decision, for, unknown to the Norwegian, the *Filefjell* and the *Pinguin* were then on diverging courses and, had he kept radio silence for a little longer, the tanker would probably have escaped into the gathering dusk. As it was, Krüder's wireless operators were keeping a diligent watch, and within minutes had taken bearings of the fleeing tanker.

The Heinkel arrived overhead again half an hour later, and without further challenge, dived on the *Filefjell* and ripped out her wireless aerial with a grapnel. This was followed with a small bomb dropped close ahead of the tanker and several bursts of machine-gun fire across her bridge. The message was plainly obvious and, without as much as a pistol to defend his ship, Nordby gave the order to heave-to.

By now the sun had set and, with the brief equatorial twilight fast turning to complete darkness, the seaplane made one more circuit and then landed on the water close to the *Filefjell*. A morse light flashed out from the plane's cockpit, staccato and demanding: 'REMAIN STOPPING HERE,' Nordby read off, 'CRUISER CUMBERLAND WILL GO WITH YOU. SHOW YOUR LIGHTS.'

Nordby was still confused as to the real nationality of the aircraft and once again the wording of the message was not right, but the second mention of HMS *Cumberland* carried weight. Moreover, the bomb and the machine gun spoke volumes. He opted to remain stopped, show his lights as instructed and await developments.

Viewed in the cold light of history, the situation was ludicrous. Here was a ship of 10,000 tons – unarmed she might have been, but she was a big, powerful ship – lying stopped in the water, having surrendered to one tiny reconnaissance seaplane carrying a handful of small bombs no more lethal than thunder flashes, and armed with one light calibre machine gun and a limited supply of ammunition. And, as it later transpired, Leutnant Werner had not landed alongside the *Filefjell* by design, but had been forced to do so by empty fuel tanks. Had Nordby taken it into his head to make a run for it, there was very little Werner could have done to stop him. However, there was the question of the 10,000 tons of volatile petroleum the *Filefjell* was carrying, which would have required only one bullet in the right place to blow the ship and her crew to kingdom come. In the end, Nordby had made the decision that was in the best interests of the thirty-one men who depended for their lives on his judgement.

Guided in by the *Filefjell*'s lights, the *Pinguin* arrived an hour and three-quarters later, by which time it was completely dark. The raider dropped two boats, and an armed boarding party led by Leutnant Warning swarmed up the tanker's side. The Norwegians offered no resistance and within fifteen minutes the *Filefjell* was in German hands. The takeover was so quickly and efficiently carried out that Captain Nordby, still uncertain as to the identity of the boarders, made no effort to destroy the ship's confidential papers and code books. These were at once trans-ferred to the *Pinguin*.

Nordby and his crew of thirty-one joined the thirty-two *Domingo de Larrinaga* survivors, who were then in their fourth week of captivity, aboard the *Pinguin*. These men had been well treated, their wounded carefully nursed in the raider's sick bay and recovering rapidly.

Later that night Josef Nordby stood on deck and watched as his late command, with a German crew on board, followed in the wake of the *Pinguin* as she set course to the south. Krüder had acquired a very valuable prize – her cargo of aviation spirit would be worth a king's ransom to the German war effort – and he was determined to send her home. But first, as they were then only 400 miles from Madagascar, which might well be in British hands, he must quit the scene of the capture as quickly as possible. He opted to go south, where in safer waters he intended to top up the *Pinguin*'s bunkers with fuel oil from the *Filefjell*.

Chapter Four

For the Allies, the Norwegian campaign had been a lost cause from the start; another example of the British Government's penchant for doing too little too late. Yet control of this thousand-mile-long peninsula fronting on the North Atlantic was absolutely vital for the successful prosecution of the war against Germany.

In 1939 Germany's steel industry was largely dependent on high-grade iron ore imported from the mines of northern Sweden, 10 million tons a year flowing south. During the summer months the ore was sent by rail to the Swedish port of Lulea, at the head of the Gulf of Bothnia, and thence direct by sea to German ports in the Baltic, a route safe from the attention of Allied warships and bombers. In winter Lulea was frozen in and for six months the only way out for the ore was through the port of Narvik, on the west coast of Norway. From Narvik south to the Skagerrak the Atlantic coast is fringed by a chain of islands, inside which are deep-water channels known as 'The Leads', all of which lie inside Norwegian territorial waters. As long as Norway remained neutral, German ore carriers were free to make use of the Leads to run south to the Baltic with their vital cargoes, again without fear of attack. Representations had been made to the Norwegian Government to put a stop to this trade, for it was estimated that one winter without iron ore would cripple Germany's war effort. However, the British pleas fell on deaf ears. Having only a small and insignificant army, Norway could not afford to upset her powerful and aggressive neighbour to the south.

In December 1939 Winston Churchill, then First Lord of the Admiralty, said: 'The effectual stoppage of the Norwegian ore supplies to Germany ranks as a major offensive operation of war. No other measure is open to us for many months to come which gives so good a chance of abridging the waste and destruction of the conflict, or of perhaps preventing the vast slaughters which will attend the grapple of the main armies.' Churchill proposed mining the Leads, but he was outvoted in Cabinet on the grounds that Norwegian neutrality must not be breached.

Adolf Hitler's opinion was expressed in a directive issued on 1 March 1940 : 'The development of the situation in Scandinavia requires all preparations to be made for the occupation of Denmark and Norway by a part of the German Armed Forces. This operation should prevent British encroachment on Scandinavia and the Baltic, further it should guarantee our ore base in Sweden and give our Navy and Air Force a wider start-line against Britain.'

For hundreds of years Norway had presented a neutral face in northern Europe, stoutly refusing to become embroiled in the recurring power struggles of the bigger nations to the south. But, due largely to her geographical position, her status was about to be forcibly changed.

Britain and Germany acted simultaneously in the spring of 1940. On 6 April a force commanded by Vice-Admiral Sir W.J. Whitworth, consisting of four mine-laying destroyers, escorted by the battle-cruiser *Renown*, the cruiser *Birmingham* and eight other destroyers, left Scapa Flow and crossed the North Sea. Their objective was to lay mines in Norwegian territorial waters, specifically to close the Leads to shipping.

Next day, the 7th, a German invasion fleet sailed from the River Weser and steamed north. Under the command of Admiral Wilhelm Marschall, the fleet consisted of two groups, the battle-cruisers *Scharnhorst* and *Gneisenau* escorting ten troop-carrying destroyers bound for Narvik, and a second group made up of four destroyers led by the heavy cruiser *Admiral Hipper*, commanded by Kapitän-zur-See Hellmuth Heye. The *Hipper*'s destroyers were crammed with troops to be landed at Trondheim.

The *Scharnhorst* and *Gneisenau* had made their mark earlier in the war by disrupting shipping in the North Atlantic and sinking the British armed merchant cruiser *Rawalpindi*. The *Hipper*, on the other hand, was still unblooded. She had been undergoing a refit when war broke out, and it was not until the end of January 1940 that she was ready for action. Her first, and only, active service cruise to date, a sweep against Allied shipping off Scandinavia in February 1940, also in company with *Scharnhorst* and *Gneisenau*, had been futile and was abandoned when the three ships were sighted by British aircraft.

The 16,974-ton *Hipper*, named for Admiral Franz Ritter von Hipper, who commanded the German battle-cruiser squadron at Jutland, was the Kriegsmarine's first heavy cruiser to be built since the Treaty of Versailles severely curtailed Germany's sea power. Designed and started before Hitler abrogated the Treaty in 1935, she was a fast and powerful ship. Her 132,000 horse-power Deschimag geared turbines, fed by nine Wagner high-pressure boilers, gave her a top speed of 32½ knots. Her fire-power was just as impressive, consisting of eight 8-inch guns mounted in twin armour-plated turrets able to fire individually or collectively, each gun being capable of delivering three rounds a minute at a maximum range of 19.5 miles. Twelve 4.1-inch guns and twelve 37mm quick-firing cannon provided defence against air attack, and to complete her armament the *Hipper* mounted twelve torpedo tubes, six a side, at the forward end of the weather deck. Three reconnaissance seaplanes launched by catapult were also carried and an early form of radar was fitted. Her crew numbered 1,600.

Although comparatively lightly armoured, the *Hipper* was a strong ship, built with longitudinal framing and subdivided into eighteen watertight compartments. But her main characteristic was her superior speed, ideally fitting her for the role her designers had in mind, that of an ocean raider dedicated to the destruction of Allied merchant shipping. She was, however, fatally flawed; her sophisticated high-pressure steam turbines were unreliable and subject to frequent breakdowns, and she had insufficient bunker capacity for sustained steaming. She carried only 3,250 tons of fuel oil, which at a consumption of 172 tons a day at 15 knots, gave her a maximum range of only 6,800 miles. At maximum speed, her endurance was under three days, with the result that she would need to be accompanied by refuelling tankers wherever she went. This was to prove her Achilles heel.

When the German invasion fleet left the Weser on 7 April the weather was fine and calm, but would soon change for the worse. A vigorous depression was moving in from the Atlantic, and by evening, as the mouth of the Skagerrak was crossed, the sky was lowering and the wind gusting to gale force. The big ships were not troubled, but the sharp-prowed destroyers, driving into heavy seas at 26 knots, were taking considerable punishment. The suffering of the troops they carried, most of whom had never ventured out to sea before, was pitiful to see. Yet Marschall, anxious to get the sea passage over as soon as possible, refused to reduce speed. When a grey dawn broke on the 8th the weather had worsened, making a mockery of any attempt at station keeping. The ships were scattered over a wide area, each fighting her own personal battle with the storm. Later in the morning, when the weather eased, the *Hipper* rounded up her four destroyers and set course for Trondheim.

Vice-Admiral Whitworth's mine-laying fleet, then nearing the Norwegian coast, was encountering similar weather, with driving sleet and fog banks adding to the misery of the morning. The British destroyers, smaller than their German counterparts, were all but disappearing from sight as green seas swept over them. Then, one of the escort destroyers, the 1335-ton 'G' class HMS *Glowworm*, lost a man overboard.

A man overboard in rough weather is every ship captain's worst nightmare, for then one man's life must be weighed against the safety of the ship and all on board. Under the circumstances prevailing, *Glowworm*'s captain, Lieutenant-Commander Gerard Roope, would have been fully justified in leaving the unfortunate man to the mercies of the sea. But Roope was a man of compassion. Putting the helm hard over, he ran back on a reciprocal course with lookouts posted at all points.

With poor visibility and the sea a raging maelstrom of white foam, it seemed like a hopeless quest, and after searching for an hour Roope was about to give up when there was a cry from one of the lookouts. There was a man in the water – and he was still alive! With a magnificent display of ship handling, Roope brought the destroyer short round and made a lee. A boat was dropped and within minutes the exhausted man was snatched from the sea.

By this time *Glowworm* was many miles astern of the main force, which was not then aware that it had lost a destroyer. Having no radar, and under orders to keep strict radio silence, Roope knew that the chances of finding the fleet again in the atrocious weather prevailing were slim, but he must try. Resuming his original course, he piled on all possible speed and the destroyer began to bury her bows deep in the oncoming seas as she forged ahead.

It was then, by some cruel twist of fate, that *Glowworm* blundered into the rearguard of Group Two of the German invasion fleet. A single destroyer was sighted at first, which, when challenged, identified herself as German. Roope immediately opened fire, straddling the enemy with two salvoes before she disappeared into the murk.

Roope gave chase, breaking radio silence to report to the Admiralty: 'Am engaging enemy'. Soon afterwards *Glowworm* ran into a hornet's nest. Emerging from a rain squall, she found herself in sight of a second German destroyer. This was the 2,400-ton *Bernd von Arnim*, one of Marschall's troop carriers. She was quickly joined by another of her class. Both German ships were armed with five 5-inch guns, while the *Glowworm* carried only four 4.7s. She was outweighed and outgunned, yet she engaged the enemy fearlessly, and a running fight ensued that was made all the more dramatic by the storm that raged around the ships.

It is more than likely that the plucky little *Glowworm* would have given a very good account of herself in this one-sided fight – at the very least, she might have got away. But then the odds against her lengthened as two more German destroyers arrived on the scene. They were followed by the *Admiral Hipper*, which came racing in to seal the fate of the lone British ship. The cruiser opened up with her 8-inch guns, hitting the *Glowworm* with her first salvo. Roope made a brave attempt to torpedo the *Hipper* but missed. He then laid smoke to cover his escape.

The *Hipper* followed *Glowworm* into the smoke and continued to hammer the fleeing destroyer with her big guns. Roope hit back with his after turret, but the destroyer was rolling and pitching heavily, and most of his shells went wide. The German cruiser, on the other hand, was a steadier gun platform and her shots went home. *Glowworm* was soon on fire and listing. But Roope was not finished. As the German heavy cruiser bore down on him, he suddenly turned under full helm and charged at her, guns blazing.

Glowworm slammed into the *Hipper* at 38 knots, tearing a hole 120 feet long in her armoured hull. The gallant destroyer then fell away, her bows a tangled mass of twisted metal, on fire from stem to stern and her decks littered with dead and dying. A few minutes later, with her battle ensigns still flying defiantly, she rolled over and sank. Only forty of her crew of 100 survived. Lieutenant-Commander Gerard Roope was not among them, but he had won the day. The *Hipper* reached Trondheim and, after temporary repairs, sailed for Wilhelmshaven. A month went by before she was fit for sea again.

Alerted by *Glowworm*'s signals, the *Renown* came looking for the enemy and at 0330 on the 9th she sighted the *Scharnhorst* and *Gneisenau* as they returned from landing troops at Narvik. The sighting was only brief, for the horizon was almost immediately blotted out by a snow squall. Another hour passed before the German battle-cruisers were seen again, and by this time it was dawn. The *Renown* then opened fire on the *Gneisenau* with her 15-inch guns at a range of 18,000 yards, scoring several hits. *Scharnhorst* made smoke to cover her damaged sister and both German ships made off to the north with *Renown* in pursuit. The enemy battle-cruisers were faster and began to draw away, but the *Renown* had the bigger guns and she continued to lob shells after them. The *Gneisenau* was hit again, but a combination of passing snow squalls, smoke and the motion of the ships made fire on both sides largely ineffectual. Eventually, as she was in danger of inflicting serious damage on herself as she ploughed into the rough seas, *Renown* was obliged to reduce to 20 knots. The two German ships finally drew out of range and then out of sight.

It was several days before the full extent of the German invasion of Norway became known in London. When the picture was clear, British forces were landed north of Trondheim on 16 April. They were later joined by French and Polish troops and, along with remnants of the Norwegian Army, succeeded in recapturing Narvik on 28 May. This was the first time in the war that Allied forces had won a victory on land – and it was to be the last for a long time to come.

Meanwhile, things were going badly for the Allies elsewhere in Europe. On 14 May German bombers razed the undefended city of Rotterdam to the ground, prompting the Dutch to lay down their arms that evening. At the same time powerful German armoured forces advanced into Belgium, sweeping all before them. The British and French armies, unprepared to meet an attack of such ferocity, fell back in disorder. By the end of the month France was ready to capitulate and what remained of the British Expeditionary Force was gathering on the beaches of Dunkirk awaiting evacuation.

Although the Allies had gained a toehold in Norway, in the light of the catastrophic events taking place to the south the effort required to maintain this presence could no longer be justified. The evacuation of Narvik was begun on 4 June and by the 8th four convoys carrying 24,000 British, French and Polish troops, along with much of their equipment and supplies, had sailed for British ports. At the time of sailing no heavy units of the German Navy were reported at sea and it was decided to allow the convoys to sail with only light anti-submarine escorts.

Berlin was well aware that the Allied position in Norway was becoming untenable, but no intelligence had reached the Germans of the impending withdrawal. On 4 June, while the British evacuation ships were assembling off Narvik, Admiral Marschall sailed from Kiel with the *Scharnhorst* and *Gneisenau*, the *Hipper* and four destroyers. His orders were to carry out a routine bombardment of British positions around Narvik.

News of the British evacuation of Narvik reached Marschall on the 7th and he immediately raced north, hoping to intercept the troop convoys. The scene was set for a major tragedy.

German hopes were raised when, at around 0600 on the 8th, some 160 miles north-west of Trondheim, two British ships were sighted. They were the 5666-ton tanker *Oil Pioneer*, escorted by the 505-ton armed trawler HMS *Juniper*, having between them only one 4-inch gun – this carried by the *Juniper*. Marschall signalled the *Hipper* to deal with the British ships.

42

Using her smaller calibre guns, *Hipper* easily disposed of the trawler, and then turned her fire on the *Oil Pioneer*. The tanker proved to be a tougher nut altogether. The German cruiser's shells quickly set her on fire, but her hull was strengthened for carrying heavy deadweight cargoes, and she stubbornly refused to sink. Eventually the destroyer *Hermann Schoemann* was sent in to dispatch her by torpedo. Twenty of the *Oil Pioneer*'s crew lost their lives, the remainder, with twenty-nine survivors from the *Juniper*, were rescued by the German ships.

Marschall continued northwards and later that morning sighted two more British ships, this time without even a trawler to protect them. But, once again, the German Admiral was disappointed. The larger of the two ships, the 19,840-ton ex-passenger liner *Orama*, had been sent to Narvik to lift off troops, but was returning empty-handed, having been surplus to requirements. The other vessel turned out to be the hospital ship *Atlantis*. Under the terms of the Geneva Convention – and both sides were then adhering to the Convention – the *Atlantis* was immune from attack. This was a far cry from the convoys of loaded troopships and supply ships Marschall had hoped to find, but, once met with, the *Orama*, at least, could not be allowed to go free. He again appointed the *Hipper* as executioner and, using her 8-inch guns, she reduced the liner to a blazing wreck. The smaller guns of the destroyer *Hans Lody* finished the job, sending the *Orama* to the bottom. Nineteen of the trooper's crew were killed and 280 taken prisoner.

The *Hipper*'s limited supply of fuel oil was now running short and Marschall ordered her to make for Trondheim with her four escorting destroyers. *Scharnhorst* and *Gneisenau* then continued north, Marschall still seeking the elusive British troop convoys. His search was in vain. However, there was some compensation, for at 1600 the British aircraft carrier HMS *Glorious* and her escorting destroyers *Ardent* and *Acasta* were sighted.

It was a meeting that could only end in a massacre. The two German battle-cruisers opened fire with their 11-inch guns at a range of 15 miles, and the British ships, none of them mounting anything heavier than a 4.7-inch, were powerless to hit back. The big-gun salvoes reduced the *Glorious* to a smoking wreck before she could get the first of her torpedo bombers airborne. *Ardent* and *Acasta* laid a smoke screen to protect the carrier, and then, showing immense determination and courage, charged in to attack the *Scharnhorst* and *Gneisenau* with torpedoes. *Ardent* was blown out of the water as she came in, but the *Acasta*, although severely damaged and on fire, closed the *Scharnhorst* and torpedoed her, before she too was sunk.

As a result of this one-sided fight the Royal Navy lost an aircraft carrier, two destroyers and 1,474 men, but the sacrifice was not in vain. *Acasta*'s torpedo blasted open the *Scharnhorst*'s side, flooding two of her engine-room compartments and putting her after gun turret out of action. With twenty-eight dead and many others wounded, she was escorted into Trondheim by the *Gneisenau*.

Admiral Wilhelm Marschall's plan to create havoc among the British troop convoy's had come to nought. If only he had known that the *Glorious* was just 200 miles ahead of the first convoy, then he might have acted differently. As it turned out, he had scored a very hollow victory and had come within an ace of losing his flagship. Meanwhile, the British convoys, carrying 24,000 troops, got through without losing a man.

And there was much worse to come for Admiral Marschall. When, a few days later, the *Gneisenau* left Trondheim with the *Hipper* and her destroyers, the British submarine HMS *Clyde* was lying in wait outside the entrance to the fjord. *Clyde* put a torpedo into the battle-cruiser's bows, causing extensive damage and flooding. The *Gneisenau* returned to Trondheim to share the repair services with her already crippled sister ship.

The Allies lost the Norwegian land campaign through lack of decent air support and because they put half-trained Territorials against first-class German professional soldiers. But they did win the war at sea. The German Navy's two premier ships, the 32,000-ton battle-cruisers *Scharnhorst* and *Gneisenau*, were out of action for six months. Its most modern heavy cruiser, the 14,000-ton *Blücher*, was sunk by coastal batteries at Narvik. The light-cruiser *Karlsruhe* was torpedoed and sunk by a British submarine off Kristiansand, while her sister-ship, the *Königsberg*, was sent to the bottom by Fleet Air Arm bombers in Bergen. Furthermore, no less than ten of its most modern destroyers were sunk in the battles for Narvik. As a result of these losses, the

German Navy was in no condition to cover the planned invasion of Britain across the Channel and was thus partly responsible for the cancellation of that invasion.

Of Admiral Raeder's big ships involved in the Norwegian campaign, only the *Hipper* was now operational and she did not venture out to sea again until late July. In August 1940 she was reported to be patrolling south of Spitzbergen looking for British shipping. She had no success.

Chapter Five

While the *Hipper*, taking full advantage of the endless daylight of the Arctic summer, carried on her fruitless search for enemy shipping, 6,500 miles to the south, in the Cape of Good Hope, it was winter. That is to say, it was the season when the sun was furthest north in its annual round, for winter at the Cape is not the dramatic event it is in the far north. From time to time gales move in from the open Atlantic, but they lack the concentrated fury of those in the opposite hemisphere; for the most part the weather is largely benign. And it was so when the Dutch navigator Jan van Riebeek first sailed into Table Bay on 6 August 1750. Van Riebeek found that the bay afforded a safe anchorage in all but winds from the north and north-west, a stream of good fresh water ran into the sea near an accessible beach, and cattle were available ashore. Taking possession in the name of the Dutch East India Company, he established a victualling station for the Company's ships trading to and from India and the Far East.

At the turn of the twentieth century, Lord James Bryce, British historian and diplomat, waxed lyrical in his description of the city Jan van Riebeek founded: 'For a few hours only before reaching Cape Town does one discern on the eastern horizon the stern grey mountains that rise along the coast. A nobler site for a city and a naval stronghold than that of the capital of South Africa can hardly be imagined. It rivals Gibraltar and Constantinople, Bombay and San Francisco. Immediately behind the town, which lies along the sea, the majestic mass of Table Mountain rises to a height of 3,600 feet, a steep slope capped by a long line of sheer

46

precipices more than 1000 feet high, and to the right and left by bold, isolated peaks. The beautiful sweep of the Bay in front, the towering crags behind, and the romantic pinnacles which rise on either side, make a landscape that no one who has ever seen it can forget.'

The noble Lord's impression of Africa's southernmost city fitted as well in August 1940 as it had at the beginning of the century. The powerful landscape was unchanged and Cape Town had once again assumed a vital role on the sea route to the East. The entry of Italy into the war had closed the Mediterranean to Allied ships, forcing them to make the long haul around the Cape. This resulted in a steady stream of merchantmen calling in at Cape Town to take on stores, bunkers and water, and, not least, to give their war-weary crews a short respite from the bloody battle raging further north in the Atlantic.

The 'deliverance of Dunkirk', as Churchill described it, had saved nearly 350,000 British and French troops, but they left behind them the bulk of their equipment; 2,300 guns, 82,000 vehicles, 8000 Bren Guns, 400 anti-tank rifles, 90,000 rifles and 7000 tons of ammunition, all lost. Britain now lay under the threat of invasion and with little means of defending herself. Hitler, brimming with confidence after seeing his troops march triumphantly through the Arc de Triomphe and down the Champs-Elysées, had in fact set the date of Operation 'Sea Lion' as 21 September.

The very survival of Britain, now more than ever, depended on her merchant ships getting through with arms and equipment from America, food from the Empire and oil from the Persian Gulf. The fall of France had been a particularly heavy blow for the Royal Navy, resulting in the loss of most of the French destroyers and convoy escort vessels. At the same time the Italians had brought in another 118 submarines to be unleashed against the convoys. The Italians were not in the same league as Dönitz's U-boats, but the sheer weight of numbers was beginning to tell. In June and July 1940, the first two months of the changed situation, nearly half a million tons of Allied shipping was lost. The carnage continued throughout August with ships going down at the rate of three a day and men dying in their hundreds in the cold waters of the Atlantic.

Far removed from all this, Cape Town, resting serenely in the lee of its Table Mountain, remained a safe haven, as it had so been since Jan van Riebeek first landed 190 years earlier. South Africa was at war, but then war in the southern hemisphere was largely only a state of mind. In Cape Town the lights still burned brightly, luxuries long since disappeared in Britain filled the shops, restaurants still served steaks and lobster, and the drink flowed freely. Moreover, the white people of the city made heroes of visiting Allied seamen. In the midst of a savage war Cape Town was a place to rest and relax, where nerves stretched beyond breaking point were soothed and healed. So it appeared to the thirty-six-man crew of the tanker *British Commander* when, on 19 August 1940, they entered Table Bay. Sailing from Falmouth at the end of July, bound for Abadan in ballast, they had left behind a country stretched on the wrack of war, then mustering its meagre forces to repel a threatened invasion and already heavily under attack from the air. Food was rationed, morale beginning to flag and, although the summer sun shone, there was a greyness in the air.

The *British Commander*, commanded by Captain J. Thornton, joined a lightly-escorted Gibraltar-bound convoy in the Western Approaches and for five days ran the gauntlet of U-boats and long-range bombers operating from their new bases in Western France. Abreast the entrance to the Straits of Gibraltar she parted company with the other ships and continued south alone.

The 6901-ton *British Commander*, built in 1922, had seen her best days and was rarely able to achieve 10 knots, and then her ageing turbines were always dangerously close to breakdown. Outwardly, she appeared well-armed for a merchant ship of her day, carrying a 4-inch anti-submarine gun, a 12-pounder HA/LA and an assortment of heavy machine guns. In compliance with the Geneva Convention, both the 4-inch and the 12-pounder were mounted on the tanker's stern, so they were only really of any use when running away from an enemy.

The stark reality of the *British Commander*'s defensive equipment was that her guns were older even than the ship and were manned by ship's personnel, whose experience with such weapons extended no further than a one-day gunnery course snatched while in port in the UK. The only professional on board was a sergeant seconded to the ship from the Royal Marines. He had worked hard to lick the scratch guns' crews into shape, but he was dealing with men who, for all their enthusiasm, had other things on their minds – mainly the day-to-day running of the ship. Furthermore, there was precious little ammunition to spare for practice shoots. Clearly, the *British Commander*'s armament was no match for the guns of Hitler's Kriegsmarine.

Once south of the Canary Islands they were in relatively safe waters, but there was always the danger that some of the long-range U-boats had extended their radius of operation. And then there was the threat of surface raiders. Captain Thornton had been warned that at least two of these converted merchantmen were at large in southern latitudes. The long watches were filled with tension and frustration.

The bunker call at Cape Town, short as it was, had afforded Thornton and his men a night's untroubled sleep, a run ashore and a glimpse of a world without war. When, on the morning of the 20th, they sailed out of Cape Town, the crisp, clear air was heady with the scent of woodsmoke, the sky washed clear blue by the rains of the night before. With them the tanker's crew carried memories of a land of plenty, of fine brandy and aromatic Rhodesian cigarettes, and long-limbed, tanned girls who had not forgotten how to laugh.

As she left the shelter of Cape Town's breakwaters, the *British Commander* met the first of the long Cape Rollers and curtseyed deep. Rounding Green Point, she rolled ponderously, crockery crashed in the pantry, doors slammed and the hull creaked noisily as the sea probed its weaknesses. Then she settled down on a southerly course, roller-coastering down to the Cape, fine spray whipping over her bows to form a shimmering rainbow each time she dipped low to the swell. Twelve hours later, having rounded the Cape of Good Hope and set course to the east, Captain Thornton watched the powerful light on Cape Agulhas dipping astern. They had passed from the troubled Atlantic into the gentler world of the Indian Ocean.

Although the Japanese threat was growing in the East, for the time being, at least, trade in the blue waters of the Indian Ocean carried on much as it had done before. No U-boats had yet reached east of the Cape and as yet only one German surface

49

raider was known to be active. And so the trade routes remained open, with hundreds of Allied merchantmen criss-crossing the ocean, mainly unescorted. It was not that it was thought no escorts were needed, but the Royal Navy's presence here was more symbolic than threatening. Based at Colombo, the India Squadron consisted of a handful of veteran cruisers and destroyers, supplemented by two ex-passenger liner AMCs. In an ocean variously measured as being between 17 million and 33 million square miles, the role of this small force was limited to patrolling potential trouble spots and showing the flag, just as it had done in the peacetime days of Empire. Escorting merchant ships, either singly or in convoy, was out of the question.

Hugging the coast until abeam of East London to avoid the full strength of the west-flowing Agulhas current, the *British Commander* then set course to pass to the south of Madagascar, before altering to the north. The shortest route to the Persian Gulf and India from the south lies through the Mozambique Channel, between Madagascar and the African mainland, but in time of war there was no better place to set up an ambush. In accordance with Admiralty instructions, all Allied shipping now took the outside route. This added some 300 miles to the passage, but at the time was thought to be a safe option.

Once clear of the South African coast, the *British Commander* moved into pleasant sub-tropical weather. To the north of Madagascar the south-west monsoon was still blowing hard and there would be rough seas and grey, rain-laden skies to come. For the time being the days were fine and clear, with light winds and calm seas; the nights dark and comforting.

On 24 August, when the tanker was mid-way across the southern entrance to the Mozambique Channel, there was a sudden flurry of excitement when a British flying boat appeared overhead. The plane circled the ship twice before flying back towards the land. There was no communication between the ship and the aircraft, but the fleeting visit served to assure those on board the tanker that someone was watching over them. Otherwise, the days passed without even a smudge of smoke on the horizon.

The first sign of trouble came two days later, on the 26th, when the *British Commander* was off Cape St. Mary, southernmost point of Madagascar, and about to enter the Indian Ocean proper. A little before sunset Radio Officer Watson picked up a distress call from the Norwegian ship *Bernes*, reporting she had been stopped by a 'suspicious vessel with two funnels'. The *Bernes* gave a position which was only 170 miles north-west of the *British Commander*. This gave rise to some concern, but within 15 minutes the *Bernes* cancelled her SOS and Thornton assumed her interceptor must have been a British AMC. The two funnels mentioned would seem to support this theory.

At around 0100 on 27 August the *British Commander* was clear of Madagascar and altered course to the north to pass westwards of the island of Reunion. The moon had not yet risen and the darkness was intense, but the glow cast by the swathes of brilliant stars that hung in the velvet sky was enough to show an empty horizon all round. The night was hot and muggy, and Thornton, who had been on the bridge of the tanker for some hours, decided he could now safely catch up on lost sleep. Leaving Second Officer Mitchison in charge, he went below.

It seemed to Thornton that he had been asleep only for a matter of minutes when a persistent knocking on his door prodded him awake again. A breathless apprentice, his voice squeaky with excitement, informed him that he was wanted on the bridge at once. Instantly alert, Thornton looked at his watch. The time was 0418: he had been asleep for almost four hours.

Tumbling out of his bunk – he was still fully clothed – Thornton made for the door, and as he did so, he heard what sounded uncomfortably like the crump of a shell landing close by. He ran for the bridge ladder.

Arriving on the bridge, Thornton saw a ship on the *British Commander*'s port quarter at a distance of about 2 miles. Minutes earlier, the stranger had signalled by lamp demanding the tanker's name, and when this had been passed, replied: 'STOP INSTANTLY. DO NOT USE YOUR WIRELESS.' This message, full of menace, had been reinforced by a shot across the bows.

Bearing in mind the *Bernes* and her cancelled SOS of the previous evening, Thornton's first thought was that he was being challenged by the same British AMC. Closer examination of the other ship through binoculars changed his opinion. This ship was low and sleek, with only one funnel, a far cry from the usual high-sided auxiliaries used by the Royal Navy. A flash and a second shell screaming through the *British Commander*'s rigging was sufficient to confirm his suspicions. Thornton ordered the officer of the watch to stop engines.

If there is a god of the sea, then he was not watching over the *British Commander* that night, for it was by pure chance that the German raider *Pinguin* had come upon the tanker. After seizing the *Filefjell*, Ernst Krüder decided to transfer the 500 tons of fuel oil found in the Norwegian's cargo tanks to his own ship. However, being then only 250 miles from Madagascar, which by this time might well be under British control, Krüder deemed it prudent to move to a more remote area before attempting the transfer. With the *Filefjell*, manned by a prize crew, following behind, the *Pinguin* set course to the south, and to an unexpected rendezvous with the *British Commander*.

At 0303 on the 27th an alert lookout at the *Pinguin*'s masthead reported sighting a ship ahead and slightly to port. Examining the stranger through his night glasses, Krüder concluded that she was another tanker, and, being in this area, almost certainly an Allied ship. He ordered the *Filefjell* to drop back and then altered course to pass astern of the stranger. Having done so, he took up station on her port quarter and began to shadow her.

An hour passed, long enough for Krüder to satisfy himself that here was another prize for the taking, an unescorted tanker, in ballast and heading north for the oilfields of the Persian Gulf. At 0400, on the change of the watch, he ordered the 75-mm gun to be manned and loaded. At 0418 the ship was challenged by lamp and immediately afterwards a shot was put across her bows.

There was a pause, then, as the echoes of the shot died away, a light winked back across the dark water. 'B-R-I-T-I-S-H C-O-M-M-A-N-D-E-R', Krüder spelled out. A midshipman at his side leafed quickly through the pages of a pre-war copy of Lloyd's Shipping Index. 'I have it, sir!' he burst out excitedly. '*British Commander*; steam tanker; 6865 tons gross; owners British Tanker Company.'

And so the interception of the *British Commander* might have ended swiftly and peacefully – had it not been for the instinctive reaction of Radio Officer Watson. The crump of the bursting shells and the sudden stillness when the tanker's engines stopped combined to bring him out of a deep sleep. In seconds he was wide awake and running for the wireless room. Throwing the switches, he waited for the main transmitter to come alive and then his hand was on the key. This was something Watson had rehearsed dozens of times in the quiet of the night watches. 'RRRR,' he tapped out urgently, using the code for 'attacked by raider', 'LAT 29.37S LONG 45.50E. STOPPED BY SUSPICIOUS VESSEL.' He repeated the message, which was quickly acknowledged by Durban Radio.

Informed that the British ship was transmitting, Krüder ordered the searchlight to be turned on her. The 15-inch lamp mounted above the *Pinguin*'s bridge hummed into life and its brilliant beam stabbed across the intervening darkness to sweep along the length of the tanker. Reaching the stern, the beam revealed a long-barrelled 4-inch gun with tiny figures moving around it. Without further hesitation, Krüder ordered his 5.9-inch guns' crews to open fire in earnest.

The first salvo went over the *British Commander*, throwing up spouts of water some 50 yards beyond the ship. Caught in the beam of the searchlight like a plastic duck in a fairground shooting range, Captain Thornton decided on swift action. Ordering the helm hard to starboard, he rang for emergency full speed on the engines and brought the tanker short round to present her stern to the enemy. He debated whether to make a fight of it, to order the 4-inch to open fire, but the weight of shells landing around his ship convinced him of the futility of resistance. The ship had not yet been hit and none of his crew injured, so it would be better not to provoke his attacker further. Thornton did, however, make a serious mistake, in that he ordered Radio Officer Watson to resume transmitting the 'RRRR' message.

Watson went back on the air and, in spite of jamming by the *Pinguin*'s transmitter, was soon able to report that Durban, Cape Town and Singapore had acknowledged receipt of his signals. The ether was in fact now alive with signals flashing back and forth between station and station, ship and shore. The outside world had been alerted to the plight of the *British Commander*.

By this time the raider was no more than a mile off the *British Commander*'s port quarter and holding the tanker in the beam of her searchlight. Watson's renewed activity on the morse key brought a swift response from the *Pinguin*'s guns, which were now finding their target and scoring hits above and on the water-line. Fires broke out on board.

Now that Watson's calls for help had been acknowledged, Thornton decided that any further show of defiance in the face of such a heavily armed enemy would serve no useful purpose other than to result in the deaths of many of his crew. Accordingly, he ordered Watson to cease transmitting, then stopped his engines and lay hove-to while preparations were made to abandon ship.

Thornton's actions had an immediate effect. The *Pinguin* ceased firing and her signal lamp flashed again: 'I will sink your ship and will give you 15 minutes to abandon.' Krüder, ever the humanitarian, also wished to avoid bloodshed.

The time was now 0456, the darkest hour before the dawn, and in the light of the flames licking at the *British Commander*'s bridge, Thornton lowered the two lifeboats on the starboard side and the ship was abandoned, swiftly but without panic. The burning ship was between the boats and her attacker, and, shipping the oars, Thornton ordered his men to row to the west. His hope was that they could slip away unseen under the cover of darkness and perhaps take advantage of the South Equatorial Current, which flows westwards at up to 2 knots in this area, to reach the coast of South Africa. It was a forlorn hope; it would be daylight in less than an hour and Thornton was realist enough to know that the enemy would never let them get away.

The survivors had not rowed more than 50 yards from the ship when a torpedo fired by the *Pinguin* slammed into her side and exploded with a deafening roar. For many ships this would have been the end, but the *British Commander*, built at the Caledon Yard in Dundee with a strong riveted hull, deep transverse frames and longitudinal bulkheads, was, like most tankers of her day, virtually unsinkable. Krüder's torpedo struck on her port side, in the vicinity of her No.3 main tank, and blew a large hole in her hull. The sea poured into the empty tank, her foremast collapsed and she took a heavy list to port. However, in spite of all this, she remained stubbornly afloat. It would take another forty shells from the *Pinguin*'s guns to set her blazing fiercely and finally sink her.

Thornton and his crew, who, realizing there was no escape

for them, had laid back on their oars to watch the end of their ship, were taken on board the *Pinguin* to join the prisoners from the *Domingo de Larrinaga* and the *Filefjell*. Thornton found himself treated with the utmost courtesy and had what he called an 'interesting interview' with Krüder. 'He called me to his cabin,' Thornton related, 'and asked me why I had sent a wireless message after he had told me not to. He said that as a master of a merchant vessel my first duty was the safety of my crew. He remarked that he had been very forebearing with me, and said that I was very fortunate not to be dead with half my crew. I replied that it was my duty to send a wireless message. He then asked me if I thought it likely that all British ships would do the same. I said that I thought they would. "Under any circumstances?" he asked, and I replied, "Yes, I think so." He seemed to be very concerned at the likelihood of distress messages being transmitted and told me that merchant seamen were not soldiers, they had no right to endanger their lives, and it would have been my responsibility had any of my crew been killed.'

In his conversation with Thornton, Krüder revealed his complete lack of understanding of the British merchant seaman, a dedicated professional who fiercely resented any attack on his ship and was prepared to fight back whenever possible. Krüder's inability to appreciate the motivation of his so-called non-combatant enemy was common throughout the German Navy and must have contributed in no small way to its inability to sever Britain's maritime supply lines.

The *British Commander* finally succumbed to the onslaught of the *Pinguin*'s shells at 0615 and rolled over to expose her rusty bottom to the rays of the rising sun before taking her last plunge. At 0650 Krüder, now being anxious to clear the area before the Royal Navy arrived on the scene, set course 110° to go deeper into the Indian Ocean.

The raider's engines had not yet worked up to full speed when another ship was sighted coming up astern. It soon became apparent from her general outline and foaming bow-wave that this was a fast, modern cargo liner. She was, in fact, the 5008-ton *Morviken*, owned by Wallem, Steckmest of Bergen, and built in Bremen in 1938. Commanded by Captain Anton Norvalls, the

14-knot motor ship was bound from Cape Town to Calcutta in ballast. She was unarmed.

Although he was anxious to put as much distance between himself and his last victim, Krüder was unable to resist such a tempting target. Altering course to port, he took the *Pinguin* around in a wide circle, crossed the stranger's stern and came up on her starboard side. Although the other ship must have been aware of the *Pinguin* and witness to her obviously predatory manoeuvre, she appeared to take no notice of the raider. She made no attempt to turn away, nor was there any sign of unusual activity on her decks. Krüder accepted this as an illustration of how complacent Allied shipping in the Indian Ocean had become. It was his intention to change all that.

Correctly surmising that the elegant-looking ship – she had raked masts, clipper bow and counter stern, and smart paintwork – was not British, Krüder hoisted the two-letter flag signal 'SN' – Stop or I will sink you! – at *Pinguin*'s yardarm. And, to add weight to the signal, Krüder put a shot across the bows of the ship with his 75-mm. This brought an immediate response. The *Morviken* ran up her Norwegian ensign, stopped her engines, went astern and, when the way was off her, lay drifting, awaiting her fate. She made no attempt to use her radio.

Leutnant Warning, who was again in charge of the boarding party, was surprised at the degree of cooperation shown by the *Morviken*'s crew when he boarded the Norwegian. His orders were obeyed without question, almost with enthusiasm. Captain Norvalls, who spoke fluent German, was beside himself at the thought of his beautiful ship being sunk, even offering to take her to Germany himself, rather than lose her. But Norvalls' pleas fell on deaf ears. Much as he would have liked to take the *Morviken* as a prize, Krüder had no time to waste. Scuttling charges were set in the engine-room and, once her 35-man crew had been transferred to the *Pinguin*, the bottom was blown out of the *Morviken*. The only booty taken from her was her motor lifeboat, a fine craft with a powerful engine, which Krüder intended to use for future boarding parties. The *Morviken* sank at 1100, her last resting place in 2,500 fathoms, 300 miles south of Cape St. Mary.

It seemed that the *Pinguin* was fated not to get away from this area, for as she put the sinking *Morviken* astern, the *Filefjell* rejoined to report a large Allied cargo ship in sight just over the horizon to the west. Krüder was sorely tempted by the prospect of another easy victim – three in the space of a few hours – but to pursue this latest arrival would mean backtracking towards the scene of the *British Commander* sinking. This would perhaps be taking one chance too many.

The German captain was correct in his assumption. As a result of the *British Commander*'s RRRR calls, the hunt for the *Pinguin* was already under way. The British cruisers *Colombo* and *Neptune*, and the AMCs *Arawa* and *Kanimbla*, all coming from different points of the compass, were homing in on the raider at full speed.

That it was time for the *Pinguin* to show a clean pair of heels was beyond argument, but before she quitted the area there was the problem of the *Filefjell* to be solved. For some time Krüder had been conscious that the captured Norwegian tanker was becoming a liability, but, much as he would have liked to send her priceless cargo of aviation spirit back to Germany, he had no time to make the necessary preparations for the long voyage. There was no other choice but to sacrifice the tanker and her cargo.

After dark that night, both ships having steamed some 140 miles to the south-east, they hove-to and the 500 tons of fuel oil were transferred from the *Filefjell* and her storerooms were cleared of all usable provisions. At 1900, after scuttling charges had been laid, the tanker was abandoned and Krüder took the *Pinguin* well away to watch the death throes of his prize.

Contrary to all expectations, the *Filefjell* did not explode in a ball of fire when the scuttling charges went off. There was a muffled thud and she was obviously holed, for she began to settle by the stern, but she did not catch fire. Five hours later, at 0100 on the 28th, she was still very much afloat and Krüder was once again forced to bring his guns to bear. The 75-mm was used first, but its small shells had no appreciable effect on the tanker. One of the 5.9s was then manned, and its second shell hit the *Filefjell* near the waterline, forward of the engine-room, with immediate and dramatic results. A great sheet of flame shot skywards, petrol gushed out of the hole in the ship's side, caught fire and then spread a sea of flames around the ship. The *Filefjell*'s other tanks now exploded one by one with a thunderous roar, each sending a giant orange fireball soaring 150 feet or so into the night sky. When dawn came the *Pinguin* was 50 miles to the south-east, but the pall of smoke hanging over the burning tanker was still visible on the horizon.

Later that morning the *Pinguin*'s wireless office picked up radio transmissions very close by; so close that no accurate bearings of the signal could be obtained. In his log Krüder wrote: 'The enemy was either a Sunderland flying boat from the land or an enemy cruiser or AMC was searching in the area where *British Commander* sunk and looking for Ship 33.'

Fortunately for the *Pinguin*, the weather had by then deteriorated, and cloud and rain were restricting visibility. She sailed on undetected. Krüder's next log entry read: 'It is my intention to stay one more week in this bad weather in the south, where we are unlikely to be seen and then move to 30 S 60 E to carry on the hunt. It should then be possible to meet steamers from the Sunda Strait and especially ships homeward bound from Australia. The aircraft will be sent up to reconnoitre when reaching 30 S.'

Chapter Six

Reaching the conclusion that the *Pinguin* could not masquerade
for much longer as the Greek steamer *Kassos*, Krüder now looked
around for a quiet spot in which to assume a new identity. He
decided to head south-east where, well away from the normal
shipping lanes, he hoped to find solitude and fair weather.

The ocean appeared empty at first, but shortly after noon on
the 29th, having steamed 540 miles on a course of 134 degrees,
Krüder was horrified to see the masts and funnel of a large ship
coming over the horizon. Within minutes she was hull-up and
showing the very distinctive lines of a Blue Funnel cargo liner of
10,000 to 12,000 tons, a possible British armed merchant cruiser.

Krüder sent his men quietly to their actions stations, but maintained his course and speed, hoping to bluff it out, for he had no
wish to be involved in a shoot-out with the enemy. When the two
ships were close, he exchanged the usual 'What ship? Where
bound?' pleasantries by lamp, ordering his yeoman of signals to
send slowly and hesitantly, in the manner of any run-of-the-mill
Greek tramp. The British ship reciprocated and went on her way.
Krüder never did establish whether he had passed up the chance
of a valuable prize or narrowly escaped a brush with the Royal
Navy.

On the 31st the *Pinguin* reached a position 600 miles to the
north-west of the uninhabited Amsterdam & St. Paul Islands, a
spot as remote as can be found in the Indian Ocean. Hove-to in
fine weather, the raider then began her second change of identity,
this time becoming the Wilhelmsen liner *Trafalgar*. Krüder's
decision to adopt this disguise was prompted by Captain Norvalls

of the *Morviken*, who said he had taken the *Pinguin* for a Wilhelmsen ship when they met. The Norwegian Wilhelmsen Line ran crack cargo liners on the Far East trade, ships renowned for their smart appearance. Suitably painted, the *Pinguin* would fit the bill.

After drifting for five days in his lonely hiding place, Krüder thought it prudent to send his aircraft up to scan the surrounding area. As luck would have it, he chose a day when the wind arose without warning, setting up a short, steep sea. Unwilling to cancel the launch, he steamed around in a wide circle, creating an area of comparatively calm water with his wake. The Heinkel was hoisted over the side and began its run. Unfortunately, the pilot ran out of calm water before he had gained sufficient speed for take-off and the seaplane crashed nose-first into the first big wave it met. The engine broke away from its mountings, petrol spewed out from a broken pipe and the plane was engulfed in flames. The pilot and observer saved themselves by jumping into the sea, but the aircraft was a total loss.

As there was a spare Heinkel in the hold, the destruction of the plane was not a complete disaster, but the loss of the portable radio telephone that went down with it was. This set, the only one on board, operated on a wavelength which British ships were unable to listen in to and had been a priceless asset in communications between the *Pinguin* and her airborne eyes.

Another five days passed then, on 10 September, the *Pinguin*'s change of identity was complete. With her hull painted black relieved by a continuous white band running around her sheer strake, her upperworks white and her funnel black with two narrow light blue bands, Wilhelm Wilhelmsen himself would have accepted her as one of his own. The name *Trafalgar*, in white on her bows and stern, looked authentic, and who was to know that the real *Trafalgar* was otherwise occupied in the North Atlantic?

Now that the *Pinguin* had a new disguise, Krüder decided to make one more sweep in the direction of Madagascar before setting off for Australian waters, where he was to lay his mines. Later that day, as the raider steamed north-westerly at 16 knots, anxious to be back at work, her wireless office intercepted an SOS from the British ship *Benarty*, reporting she was under attack

60

by an enemy aircraft some 800 miles to the north-east. Krüder assumed, and correctly so, that this was the work of the *Atlantis*. Not only had Rogge sunk the 5800-ton *Benarty*, but he had also gathered a rich harvest of secret mail and papers found on board. Unknown to Krüder, he too was soon to make the acquaintance of the prestigious Ben Line.

Founded in 1820 by Alexander and William Thomson, Ben Line grew from one sailing vessel carrying marble from Leghorn for the family business in Edinburgh into a proud Scottish institution operating, in 1939, a twenty-strong fleet of crack steamers totalling 145,750 tons gross. These ships, always maintained to the highest standards, traded between British ports and Malaya, Singapore, the Philippines, Hong Kong, China and Japan. On a prestige trade, carrying prestige cargoes, they enjoyed a reputation for service and efficiency second to none. Ben Line's great strength lay mainly in its adherence to its Scottish roots, firmly based in the port of Leith and manned almost exclusively by Scottish officers and deck ratings, with Chinese in the engine-room and catering departments as a concession to its Eastern interests. A berth in one of these ships was much sought after, for Ben Line looked after its men, who in turn looked after its ships.

The 5872-ton *Benavon* sailed from Penang on the morning of 31 August, bound for London, via Durban, with a cargo of hemp, jute and rubber. She had previously loaded in Manila and Singapore. Commanded by Captain A. Thomson, the 10-year-old ship had a total complement of forty-eight, the usual mix of Scots and Chinese, with six of the deck crew being Shetland islanders.

From the time of sailing from Penang, Captain Thomson was aware that a German surface raider was at large in the Indian Ocean, but had not been unduly troubled by the news. The ocean was big and the likelihood of the *Benavon* meeting the raider was remote. When news of the attack on the *Benarty* came through on the 10th, the *Benavon* was already off Réunion and nearly 600 miles to the south-west of the position given. Thomson felt safe to assume that he had slipped past the danger. He was also assuming that only one German raider was at work.

At 6.45 on the morning of the 12th the *Benavon* was 330 miles due east of Cape St. Mary and making 12 knots on a west-south-westerly course in fine weather. The normal day's routine was then already under way. Chief Officer James Cameron was in the chartroom working out his morning star sights, while Cadet Graham Spiers kept a lookout in the wheelhouse. At the helm Able Seaman Magnus Slater contemplated the breakfast that would be waiting when his watch finished at 8 o'clock, using only a spoke or two each way to keep the ship on course in the calm sea. Boatswain Andrew Ollason was on his way up to the bridge to discuss the day's work with Cameron. Deep in the engine-room, where the *Benavon*'s Scottish-built engine reeled off the miles with a steady beat, Second Engineer Crawford paced up and down near the controls, his mind on nothing in particular.

God was in his heaven and all was well with the *Benavon*. Then Cadet Spiers saw the other ship, broad on the port bow and on a converging course.

Called to the wheelhouse, Chief Officer Cameron studied the stranger through his binoculars. As the morning haze cleared, he saw she was flying the Norwegian flag. Her sleek lines and paint-work suggested she was one of Wilhelmsen's – probably bound for the Malacca Straits, Cameron concluded. Through his binoculars he made out the name *Trafalgar* painted on the bows. She was a Wilhelmsen ship all right.

As a routine precaution, Cameron took compass bearings of the approaching ship and soon established that she was on a collision course with the *Benavon*. Such a situation is common at sea and is catered for by the International Collision Regulations, which clearly state: 'When two steam vessels are crossing, so as to involve risk of collision, the vessel which has the other on her own starboard side shall keep out of the way of the other.' In this case the *Benavon* was clearly the 'stand-on' ship, so Cameron maintained his course and speed.

The minutes ticked by and, as the other ship bore down on the *Benavon*, making no effort to alter course, Cameron became increasingly uneasy. The situation was ludicrous: two ships, in sight of each other and alone on an empty ocean, were in danger of colliding. Yet the rules were unambiguous. In order to avoid confusion which might lead to a collision, the *Benavon* must stand on, for the time being, and wait for the other ship to get out of the way.

The fact that the Norwegian ship might not be as innocent as she appeared had not occurred to James Cameron, and he was prepared to excuse her conduct by assuming her chief officer was, as he had himself been, busy working out morning stars and had not posted a lookout. But, by the time the two ships were only just over a mile apart and still closing, Cameron became thoroughly alarmed. He blew a long blast on the *Benavon*'s whistle. The other ship continued to close.

The throaty roar of the steam whistle brought Captain Thomson to the *Benavon*'s bridge, still in his pyjamas. He summed up the situation quickly and ordered the helm hard to starboard. The spokes of the wheel spun through Magnus Slater's hands and the *Benavon* sheered away from the danger, presenting her stern to the other ship.

The *Trafalgar* now dropped all pretence of innocence. The German naval ensign, with its menacing black swastika, was hoisted to the gaff and the signal to stop, 'SN', broken out at the yardarm. The flags confirmed Thomson's already growing suspicions. He punched the alarm button and the bells shrilled out, sending the *Benavon*'s crew to their action stations.

Chief Engineer R.C. Porteous, who habitually slept with half an ear cocked for a change in the beat of his beloved engine, was wide awake as soon as the *Benavon*'s propellor began to race as she turned under full helm. He was out of his bunk and running aft along the alleyway when the first shell hit the water with a sharp crack. Bursting out onto the deck, he saw a ship lying across the *Benavon*'s stern no more than 500 yards off. A small cloud of blue smoke hung over her bows.

Porteous returned to his cabin, threw on some clothes and ran for the bridge. As he climbed the second ladder from the deck two rungs at a time, another shell landed in the water close alongside. He stopped momentarily, ducked as shrapnel whined over his head and then continued on up. At the top of the ladder he found the pyjama-clad Captain Thomson in complete control of the situation and, if necessary, determined to make a fight of it. His first words to Porteous were: 'I want everything you've got, Chief. Now!' Porteous slid down the ladder on the handrails, his feet not touching the rungs. On reaching the engine control platform minutes later, he spun the main steam valve wide open and the gleaming piston rods of the *Benavon*'s triple-expansion steam engine accelerated their beat. The ship surged forward, and the chase was on.

Aft, on the *Benavon*'s poop deck, Second Officer J. Robertson and his gun's crew hastily loaded the 4-inch and prepared, for the first time, to fire a shot in anger. On the bridge of the *Pinguin*, Krüder observed their preparations and, with some regret, ordered his 5.9s to open fire.

The fight almost came to a sudden end when the first shell fired by the *Benavon*'s 4-inch ricocheted off the water and penetrated the *Pinguin*'s hull near her after cargo hatch. The shell failed to explode, bounced off a ventilator shaft and ended up in the stokers' mess. With great presence of mind, and almost comical nonchalance, Bootsmann (Petty Officer) Streil, who was in the mess, took off his cap, used it to pick up the still hot shell, and heaved it back out through the hole it had made in the ship's side.

Thanks partly to the bravery of Bootsmann Streil, but mainly to the inexperience of the *Benavon*'s gun's crew, who had omitted to fuse the shell, the *Pinguin* and her crew narrowly escaped sudden extinction. The stokers' mess, adjacent to the raider's mine compartment, at that time contained row upon row of horned mines, each packed with enough explosives to blow the ship apart.

Angry now that he should have been fool enough to allow the enemy to strike the first blow, Krüder ordered his guns to open fire in earnest. The *Benavon*, having worked up to a speed that strained every rivet in her hull, was zig-zagging wildly, her 4-inch lobbing shells at the pursuing *Pinguin*. But this was little more than a brave show of defiance. With the exception of one DEMS gunner, the men who manned the gun were only enthusiastic amateurs. Their first shot had been a fluke and they were unlikely to repeat it. Nevertheless, Krüder was not to have it all his own way. Eight salvoes were fired by his 5.9s before they scored a hit on the fleeing merchantman. Unfortunately for the *Benavon*, one of the raider's shells hit the ready-use ammunition locker on her poop. When the smoke and flames cleared, the 4-inch gun and its gallant crew had disappeared.

Having found the range, the *Pinguin*'s gunners pounded the British ship with determination, using every gun that could be brought to bear. First her mainmast went, toppling like a tall tree, and bringing the wireless aerials down with it. This successfully silenced Radio Officer Charles Clarke, who throughout the fight had stuck to his morse key sending out urgent calls for help. Then the *Benavon*'s funnel, taking a direct hit at the base, crumpled and fell. With her boiler furnaces starved of draught, she began to lose way.

It would have done Ernst Krüder great credit if he had now ceased fire, but the German commander was so angry at the defiance showed by the British merchantman that he continued to punish her. Shell after shell smashed into her hull and upperworks, her lifeboats were reduced to matchwood, fires broke out, men died as they ran for cover.

The situation aboard the *Benavon* soon became hopeless; fires raged out of control on deck and in the accommodation, and her engine-room was filled with steam and smoke. Reluctantly, for he too was angry, Captain Thomson gave the order to abandon ship. No sooner was the word passed below than one of the *Pinguin*'s murderous salvoes struck the bridge, killing Thomson and his entire complement of deck officers. Chief Officer Cameron, Second Officer Robertson, Third Officer Milne and Radio Officer Clarke all died in the carnage, while the helmsman, Magnus Slater, was seriously wounded. Only then did Krüder cease fire.

Chief Engineer Porteous, driven out of his engine-room by fire, reached the deck to find himself, as the senior surviving officer, in command of the *Benavon*; that is to say he was charged with saving all who could be saved. The lifeboats were smashed, but with the assistance of Second Engineer Crawford and Boatswain Ollason, Porteous launched a wooden liferaft and helped the survivors, many of whom were wounded, over the side. They were twenty-four in all, the wounded aboard the raft, the others in the water clinging to its sides. As the raft drifted away from the ship's side, Third Engineer Johnson, who had been very seriously injured, died.

Krüder was still smarting from the blow inflicted on his pride and, although the *Benavon* was ablaze from stem to stern, with survivors clearly visible in the water, he waited for a full hour before sending a boat. A boarding party found five more men, three of them injured, in the burning shambles of the once elegant ship. A total of twenty-eight survivors were picked up and brought back to the *Pinguin*. Of these, three, including Magnus Slater, died on board the raider, despite the efforts of the German ship's surgeons.

The unequal battle between the *Pinguin* and the *Benavon* lasted for over an hour, during which time the raider fired fifty-nine shells from her 5.9s, finally reducing the British ship to a burning hulk manned by the dead and dying. In retrospect, it might be said that Captain Thomson, through his stubborn refusal to surrender, brought upon himself and his ship this dreadful end. This was, indeed, Ernst Krüder's opinion, but Thomson and his men would not have had it any other way. They had been given guns with which to defend themselves against attack and had used them. They great pity was that the Admiralty, which supplied the guns, did not see fit to train these men to use them. Had this been done, the *Pinguin* may well have met her end on that September day in the Indian Ocean.

The *Benavon* was left to burn herself out, the rubber in her cargo sending clouds of black, oily smoke rolling out over the blue waters to form her funeral pall. Within sight of her, Krüder stopped the *Pinguin* and buried, with full military honours, the three brave men who died aboard his ship. The twenty-five survivors, seven British and eighteen Chinese, joined those prisoners already below decks.

Krüder was by now receiving signals from Berlin indicating that he had overstayed his welcome in these waters. It was time for him to move eastwards, to attend to the important business of mining the approaches to Australian ports. But Krüder had tasted success and wanted more. He did sail east, but kept as close as possible to the Australia–Cape trade route in the hope of falling in with more homeward-bound British ships.

At first he was disappointed, four days passing without a sighting of any sort, possibly as a result of the panic caused by two German raiders being active in the area. Then, on the 16th, along came another easy victim, again a Norwegian.

The 4111-ton motor vessel *Nordvard*, an ex-German ship built in 1925, was on her way from Fremantle to Port Elizabeth when she ran straight into Krüder's open arms. Being down to her winter marks with 7,500 tons of grain, the *Nordvard* had little chance of running away when the *Pinguin* came over the horizon – not that she had any such intention. She offered no resistance, stopping and surrendering without a shot being fired.

A quick examination of the Norwegian ship showed her to be the answer to a problem which had been troubling Krüder for some time. He then had on board the *Pinguin* 170 prisoners – the *Norvard*'s crew of thirty would make this up to a round 200 – an ever-increasing strain on the raider's accommodation and her food and water supplies, to say nothing of the constant threat of unrest breaking out on board. Krüder decided to send the *Nordvard* home, taking with her a valuable cargo of grain that would be much appreciated in Germany, and most of the prisoners. For some reason not explained – possibly because he regarded these men as potential trouble makers – he elected to keep on board the *Pinguin* Captain Thornton of the *British Commander*, Captain Chalmers of the *Domingo de Larrinaga*, their six deck officers, along with the Third Radio Officer, Gunner and Messroom Steward of the *British Commander*. A prize crew took over the *Nordvard* and she was prepared for the long voyage back to Europe. This involved transferring from the *Pinguin* 270 tons of diesel oil, 100 tons of fresh water and provisions for 200 men for two months. The prisoners were sent over and, on 19 September, the *Nordvard* sailed for Bordeaux under the command of Leutnant Hans Neumeir, an ex-merchant service officer.

Krüder considered the delay involved in preparing the *Nordvard* was well justified by the need to get rid of his prisoners, but it played havoc with his timetable for laying mines in Australian coastal waters. His orders specified that the mines were to be laid in the new moon period at the end of September, but this was now clearly out of the question. The operation would have to be postponed until the end of October, when similar conditions would prevail. In which case Krüder had plenty of time on his hands and he intended to put this to good use by heading north-eastwards to cross the busy shipping routes between Australia, the Sunda Strait and India. Meanwhile, the *Pinguin*, having disposed of six Allied ships of 34,865 tons in six weeks, had earned the right to rest on her laurels.

Krüder's decision to move on proved to be a wise one. In the early hours of the following day an SOS was intercepted from the 10,000-ton French passenger liner *Commissaire Ramel*. 'RRRR 28-25S 74-23E COMMISSAIRE RAMEL GUNNED,' the French ship tapped out urgently, a call for help becoming all too familiar in these waters. The position given was only 90 miles north of the *Pinguin* and the attacker was almost certainly Rogge's *Atlantis*. The two raiders were operating much too close to each other.

Steaming at an economical speed of 7 knots, which more than halved the *Pinguin*'s daily fuel consumption, Krüder cruised north-eastwards, killing time while his crew basked in the warm sunshine. On the 27th, with the ship on the Tropic of Capricorn and 760 miles due north of Amsterdam & St. Paul, the spare Heinkel was brought up on deck and assembled. Krüder intended to make good use of the time in hand, mounting a daily all-round air reconnaissance to search for Allied shipping. But the days went by and September moved into October without so much as a lonely seagull being sighted. So far as was possible Krüder kept his men occupied with ship maintenance, while a supply of films on board helped to while away the long, warm evenings, but it was difficult to hold boredom at bay.

By 7 October, having steamed across 2,800 miles of empty ocean at reduced speed, the *Pinguin* was south of Christmas Island and had come as far east as she could without running out of sea room. Then, as the first rays of the rising sun fingered the horizon, yet another unsuspecting Norwegian crossed the raider's path. She was the 8998-ton motor tanker *Storstad*, bound from Borneo to Melbourne with 12,000 tons of diesel and 500 tons of heavy fuel oil.

The *Storstad*, owned by Skibs A/S Sommerstad of Oslo, was unarmed and the usual flag hoist and a shot across her bows with the 75-mm was sufficient to bring about her immediate surrender. The boarding party was offered full cooperation by the Norwegian's 36-man crew and within the hour the *Storstad* had a prize crew on board and was following obediently in the *Pinguin*'s wake.

For some time Krüder had been convinced that the minelaying plan devised by Berlin was too ambitious to be carried out by one ship alone and he had been on the lookout for an auxiliary. A thorough inspection of the captured tanker revealed her to be suitable for the role. She was taken to a deserted spot midway between Java and Australia's North-West Cape, where her after-accommodation was stripped out and converted into a mine deck, complete with rails for launching. A total of 110 mines were then transferred from the *Pinguin* using the motor cutter so kindly donated by the *Morviken*'s crew. At the same time 1,200 tons of diesel oil were pumped across from the *Storstad* to top up the *Pinguin*'s tanks.

Showing a flair for the dramatic, Krüder renamed his new acquisition *Passat*, the old German name for the North-East trade wind of the Atlantic. One of the big four-masted German barques still trading up until the outbreak of the war also carried this name, but she was presently laid up in Hamburg. Leutnant Erich Warning, temporarily promoted to Kapitänleutnant by Krüder, took command of the *Passat*, taking with him from the *Pinguin* two navigating officers, one engineer officer, eight petty officers and nineteen ratings. Five members of the tanker's Norwegian crew volunteered to stay on board to man the engine-room.

At 0300 on 12 October the *Passat* took her leave, her orders to lay mines in the Bass Strait near the approaches to Melbourne, and in the Banks Strait, which runs between Flinders Island and Tasmania. While she was thus occupied, the *Pinguin* would lay her mines in the busy approaches to Sydney and Newcastle on the east coast, and subsequently off the southern Tasmanian port of Hobart. Their tasks completed, the two ships were to rendezvous in a position 700 miles west of Perth in a month's time.

This ambitious mining operation in Australian coastal waters, regarded with some trepidation by those involved, proved to be a great deal easier than anticipated. In fact, the two German ships experienced little difficulty in sowing their lethal crops. Like South Africa, Australia, 12,000 miles removed from the war, was quietly confident that the conflict would never come to her door. No attempt was made to guard the ports, street lights shone out across the harbours and all lighthouses were operating at full power. The *Pinguin* and *Passat*, both sailing blacked out, laid their mines at night quickly, accurately and totally without interference. Ironically, it was the mines laid by the *Passat*, the makeshift auxiliary, that proved to be the most effective.

The Federal Steam Navigation Company's 10,846-ton refriger-ated cargo liner *Cambridge* was the first reported victim. On her thirty-first, and last, voyage to Australia, the *Cambridge* was on passage from Melbourne to Sydney carrying 3,500 tons of tin plate when she hit one of the *Passat*'s newly-laid mines. Late on the evening of 7 November she was 2¼ miles off Wilson's Promontory, in the Bass Strait when, in the words of her master, Captain A.J. Angell: '. . . there was a loud explosion, which sounded to me like the firing of the 4-inch gun. I was not shaken by the explosion, neither was anyone else who was amidships, but the stern of the ship was lifted up and started to go down immediately. It was very dark and very little could be seen, but some of the crew said afterwards that a considerable amount of water was thrown onto the deck, there was no smell and no flame. I think the explosion occurred under No.5 hold on the centre line of the ship, near the after bulkhead of the engine-room, 350 feet from the bow. All the holds were insulated and four of these insulated beams from No.5 hold were thrown up onto the deck, and the hold rapidly filled with water. All the lights went out, the dynamos being situated in the after end of the engine-room.'

With part of her stern blown off, and weighed down by the heavy tin plate in her holds, the *Cambridge* sank within half an hour of striking the mine. At the time the wind was blowing SW'ly force 6, and the sea was rough, but, having signalled their plight to the lighthouse keeper on Wilson's Promontory, the British ship's crew of fifty-six took to the boats with the loss of only one man. They were picked up eleven hours later by the minesweeper HMAS *Orara*.

Two days later, on 9 November, the American Pioneer Line's *City of Rayville*, commanded by Captain Arthur P. Cronin, was unfortunate to run into another of the *Passat*'s mines. This happened at the western end of the Bass Strait, near Cape Otway, in the dead of night and in bad weather. The explosion broke the 5883-ton motor vessel's back, her forward half sinking almost immediately. Fortunately, the stern section stayed afloat for another 45 minutes, allowing the *City of Rayville*'s crew of thirty-seven to abandon ship. Again, only one man, in this case Third Assistant Engineer Mack Bryan, lost his life.

With the sinking of the *City of Rayville*, Erich Warning had

70

unwittingly written a new page in the history of the Second World War. The *City of Rayville* was the first American merchant ship to be sunk, while the unfortunate Mack Bryan was the first American merchant seaman to be killed. The loss of neither helped the German cause.

The *Pinguin*'s mines would take much longer to reveal themselves, and then their yield was of no real account. On 5 December the *Nimbin*, an Australian coastal ship of 1052 tons, was mined and sunk off Sydney with the loss of seven men. Two days later another of Federal Steam's meat carriers, the 10,923-ton *Hertford*, was damaged by a mine in the approaches to Adelaide. Three months went by before the *Pinguin*'s next mine claimed a victim, sinking on 26 March 1941 the 287-ton trawler *Millimulmul* while she was fishing off Sydney. Only one man was lost.

And so Krüder's month-long mining operation, involving two ships and the laying of 230 mines, failed to wreak the devastation aimed at. Only two ocean-going ships were sunk – one of which was neutral – and one damaged; the loss of the *Nimbin* and the *Millimulmul* would not leave its mark on the war. However, the ramifications of this audacious expedition were serious and long-lasting. Soon after the sinking of the *Cambridge* and the *City of Rayville* the Bass Strait and the vital port of Melbourne were closed to all shipping until safe channels were cleared through the minefields, an operation which resulted in the loss of the minesweeper HMAS *Goorangai* and all her crew. Over the next few months, as the mines made their presence felt, Sydney, Newcastle, the Spencer Gulf and Hobart were either closed to shipping or seriously disrupted. At first the Australians thought that U-boats were responsible for the sinkings, and it was not until it became obvious that a German surface raider was at work that the light cruiser HMAS *Adelaide* was sent out to search for the enemy. By then the *Pinguin* and her auxiliary were long gone.

Chapter Seven

The two German ships, *Pinguin* and *Passat*, met up again on 15 November in a position 750 miles due west of Perth. Having been apart for thirty-three days and keeping radio silence, the coming together was a cause for great celebration. The risks they had taken in their separate minelaying operations were huge, but they had come through, and without a single casualty. The day was made all the more memorable by a signal from Admiral Raeder congratulating them on the completion of the mission and awarding five Iron Crosses, First Class, and fifty Second Class, to be distributed as Kapitän Krüder thought fit. The schnapps was broken out and the cheers rang between the two ships.

And now there was serious work to be done. Krüder's orders from SKL were to attack the British and Norwegian whaling fleets at the end of December, when it was known they would be working off South Georgia. This involved a passage of over 6000 miles, but even so Krüder had time to waste. He proposed to use this to overhaul the *Pinguin*'s engines, which had been running almost continuously for five months. The job could be done by shutting down one engine, which would give a speed of around 10 knots, while work was carried out on the other. But first there was the question of what was to be done with the *Passat*.

It had been Krüder's original intention to transfer the seventy mines remaining aboard the *Pinguin* to the other ship and then send her north to lay them on the west coast of India. However, the *Passat*'s engines were in an even worse state than the *Pinguin*'s and her hull heavily fouled with barnacles and weed. She was in no condition to go north on her own.

Next day the *Passat* was decommissioned as an auxiliary and once more became the Norwegian tanker *Storstad*. Her German crew was reduced to eighteen and her Norwegian crew increased to twenty with volunteers from the *Pinguin*'s prisoner accommodation. Oberleutnant Levit was given command, with orders to act as scout for the *Pinguin*. The two ships then set off, the *Pinguin* running on one engine and the *Storstad* positioning herself some 70 miles ahead. Communication was by Hagenuk radio, an ultra-short wave system with a range of only 100 miles. With this Krüder hoped to be able to communicate without revealing his presence to radio stations ashore and patrolling British warships.

First sailing north to the latitude of 30 degrees South, and then altering to the west, the next thirty-six hours passed pleasantly, the weather being fine and warm. No other ships were sighted until, at sunset on the 17th, a stranger appeared on the horizon ahead. She was soon identified as a large cargo vessel steering a westerly course.

At the time the *Pinguin* was on one engine and making 10½ knots. Fortunately, the maintenance on the second engine was at a stage which enabled it to be brought back into use at once and within the hour the *Pinguin* was up to 15 knots and in pursuit. Night was falling fast, however, and the other ship was soon swallowed up by the darkness. It was after midnight before she was sighted again.

The men were sent to their action stations at 0032 on the 18th. It was a very black night, with no moon, but there was not a cloud in the sky and the light cast by the stars was sufficient to reveal the silhouette of the ship on the horizon. Krüder, who had not left the bridge since the first sighting, examined her through his binoculars and judged her to be a fully loaded vessel of around 7000 tons. He altered course to close her and called for more speed.

At 0239 the *Pinguin*'s searchlight clicked on and its powerful beam sliced through the darkness to bathe the other ship in light. The 75-mm barked, throwing a shell across the stranger's bows, and the *Pinguin*'s signal lamp clattered, 'STOP YOUR SHIP. DO NOT USE YOUR W/T OR I OPEN FIRE.'

The British India Steam Navigation Company's motor vessel

Nowshera was taken completely by surprise. Eight days out of Adelaide and homeward bound via Durban, no one aboard the 7920-ton cargo liner had considered it remotely possible that they would meet up with the enemy in this lonely part of the ocean. Ironically, the first to react to the raider's challenge were two of the *Nowshera*'s most junior officers, Fifth Engineer Bellew and Cadet Simpson. The *Pinguin*'s warning shot brought them tumbling out of their bunks and, stopping only to snatch up their lifejackets and steel helmets, they ran aft to their action station on the poop. The *Nowshera*'s DEMS gunner was already there and the three men manned the old Japanese 4-inch, loaded with commendable speed, and trained the gun round to aim down the beam of the *Pinguin*'s searchlight. Before they could fire, the order came from the bridge to stand down.

In preventing his over-eager gun's crew from opening fire, Captain J.N. Collins undoubtedly saved the lives of many of his crew. Momentarily, he had been tempted to resist, to turn and run. The *Nowshera* was a twin-screw ship with a good turn of speed, but he had no means of judging the firepower of his assailant. His own armament, the superannuated 4-inch on the poop and an even more ancient Lewis gun on the bridge, would do no more than attract retribution from a powerful enemy. With regret, for no man in command surrenders his ship with good grace, Collins ordered the radio-room not to transmit, dumped his code books and confidential papers over the side and rang the engine-room telegraphs to stop.

The armed boarding party led by Leutnant Erich Warning took over the *Nowshera* without resistance and within fifteen minutes the lifeboats containing Captain Collins and his crew were being towed across to the *Pinguin*. The operation was marred by the loss of Second Engineer R.A. Philp, who fell into the sea and drowned when abandoning ship.

Krüder received his prisoners with mixed feelings. The *Nowshera* carried an exceptionally large crew, a total of 113, of which ninety-three were Lascars. Their arrival signalled a return to all the problems which had plagued him before the *Nordvard* was sent home. The prisoners would have to be fed and watered and guarded day and night, placing a heavy burden on the

Pinguin's limited resources. The large number of Lascars posed an added problem in that, being Muslims, they would not eat pork, which was the staple diet on German ships.

The *Nowshera*'s cargo papers, brought aboard by Leutnant Warning, showed that she carried 4000 tons of zinc ore, 3000 tons of wheat and 2000 tons of wool, along with a quantity of piece goods. With Germany under blockade, such a cargo was priceless and Krüder was sorely tempted to send the British ship home, but the preparation for the long voyage would take more time than he had to spare. But there was time enough to plunder the *Nowshera* of cases of smoked meats, wines and spirits, Christmas puddings, woollen jumpers, gloves, scarves and underwear. The *Pinguin*'s crew would be well equipped for their coming operations in Antarctica.

At 1409 on 18 November British India's *Nowshera* was sunk in position 30° 00' S 90° 00' E, using fourteen time bombs placed at intervals around her hull. Her passing was unknown to the outside world, for she had sent no SOS, an omission that was to have dire consequences for ships following in her wake.

Pinguin continued her passage, again on one engine, but steering a more southerly course. Two days later, at sunrise on the 20th, her lookouts sighted a smudge of smoke on the horizon to port. The engine-room reported that the overhaul of the idle engine would be finished within the hour, so Krüder decided to bide his time, altering course slightly to keep the smoke in sight. He was of the opinion that it came from a westbound ship, almost certainly a loaded Allied merchantman.

By 0800, with the sun well up, the *Pinguin* was back on two engines and making 14 knots. Soon, the masts and funnel of the other ship were visible and she was confirmed to be a merchant ship heading west. When, half an hour or so later, her hull lifted above the horizon, she suddenly altered course away from the *Pinguin*, indicating that the raider had been sighted from her bridge. Krüder was content to let her disappear back over the horizon. She did not use her radio, but throughout the night and into the morning there had been considerable W/T traffic between Australian shore stations and naval units at sea. Krüder had no intention of rushing into a trap.

Krüder's new quarry was Shaw Savill & Albion's *Maimoa*, an

8,011-ton twin-screw refrigerated ship built in 1920. She was carrying 1,500 tons of butter, 170,000 cases of eggs, 5000 tons of meat and 1,500 tons of grain from Australian ports to the United Kingdom. Commanded by Captain H.S. Cox, she was manned by a British crew of eighty-seven, which included a large contingent of men from the Western Isles of Scotland. When the other ship was sighted, the *Maimoa* was two days out of Fremantle and making an unhurried 11 knots towards Durban, where she was to take on coal bunkers.

On being called to the bridge, Captain Cox was immediately suspicious of the stranger and altered course to put her astern, notifying the engine-room to increase to maximum sea speed. However, not wishing to raise the alarm unnecessarily, Cox delayed sending out a QQQQ message (see p 2). The other ship had the lines of a German raider, but equally she could be just another Allied merchantman going about her legitimate business.

As the morning wore on and the unidentified ship dropped back below the horizon and did not reappear, Cox began to think that he had taken the right action in the circumstances. But he was still uneasy, an unease, characteristically, he did not communicate to his officers, but to his steward, Alfred Nash, who brought the captain's breakfast to the bridge.

At 1343 Nash was in the officers' dining saloon clearing away after lunch and looking forward to a well earned afternoon siesta, which was his due. Then the *Maimoa*'s steam whistle sounded a series of short blasts, the general alarm. Grumbling aloud, for he was convinced this was just another drill, Nash made his way aft to his action station at the 4-inch gun. As he emerged on deck, there was a deafening roar overhead and he ducked as the *Pinguin*'s Heinkel, its false British markings clearly visible, swooped low over the ship, passing between the masts.

The Heinkel, piloted by Leutnant Werner, with Leutnant Müller in the observer's cockpit, was trailing a weighted wire with the object of cutting the *Maimoa*'s W/T aerial. She missed at the first attempt, came in low again and dropped a bag containing a message on the bridge. The message read: 'Stop your engines immediately. Do not use wireless. In case of disobedience you will be bombed or shelled.'

The *Maimoa*'s reply was unequivocal, her radio, which until then had been silent, bursting into life to warn the world that she was being attacked from the air. The Heinkel retaliated by dropping two small bombs ahead of the ship, did a tight turn and swooped yet again, its BMW radial engine snarling viciously. This time it was met with a hail of fire. Fourth Engineer Ernest Howlett, standing completely exposed on deck, hit back with a .303 service rifle, while the *Maimoa*'s Gunner was behind the Lewis gun on the upper bridge. Leutnant Müller replied with his machine gun, ironically slightly wounding two other crew members, John Gillies and Malcolm Maclean.

This time the Heinkel succeeded in carrying away the *Maimoa*'s aerial, but she paid a heavy price, being hit in the petrol tank and one float. Her engine spluttered and died, Werner being forced to land on the sea. Wallowing helplessly in the swell and with the smell of escaping petrol filling their nostrils, Werner and Müller crouched low in their cockpits waiting for the enemy to finish them off. To their relief, and utter amazement, the *Maimoa* steamed contemptuously past without opening fire. There was even what appeared to be a friendly wave from the bridge.

The truth was that Captain Cox, realizing that a German raider must be close by, had no time to waste on the Heinkel. Watches had been double-banked in the *Maimoa*'s stokehold and, with her furnaces roaring, she was building up to a speed she had not experienced since her first sea trials two decades earlier. At the same time, with a jury aerial rigged, her radio officer was sending out a continuous stream of SOS messages.

Fortunately for Werner and Müller, the *Pinguin* was only just below the horizon and racing in at full speed to their aid. She reached the Heinkel just as it was beginning to heel over under the influence of its waterlogged float. Slowing down only very briefly, Krüder dropped his motor cutter with a repair party on board and carried on in pursuit of the *Maimoa*.

The *Maimoa*'s smoke was visible from the *Pinguin*'s bridge within half an hour, but the British ship was in full flight. For the next two and a half hours, as he struggled to overhaul her, Krüder listened in growing annoyance to reports from his wireless office that his quarry was broadcasting in graphic detail the appearance of the ship chasing her. Every British naval ship and shore station within listening distance must be gearing up to make war on the *Pinguin* and there was nothing Krüder could do about it.

At last, at 1645, with sunset only two hours away, Krüder had closed the range to just over 12 miles, the maximum range of his big guns. The *Maimoa* was frantically making smoke, but the wind direction was such that the smoke was quickly blown clear and provided no cover. Krüder now ran up his battle flag and opened fire.

The first salvo of four 5.9-inch shells screamed over the *Maimoa*'s stern, landing just beyond and throwing up tall columns of water. The second salvo dropped slightly short, but in line with the fleeing merchantman's stern. Captain Cox, whose own 4-inch gun was useless at the range, feared that the third German salvo must strike home and decided to save his crew. He struck his flag and rang his engines to stop. The *Maimoa*'s bow wave flattened and she slowly drifted to a halt.

When the boarding party reported back to Krüder that the British ship's holds were crammed full with the finest produce of Australia's farms, he was again sorely tempted to put a prize crew aboard and send her back to Germany, where her cargo would be put to such good use. But the *Maimoa* was a coal-burner and her bunkers were already half-empty. By the time she reached the Cape she would be burning her wooden hatchboards with no friendly port south of Biscay in which to replenish her bunkers. Furthermore, with the whole of the Indian Ocean alerted by the *Maimoa*'s calls for help, it was time for the *Pinguin* to make herself scarce.

Charges were laid in the *Maimoa*'s hull and, as darkness closed in, she slid beneath the waves, taking her precious cargo with her. Krüder, watching with some regret the last moments of his prize, took comfort from the fact that there were no Lascars in her crew of eighty-seven, now his prisoners. The Lascars from the *Nowshera* already on board the *Pinguin*, with their insanitary habits, demands for special food and loud bleatings for medical attention that bordered on mass hypochondria, were already a constant source of aggravation.

It was in the early hours of next morning before Krüder located the downed Heinkel and the motor cutter. The plane was still afloat, bandages having been used to make the damaged float watertight, but by now the wind and sea had risen considerably.

Hoisting the aircraft and the boat aboard the *Pinguin* was a difficult operation that lasted almost until daybreak.

While the *Pinguin* was so engaged, the 8739-ton *Port Brisbane*, commanded by Captain Harry Steele, was attempting to make good her escape. The *Port Brisbane*, homeward bound via Durban with 8000 tons of refrigerated cargo and wool, had been only 60 miles north of the *Maimoa* when she was under attack and had listened in to her plaintive cries for help. With a suspicious-looking tanker in sight – the *Storstad* was already shadowing the *Port Brisbane* – Captain Steele had sheered away to the north and increased speed until the tanker dropped out of sight.

But for her lack of speed, the *Port Brisbane* might well have proved to be a significant threat to both the *Storstad* and the *Pinguin*. Built in Belfast in 1923 at a time when the Great War was still fresh in the minds of the Admiralty, her decks had been strengthened and mountings for seven 6-inch guns fitted. When war came again – and it was *when*, not *if*, in the minds of the Admirals – she would slip easily into the role of armed merchant cruiser without too much further modification. However, by the time war did break out again in 1939, the *Port Brisbane*, a coal burner with a heavy daily consumption and a top speed of 11 knots, was hopelessly outdated. She remained a merchant ship but, perhaps to justify in part the money spent on her by the taxpayer earlier, she was fitted with two 6-inch guns on her after-deck and a 12-pounder anti-aircraft gun forward. Although this was heavy armament for a merchantman, her firepower was really no more than a sham. Her 6-inch guns had been supplied with only ten rounds apiece, in which case any realistic gun drill was out of the question. She carried only one trained gunner, who had done his best to produce guns' crews from amongst the ship's crew, but without the opportunity for 'live' shoots his task had been a thankless one.

Captain Steele, who had left Australia with orders to run at maximum speed for Durban, had received no intelligence regarding enemy vessels in the area, but he was not prepared to tempt fate. He held his northerly course until well after dark, making all possible speed and with his crew doubled up at action stations. However, having seen nothing of the suspicious tanker by 2100, he concluded that she might, after all, have been just another homeward-bound Allied ship. He resumed his original course and speed and stood his men down.

Steele's decision to return to normality proved fatal for the *Port Brisbane*. When the sun rose next morning the *Storstad* had re-appeared, and Levit was reporting back to Krüder by ultra-short wave radio. By 0900 the *Pinguin*, homing in on the *Storstad* at maximum speed, had the *Port Brisbane*'s smoke in sight, but Krüder, mindful that the *Maimoa* had broadcast a detailed description of his ship only twenty-four hours earlier, decided to wait until after dark before he closed in. He slowed down and turned onto a parallel course with his intended victim. The British ship was always attended by a cloud of thick black smoke and was easily kept in sight. The *Pinguin*, on the other hand, a motor ship, gave off only a light haze which was quickly dissipated by the wind. Throughout the day the raider kept station on the *Port Brisbane* without being seen. The *Storstad*, her task completed, dropped back below the horizon again.

Sunset was at 1840 and, as is the case in the lower latitudes, it was completely dark within twenty minutes. The night was black, with an overcast sky and no moon or stars visible. Under cover of the dark, Krüder altered course to close the *Port Brisbane* and increased speed.

At 2130 the *Pinguin*'s lookouts, their eyes well accustomed to the night, reported a dark silhouette on the starboard bow. Krüder adjusted his course to put the ship right ahead and reduced speed, creeping up silently on his quarry. A little before midnight the *Port Brisbane*, clearly identifiable as a loaded merchantman, crossed the raider's bow at 800 yards and Krüder gave orders for the interception. The big searchlight clicked on, capturing the *Port Brisbane* in its brilliant blue-white beam, the 75-mm put a shot across her bows and the signal lamp flashed the order to stop.

And that should have been the end to the matter, but the *Pinguin*'s searchlight had revealed the big guns on the other ship's after-deck. Men could be seen gathering about them.

Convinced that he had inadvertently challenged a British armed merchant cruiser, Krüder immediately ordered all his guns to open fire. The result was devastating, all eight 5.9-inch shells in the first salvo finding their mark. The *Port Brisbane*'s radio-room received a direct hit, killing outright her Radio Officer J.H. Magee, who was in the act of sending out an RRRR message. Another shell slammed into the bridge, setting it on fire, while others ploughed into the funnel, the upper-deck accommodation and, crucially, her steering gear. With the flames spreading rapidly and her rudder jammed hard over, the *Port Brisbane* circled helplessly, trailing a cloud of black smoke. Captain Steele stopped his engines and prepared to abandon ship.

Within the hour Krüder was welcoming aboard his latest batch of prisoners, sixty men and one woman, a passenger, all British. A roll call was then taken and twenty-seven other crew members were missing. Their story is best told by Second Officer Edward Dingle: 'I was woken on November 21st at 0052 hours by gunfire. I rushed on deck and saw the raider, an armed merchant ship, standing about a mile and a half off. The *Port Brisbane* was hit about eight times on the upper deck level, but as far as I could discover none of the crew was killed or wounded.

'I persuaded the men in the boat with me to show no light. They agreed and declared they would sooner take a chance with me than suffer the fate of the *Altmark* prisoners. I watched the raider torpedo the *Port Brisbane*. She was burning fiercely when she slid under the water. That was at about two o'clock in the morning.

'When daylight came I fixed our position and proposed that we make for Australia although in the prevailing wind conditions we had not much hope of getting there. That afternoon we decided to take advantage of the favourable winds and make for Mauritius instead. I warned the men to make up their minds to undertake a passage of about forty days.'

Edward Dingle, known throughout Port Line as 'Steady Eddy', lived up to his reputation for unflappability in the face of adversity. His decision to slip away under the cover of darkness and evade capture was made with the knowledge that the only navigational aids in the lifeboat were an unreliable magnetic compass and a set of nautical tables, and the only provisions twenty-four tins of condensed milk, a few tins of biscuits and fifteen gallons of water. As luck would have it, this lack of the necessities for survival was not important. Dingle and his men were picked up next day by the heavy cruiser HMAS *Canberra*, which had been sent out to look for the raider.

Having disposed of the *Port Brisbane* with a torpedo, Krüder spent the rest of the night searching for the missing lifeboat, not from any humanitarian motive; he was loath to leave behind a boat-load of witnesses to his activities. The search was in vain and, as dawn was breaking, he made off to the south-west at full speed, which was a very wise move. The *Canberra*, 31-knots and armed with eight 8-inch and eight 4-inch guns, was by then close by.

Four days later the *Pinguin* was some 500 miles north of the Kerguelen Islands, when SKL came through with specific orders for her future operations. Krüder was instructed to steer a westerly course, which would take him across the Fremantle–Cape route, until he reached 35° S 50° E, sinking everything that came his way. Thereafter, he was to go south-west to Bouvet Island and attempt to find the Norwegian whaling fleet, which was known to be fishing somewhere in the area. In the land of the penguins, for which she was named, the primary task of the raider's long voyage was about to begin.

The *Storstad* was still scouting ahead and at 11.30 on the morning of 30 November she reported a loaded steamer on a westerly course in sight. Krüder at once began the pursuit, adopting the proven tactic of first sighting the enemy's smoke and then shadowing her on a parallel course, but out of sight. Mindful of the 6-inch guns carried by the *Port Brisbane*, he planned to come up on the ship after dark and open fire without warning. This was contrary to Krüder's usual code of conduct, but he was aware that the net must be closing in around the *Pinguin*. The time for chivalry was past.

Ernst Krüder was not then aware that the ship he was stalking was a sister to the *Port Brisbane*, another link in the endless food train that joined Britain to New Zealand and Australia. Like her sister, she had also been built with an eye to conversion to an armed merchant cruiser in wartime and was similarly armed with two 6-inch guns and a 12-pounder. She had, however, one advantage over the *Port Brisbane*, in that she carried three Royal Australian Navy gunners, men trained in the art of war.

The 8301-ton *Port Wellington*, a twin-screw cargo liner built in Belfast in 1924, was bound from Adelaide to the United Kingdom via Durban, having on board a cargo of 10,000 tons, made up of lead ingots, frozen lamb, cheese, butter and wool, the latter being stowed four bales high on deck. Commanded by Captain Emrys Thomas, she carried a total crew of eighty and ten passengers. The passengers, three men and seven women, were Salvation Army personnel returning from escorting a party of school children evacuated from Britain to Australia.

Before sailing from Adelaide Captain Thomas had been warned that German surface raiders were operating in the South Indian Ocean and was well aware that he was sailing into extremely dangerous waters. Nevertheless, life on board the *Port Wellington* proceeded much as normal. The weather on passage was fine and Chief Officer Bill Bailey took full advantage of it, working his deck crew long hours overhauling cargo gear and freshening up paintwork in the time-honoured manner of a homeward-bound ship. Even the three Australian gunners were given paint brushes and set to work on deck. When the RRRR messages were intercepted, first from the *Maimoa* and then the *Port Brisbane*, Thomas was faced with three possible alternatives. He could either alter course to the north or south and hope to skirt around the danger, return to Fremantle, take bunkers and sail again when things had quietened down, or simply carry on. After some deliberation, his inbuilt commitment to his owners and their cargo prevailed. He opted to hold his course.

Unfortunately, the determination to carry on ship's routine as normal proved to be the *Port Wellington*'s undoing. On 30 November, when the ship was some 360 miles north of the Amsterdam & St. Paul Islands, and at the mid-point of her passage across the Indian Ocean, Chief Officer Bailey decided to paint the foremast. The men were sent aloft early and by late afternoon the job was finished, but the oil-based paints of the day were slow-drying and it was not possible to put a lookout in the crow's nest. Consequently, the *Storstad* was not sighted until she was just 7 miles off. Captain Thomas, perhaps lulled into a false sense of security by the long days at sea without incident, took little notice of the tanker, unaware that his ship was being closely examined by half a dozen pairs of powerful binoculars.

When night fell the fresh paint on the foremast was still wet and the crow's nest lookout man was posted on the forecastle head, thus reducing his effectiveness by at least fifty percent. But it was a fine night, very dark, but clear, and the temporary handicap was not a cause for concern. Bowling along at 12 knots and lulling those off watch to sleep with her long, lazy roll, the *Port Wellington* sailed on.

On the bridge a relaxed atmosphere prevailed. Chief Officer Bill Bailey having gone onto daywork to oversee the maintenance on deck, the other officers had moved up a watch. Fourth Officer Edward Gilham, who was normally Bailey's assistant on the 4 to 8, had charge of the 8 to 12. In the last hour of his watch, the hour leading up to midnight, proud of his new-found responsibility, Gilham paced the starboard wing of the bridge with a measured tread. At the helm Quartermaster Jim Waggott hummed softly to himself and answered the click-click of the gyro compass with economical movements of the wheel, checking the ship's head against the pull of the current. Both men were counting the dying minutes of the day.

At a quarter to midnight Waggott leaned forward and struck the bridge bell once, signalling to the stand-by man that it was time to call the next watch. Gilham stopped his pacing and raised his binoculars to scan the horizon ahead. Nothing in sight. He then turned to look aft and was astonished to see the dark outline of a ship on the quarter. She was close, no more than a quarter of a mile off, and silently creeping up on the *Port Wellington*.

Acting instinctively, Gilham altered course to put the other right ship astern and then lunged for the Captain's voicepipe.

The *Port Wellington* leaned as she answered to her helm, but as she came round the *Pinguin*'s powerful searchlight reached out and held her in its brilliant beam. The raider's 5.9s opened fire, lighting up the night sky with a ripple of flashes.

The first shell, aimed with an accuracy born of long practice, destroyed the *Port Wellington*'s radio-room, killing First Radio Officer Arthur Haslam as he warmed up his transmitter to send an SOS. The second set on fire the late radio officer's cabin and the officers' smokeroom.

Captain Emrys Thomas was climbing the bridge ladder when

84

the third shell hit the funnel, spraying out shrapnel which smashed both his legs. As he lay in a pool of blood, other shells hit the passenger accommodation, blew the starboard 6-inch gun over the side and destroyed the 12-pounder.

Krüder's attack without warning was an unqualified success. It had crippled the *Port Wellington*'s armament, set her on fire, killed her radio officer before he could raise the alarm and disabled her commander.

As he lay dying of his wounds, Captain Emrys Thomas made a last attempt to save his ship, ordering Chief Officer Bailey to zig-zag away from the enemy at all possible speed. Shortly afterwards he lapsed into unconsciousness. Bailey then assumed command and, realizing the hopelessness of the situation, stopped the ship and surrendered. Quartermaster Jim Waggott described what happened next:

'Illumination provided by the flames erupting from the burning ship turned the night into almost daylight. It was then ascertained that it had only been possible to launch two of the ship's boats, the two on the port side being badly damaged by shell fire. On making a roll call it was found that the two boats collectively contained eighty crew members, six Australian Navy gunners and eight passengers, ninety-four in total, the Chief Radio Officer being the only crew member to have lost his life. There were several of the crew suffering from injuries and limb fractures.

'Captain Thomas was in a critical condition, having been nursed by the female passengers during the action and then lowered into a boat. It was almost impossible to provide medical attention for him in the cramped boat. The boats were taking in water owing to the buoyancy tanks being damaged during the action. It was fairly obvious that the boats were not going to be capable of a long voyage with a large number of survivors.

'The boats were within hailing distance of each other, and a discussion was taking place among the senior officers regarding the course to steer which would take us towards land, or better still, a shipping lane, when the sound of approaching motor launches was heard. They were manned by German Navy personnel armed with machine guns, who in faultless English instructed us to row towards the German raider, where their Captain it was said wished to speak to us.

'Later that day (1 December) we were informed of the death of our skipper Captain E.O. Thomas despite the very good medical attention he had received in the German ship's hospital bay. He was buried at sea the following day with full naval honours, some of the crew being allowed to attend the committal.'

The *Port Wellington* was boarded and scuttling charges laid in her engine-room, but all attempts to raid the ship's refrigerated holds for fresh provisions were thwarted by the fires raging on deck. In the end, the boarding party came away empty-handed, except for a range finder rescued from the British ship's bridge.

The *Port Wellington* sank at 0331 on 1 December in 31° 10'S 70° 37'E, bringing the *Pinguin*'s total of enemy ships sunk or captured to eleven of 74,974 tons gross. Krüder had cause to be well satisfied with his achievements, but with 405 prisoners on board problems were looming.

Chapter Eight

The war was just five weeks old when, on 8 October 1939, Hamburg South America Line's *Cap Norte* emerged from the cold, damp mists of the Denmark Strait and entered the Norwegian Sea. The 13,615-ton ex-immigrant liner, a twin-screw ship with a speed of 15 knots, was nearing the end of a long and hazardous passage from Pernambuco, Brazil. She carried in her passenger accommodation a large contingent of German reservists returning home to join in Hitler's struggle for *lebensraum*.

The *Cap Norte*, by dint of careful navigation, had so far escaped the attentions of the Royal Navy and was then only 72 hours' steaming from safe waters. The weather, typical for the time of the year in these high latitudes, was in her favour, with a low, heavily overcast sky, rough seas and frequent squalls of sleet and snow. The visibility was rarely over half a mile and the cold was bone-chilling, making watchkeeping above decks a nightmare, but this was a small price to pay for nature's cloak of anonymity.

The German liner finally came to grief next day when she was passing north of the Faroe Islands. Emerging from a squall, she sailed straight into the arms of the Royal Navy, but even then, being a 15-knotter, she might have made her escape. Unfortunately for her, the British guard ship off the Faroes on that day was not the usual slow, inferior-gunned AMC, but the 32-knot light cruiser HMS *Belfast*, armed with twelve 6-inch and twelve 4-inch guns. Very wisely in the circumstances, the *Cap Norte*'s captain stopped his ship and surrendered. However, by the time the *Belfast*'s armed boarding party reached the German ship's deck, her engines had been sabotaged by her engineers. She was towed into the Tyne and repaired, but her engines would never again be completely reliable and some fourteen months later they would prove instrumental in precipitating what could well have been a major disaster for Britain's war effort.

In the summer of 1940, after the twin humiliations of Dunkirk and Norway, Britain's morale was flagging and she was sorely in need of a victory on land. A return to Europe was out of the question for some time to come; only North Africa offered any hope of glory. The Germans had not yet entered the fray in this theatre, but the Italians posed a considerable threat. In Libya Marshal Graziani had 250,000 troops at his disposal and was intent on marching on Alexandria, then on to the Suez Canal. Other Italian forces occupying Ethiopia and Eritrea were a continuing danger to British oil supplies in Iraq and Iran. To counter these threats, the British commander in the Middle East, General Sir Archibald Wavell, was able to muster a total force of only 86,000 men, of which 36,000 were in Egypt. Wavell was confident he could throw the Italians back, but before he made any significant move he needed more men, more tanks, more guns.

From the time Italy entered the war, in June 1940, the Mediterranean had become largely untenable for Allied merchant shipping. A large, modern Italian navy and squadrons of land-based bombers obliged all but the fastest ships bound for Egypt to make the long haul around the Cape to the Red Sea, thereby adding 16,000 miles and another two months to the round voyage. The run-of-the-mill cargo ships had the protection of a convoy between the United Kingdom and Freetown, but otherwise they sailed independently and unescorted. No such risk could be taken with troopships and vessels carrying war supplies to the Middle East, and towards the end of June 1940 the 'WS' convoys were started. Known as 'Winston Specials' – they were instigated by Prime Minister Winston Churchill – these convoys were under heavy escort throughout the long voyage around the Cape to Suez. Sailing at the rate of one a month, the 'Winston Specials' had by early December 1940 carried sufficient men and equipment to enable General Wavell to rout Graziani, who by then had crossed into Egypt, and to pursue him deep into Libya. The victory was sweet and, for the time being at least, the threat to Britain's Middle Eastern interests had been lifted.

Hitler, who had meanwhile turned his face towards Russia, now became concerned that the British, hitherto considered to be beaten into submission, were staging a recovery. He therefore ordered Admiral Raeder to step up operations against Britain's Atlantic supply lines. The U-boats were already heavily engaged, sinking up to forty Allied ships a month, but the High Seas Fleet, Raeder's preferred option, was in a parlous state. The battle-cruisers *Scharnhorst* and *Gneisenau* were still in dock repairing damage sustained in the Norwegian campaign, as was the pocket-battleship *Lützow*. That left only two surface ships capable of hitting the convoys, the pocket-battleship *Admiral Scheer* and the heavy cruiser *Admiral Hipper*. The *Scheer* had broken out into the Atlantic via the Denmark Strait on 31 October and five days later showed her immense capability by savaging the 37-ship convoy HX 84.

HX 84 sailed from Sydney, Cape Breton on the evening of 27 October 1940, and on 2 November, at a rendezvous 500 miles south-east of Newfoundland, was joined by ships from ports south of the Chesapeake River and Canada's west coast. The merger resulted in a total of thirty-seven ships carrying over a quarter of a million tons of cargo for the United Kingdom.

Steaming in nine columns abreast, HX 84 had just one escort, the armed merchant cruiser HMS *Jervis Bay*. The 14,164-ton *Jervis Bay*, an ex-Aberdeen & Commonwealth liner built in 1922, was armed with eight 6-inch guns and had a top speed of 15 knots. She was commanded by the charismatic Captain E.S. Fogarty Fegen, RN, who came of five generations of naval officers. Fogarty Fegen was about to write another glorious page in the history of the Royal Navy.

The *Admiral Scheer*, under the command of Kapitän-zur-See Theodor Krancke, had sailed from the Elbe at about the same time as HX 84 left Sydney and on 5 November was only 50 miles to the north-east of the convoy on a reciprocal course. The *Scheer*'s reconnaissance Arado sighted the smoke of HX 84 that afternoon.

When the *Scheer* came in sight, at around 1600, Captain Fogarty Fegen ordered the convoy to scatter, and then, without hesitation, turned to meet the attacker, knowing full well that he was up against a ship with 11-inch guns. His own ancient 6-inch calibre guns, firing over open sights, thundered defiance, but they were hopelessly outranged, their shells falling far short of the target. Krancke opened fire at 18,000 yards, his first salvo scoring direct hits on the *Jervis Bay*. The AMC's steering gear was smashed, her wireless room destroyed. The blast also shattered the fire mains on deck and there was no water to fight the fires that broke out.

The *Admiral Scheer*'s second salvo ploughed into the *Jervis Bay*'s bridge, reducing it to a burning shambles. Fogarty Fegen was mortally wounded, but he carried on the fight until his blazing ship sank under him. He died, along with 185 of his gallant crew.

The heroic sacrifice of the *Jervis Bay*, whose guns did not so much as blister the paint of the *Admiral Scheer*, seemed a pointless gesture, but Captain Fogarty Fegen had achieved his purpose. While the *Scheer* was engaged in fending off the AMC, the convoy had scattered, and in the approaching darkness all but four of the thirty-seven merchantmen escaped the pocket-battleship's guns.

Despite the *Scheer*'s mediocre showing, Raeder was well satisfied and put in hand plans for more such sorties.

On 29 November RAF reconnaissance planes photographed the *Admiral Hipper* lying in Brünsbüttel, at the North Sea end of the Kiel Canal. The significance of this seemed to escape the Admiralty and the German cruiser was not kept under surveillance. The next day the *Hipper*, commanded by Kapitän-zur-See Wilhelm Meisel, was gone, having slipped down the Elbe at night and gained the shelter of the Norwegian Leads after a high-speed dash across the Skagerrak. Hidden behind the off-shore islands, she made her way up the coast, and when she had the cover of bad weather, steamed at full speed for the Denmark Strait.

The bad weather held and, with the cloud base almost down to sea level and the visibility seriously reduced by sleet and snow squalls, all British aircraft in the area were grounded. On the night of 6/7 December Kapitän Meisel took the *Hipper* through the Strait unseen and out into the Atlantic.

Once in open waters Meisel's orders were to build on the *Admiral Scheer*'s limited success and cause as much mayhem as possible amongst the Halifax–Liverpool convoys, Britain's main lifeline to the Americas. As these convoys were largely escorted only by corvettes and armed merchant cruisers, the 32-knot *Hipper* and her 8-inch guns presented a major threat. When his fuel was running low, Meisel had orders to head for the French Biscay port of Brest, where the cruiser would from then on be based. With the help of four supply tankers strategically placed, it was planned that the *Hipper* would make regular hit-and-run raids on Allied shipping in the North Atlantic.

One of the most important 'Winston Specials' of the war, WS 5A, sailed from the Clyde and Liverpool in December 1940. The objective of this convoy was twofold: to carry troops and their equipment to Suez via the Cape, and to deliver supplies to Malta and Greece via the Straits of Gibraltar.

WS 5A (Slow), the larger section of the convoy, assembled in the North Channel on 19 December and comprised fifteen merchant ships carrying troops, their guns, ammunition and vehicles to the Western Desert. In its ranks were some of the finest liners then afloat, including Pacific Steam Navigation Company's 16,000-ton *Orbita*, the *Llandaff Castle* of the Union Castle Line, the *Elizabethville* and *Leopoldville* from the Belgian Congo service, Holland-America's *Volendam* and the *Rangitiki* of the New Zealand Shipping Company. Initially, this army afloat was escorted by the Dido-class anti-aircraft cruiser HMS *Bonaventure*, four destroyers and the sloop HMS *Wellington*. The *Bonaventure*, commanded by Captain Jack Egerton, was a modern 33-knot cruiser of 6,850 tons, mounting eight 5.25-inch semi-automatic guns and was equipped with RDF. The latter was an early-type radar of very limited ability. It had a fixed aerial on the foremast and covered only a small arc on either side of the bow, requiring the ship to weave constantly to search for targets. Unlike the modern radar, which presents an accurate picture on-screen of what is happening all around the ship, it gave only a rough bearing and range of targets ahead. Discrimination was poor and, except in calm weather, the RDF was of little use against U-boats, but it was invaluable for station keeping in poor visibility. Although she would be able to give a good account of herself in any circumstances, the *Bonaventure*'s primary role was to meet the threat of attack by long-range Focke-Wulf Kondors, known to be flying out of a base near Bordeaux.

Liaison between the merchant ships and their escort was in the hands of the Convoy Commodore Rear-Admiral C.N. Reyne, who sailed with his staff of signallers in the 12,405-ton Shaw Savill & Albion twin-screw steamer *Tamaroa*. Reyne, like most convoy commodores, was a retired Flag Officer who had returned to sea to make his contribution to the war. Merchant ship captains were notoriously independent of mind and it required a man of Admiral Reyne's long experience of ships sailing in disciplined company to persuade them to cooperate with each other and with the escorts. A convoy commodore's lot was not an easy one.

Darkness was closing in on the afternoon of the 20th, when a latecomer joined the convoy off the north coast of Ireland. She was none other than the *Cap Norte*, now renamed *Empire Trooper* and sailing under the house flag of the British India Steam Navigation Company. Having spent some months on the Tyne repairing and converting to a troopship, the *Empire Trooper* was a useful addition to the Ministry of Shipping's fleet. However, she had never fully recovered from the damage inflicted on her engines in the heat of the moment off the Faroes in the autumn of 1939. Slow passages and poor station keeping was a cross she would have to bear for all time.

But once in the ranks of the convoy, the ex-German liner behaved impeccably. The trouble came from a more unlikely source, Andrew Weir's motor vessel *Ernebank*. The 5388-ton *Ernebank*, only three years out of Harland & Wolff's Belfast yard, suffered an engine breakdown in the forenoon of the 21st, quickly dropping astern, but rejoining the convoy later. She again broke down at 1600 and fell astern, this time with little prospect of rejoining for some considerable time. Reluctantly, Captain Egerton ordered the destroyers HMS *Witch* and HMS *St. Mary's* to stand by her. In the event, all the escorting destroyers were by now running short of fuel and due to return to Londonderry. *Witch* and *St. Mary's* turned back at 1800, the others left at 2300, leaving only the sloop *Wellington*, with her two 4.7-inch and one 3-inch guns to support Egerton's *Bonaventure*. The sixteen-ship convoy was beginning to look highly vulnerable, and none more so than the unfortunate *Ernebank*.

An easterly gale blew up during the night and two emergency

1. "In command of HK 33 was 43-year-old Kapitän-zur-See Ernst-Felix Krüder, a slim, taciturn man who had risen to command from the ranks" (p.11). *(Bundesarchiv, Koblenz)*

2. The German auxiliary cruiser *Pinguin*, (ex-*Kandelfels*). "From harmless merchantman to ship of war."

3. "The heavy cruiser *Admiral Hipper*. "An ocean raider dedicated to the destruction of Alllied merchant shipping."

4. HMS *Renown* at speed in heavy weather. *(Central Press)*

5. Third Assistant Engineer Mack Bryan, the first US seaman to be killed in the Second World War (see p. 70). *(Ian Millar)*

6. Kapitän-zur-See Wilhelm Meisel, Captain of the *Hipper*. *(Bundesarchiv, Koblenz)*

7. "The *City of Rayville* was the first American merchant ship to be sunk" (p. 71). *(Ian Millar)*

8. The crew of the *Port Brisbane*, plus one lady passenger, on board the *Pinguin*. Captain Harry Steele is in the centre of the second row (see pp 79-83). (*John D. Stevenson*)

9. Some of the *Pinguin's* prisoners in POW camp Marlag und Milag Nord in 1942. (*John D. Stevenson*)

10. "Leading Stoker Harry Penter... improvised by shutting down the air flaps on the furnaces" (p. 104). *(Harry Penter)*

11. "Fortunately for the little *Clematis*, all the enemy shells that came her way missed and she was unharmed" (p. 104). *(Harry Penter)*

12. "First Radio Officer John
Cave was on the bridge of
the *Margot*" (p. 142).
(John Cave)

13. "The 6078-ton British steamer *Jumna*, owned by Nourse Line of London, under
the command of Captain N. R. Burgess" (p. 106). *(Fred Hortop)*

S.S. CLUNE PARK AT MADEIRA, FEB. 1941.

14. "Some ships were abandoned without good cause, among them Denholm Line's 3419-ton *Clunepark*" (p. 145). She is seen here anchored off Funchal, Madeira. *(Fred Hortop)*

15. The grave of Gunner Norman Thomas of the *Gairsoppa* in St Winwallow churchyard at Gunwalloe, Cornwall. His body had not been identified when the headstone was put up (see p. 180). *(Author)*

16. The grave of Radio Officer Robert Hampshire, also of the *Gairsoppa*, at Gunwalloe. *(Author)*

17. *Admiral Hipper* moored in Altenfjord, Norway, July 1942.

18. *Admiral Hipper* consigned to the breakers by RAF bombers, May 1945. *(IWM)*

turns ordered by Rear-Admiral Reyne following possible U-boat contacts resulted in the convoy being scattered around the horizon by dawn on the 22nd. One ship, Lampert & Holt's 6054-ton *Delane*, was missing, while the *Ernebank* still wallowed somewhere astern. *Wellington* was detached to round up the two ships, leaving the *Bonaventure* to provide what cover she could for the remaining fourteen.

There was no shortage of escorts for the other section of the convoy WS 5A (Fast). This was made up of only five fast merchantmen, the 10,917-ton *Northern Prince*, Cayzer Irvine's *Clan Cumming* and *Clan Macdonald*, the 11,063-ton *Essex* of the Federal Steam Navigation Company, and the twin-screw *Empire Song*, the latter managed by Cayzer Irvine and on her maiden voyage. The five ships, chosen for their superior cargo-handling equipment and turn of speed, carried tanks, ammunition and food, and were bound Gibraltar. From there, as part of Operation 'Excess', they would attempt to break through to Malta and Piraeus. In attendance on this small, select fleet were the anti-aircraft cruiser *Naiad*, sister-ship to HMS *Bonaventure*, the destroyers HMS *Beverley*, *Kelvin* and *Kipling*, HMCS *Ottawa* and *St Laurent*, and *Le Triomphant* (Free French) and *Piorun* (Polish), and the Flower-class corvettes HMS *Clematis* and *Cyclamen*. In command of this large escort force was Rear-Admiral E. King, Rear-Admiral Commanding, Fifteenth Cruiser Squadron, who flew his flag in HMS *Naiad*.

Also in company with WS 5A, and swelling the numbers of the escort, were the old First World War aircraft carriers *Furious* and *Argus*. These were ships with a long and proud history, trail blazers in the field of aviation at sea. HMS *Furious*, originally designed as a fast battle cruiser, had in July 1918 carried out the first ever carrier-based landplane strike, flying off seven Sopwith Camels to attack the Zeppelin sheds at Tondern in North Germany. The *Argus*, one year younger, was a converted foreign merchant ship. The Sopwith Camels were gone, replaced by Blackburn Skuas and Fairey Swordfish for anti-submarine patrols, but the defence of the convoy was not the primary role of the carriers. *Argus* was to go with Operation 'Excess' to fly off Hurricanes for Malta, while *Furious* also carried Hurricanes below deck, but for a very different destination.

The need for replacement fighter aircraft in the Western Desert was urgent and, as the Cape route was so long and the Mediterranean so fraught with danger, since August 1940 deliveries were being made overland through the West African port of Takoradi. An airfield and workshops had been built near the port, and aircraft landed from ships were serviced and then flown overland to Cairo, a distance of 3,700 miles, with stops for refuelling at Kano and Khartoum. In theory, this was a simple answer to the problems encountered at sea, but in reality the difficulties to be overcome ashore were enormous. Takoradi, on the Gold Coast, built to handle bags of cocoa and logs from the plantations up country, was not geared up to the pressures of war. Work on preparing the aircraft went at a snail's pace and the combination of heat, sand and extremes of weather met with on the long flight north resulted in frequent engine breakdowns. The Takoradi to Cairo route was consequently soon littered with grounded aircraft. The thirty Hurricanes *Furious* would off load at Takoradi were to help make up the deficit.

WS 5A (Fast) cleared the North Channel at daylight on 20 December. Twenty-four hours later the escort force was further swollen when the destroyers HMS *Highlander*, *Harvester* and *Vesper* joined after having been fogbound in Londonderry. The newcomers took up their positions in the defensive ring as the first grey light of dawn crept in from the east. The convoy was by then deep into the Atlantic, 150 miles south-west of Rockall and steaming at reduced speed in poor visibility and rough seas – Winter North Atlantic at its miserable best. The merchantmen, broad in the beam and long familiar with such weather, ploughed on untroubled. The racehorse-like destroyers corkscrewed from crest to trough, their decks continually awash; the tiny corvettes were rarely visible in the swirling foam; the high-sided carriers simply wallowed. And in the midst of all this, the *Argus*, sailing second ship in the centre column, sighted a U-boat.

The carrier sent a rocket soaring skywards to burst in a shower of white stars and at the same time broke radio silence to report a U-boat on the surface in the middle of the convoy. *Argus* then turned to ram, while *Furious*, leading the port column, fired a Very light to signal an emergency turn 40 degrees to port.

There was a confused response from the merchant ships, who

were not aware that the convoy commodore, Captain Buckley in the *Northern Prince*, having no Very lights on board, had arranged with the *Furious* to make the necessary signals in the event of an emergency. Some ships made the turn, others, believing the lights had been fired in error, maintained their course.

Meanwhile, the U-boat, seeing the huge bulk of the *Argus* bearing down on her, had dived deep. She was long gone by the time the situation became clear and the destroyer *Harvester* fired star shell and dropped back to search for her. The *Harvester* combed the area for over an hour, but made no contact.

When the furore had died down, *Argus* reported to Rear-Admiral King in HMS *Naiad* that two officers and several ratings had sighted the surfaced U-boat, but King was sceptical. In a written report to the Admiralty made later, he stated: 'I think that a U-boat would hardly have reached such a position without affording some tangible proof of its presence by making an attack. The U-boat would, moreover, have had to pass right through the line of escorting destroyers. . . . It was dark at the time and visibility was poor and the sea was "lumpy". Nothing was seen by the *Naiad* who was about 5 cables astern of the *Argus*.'

In hindsight, it is difficult to follow Rear-Admiral King's reasoning. Citing poor visibility and rough seas, he was not inclined to believe the reports of not just one, but a number of reliable witnesses aboard the *Argus*. He then ignored the possibility that the convoy was being shadowed. And then there was the question of *Argus* breaking radio silence to report the U-boat sighting. This could well have betrayed the presence of the convoy to listening enemy ears, yet King took no evasive action. Instead, he chose only to admonish *Argus* for her indiscretion and carried on as before.

Early on the 21st King received orders from the Commander-in-Chief, Western Approaches to detach much of his escort force for other duties. The convoy was at this point 500 miles west of Ireland and in deteriorating weather. Reluctantly, King complied with the order, detaching the destroyers *Harvester*, *Highlander* and *Beverley* late that night, and *Ottawa*, *St Laurent*, *Vesper* and *Le Triomphant* before dawn on the 22nd. The two remaining destroyers, *Kelvin* and *Kipling*, left at 1000 that morning, leaving only HMS *Naiad* and the two corvettes *Clematis* and *Cyclamen* guarding the convoy. What had once seemed a surfeit of escorts was at a stroke reduced to a bare minimum.

The ships were then on a southerly course and running into the teeth of a rising south-easterly gale. By noon they were battling against very rough seas and a heavy swell. One of the merchantmen, Federal Steam Navigation Company's *Essex*, carrying uncrated aircraft on her foredeck, was forced to reduce to 9½ knots to avoid damaging the planes. She could not be allowed to fall astern, so the whole convoy slowed to keep pace with her. Stripped of much of his escort force, and reduced to a crawl in appalling weather, Rear-Admiral King was not a happy man.

At 1400 consternation was caused when an unidentified warship suddenly appeared out of the gloom ahead. It was HMS *Wellington*, detached by Captain Jack Egerton to stand by the disabled *Ernebank*. The sloop signalled by lamp that the ships of the slow section of WS 5A were just 80 miles to the south and widely scattered by the weather. The *Ernebank* was not to be found. Satisfied that contact would soon be established between the two sections of the convoy, King ordered *Wellington* to resume her search for the missing ship.

Later that afternoon the Admiralty signalled *Naiad* warning that there was a possibility the convoy might have been sighted reported by a U-boat. This served to confirm what many minds in the convoy were already thinking, but was contrary to Rear-Admiral King's assessment. King did, however, bow to the Admiralty's judgement and ordered an alteration of course 30 degrees to starboard and an increase in speed. This did nothing to improve the suffering of the ships, the change of course putting them beam-on to wind and sea, and increasing speed, first to 13, and later to 14 knots, put the heavily loaded merchant ships under immense strain. Rolling crazily, with the seas breaking over their weather bulwarks, they clawed their way to the south-east and, it was hoped, away from the danger.

At 1920 a further signal came in from the Admiralty, this time advising that the convoy was probably being shadowed by a U-boat. This should have been proof enough that *Argus* really had sighted a U-boat early that morning and was indicative that the Germans were adopting their usual tactics. Admiral Dönitz's standing orders were for any lone U-boat sighting a convoy not to attack at once, but to drop back out of sight and shadow on the surface until other boats could be called in to mount an attack in force.

Although the Admiralty did not say as much, it should have been obvious from their signals that they had been monitoring W/T traffic from a U-boat in the area for some time. Yet Rear-Admiral King still refused to believe his convoy was under any immediate threat. In his own words, he 'considered it improbable that a U-boat could shadow the convoy at 14 knots during the night.' By now the weather had moderated somewhat and, with amazing complacency, King resumed a southerly course and pressed on.

The night passed uneventfully and on the morning of the 23rd, when it was full daylight, the fast section of WS 5A, led by HMS *Naiad*, overtook and merged with the slow section, much to the relief of Captain Jack Egerton in the *Bonaventure*. For more than thirty-six hours he had steered a very lonely course, with only his light cruiser and – when she was not away chasing up stragglers – the little *Wellington* standing between his large flock and the many predators of the German Navy and Air Force.

By noon that day, despite continuing poor visibility and rough seas, Convoy WS 5A had become one and was composed of nineteen merchant ships – the *Delane* was still missing – led by Rear-Admiral Reyne in the *Tamoroa*, and steaming at 12 knots, a speed which all the ships could reasonably maintain. WS 5A, carrying 40,000 troops, around 150,000 tons of arms and equipment, including several squadrons of fighter aircraft, was a target the likes of which had rarely been seen at sea in time of war, a prize the Germans were now aware of and intended to take action against. The combined escort force for WS 5A consisted of the two anti-aircraft cruisers *Naiad* and *Bonaventure*, the sloop *Wellington*, the Flower-class corvettes *Clematis* and *Cyclamen*, and the two carriers *Argus* and *Furious* playing a dual role as transports and escorts. It was little enough for such a vital convoy sailing in dangerous waters.

Within an hour of the convoy forming up the Admiralty signalled Rear-Admiral King that six Focke-Wulf Kondor long-range bombers had left Bordeaux in mid-morning and were heading his way. Throughout the rest of the day guns were fully manned and lookouts doubled in all the ships, naval and merchant, while Skuas from the *Furious* patrolled the skies above them. As the hours dragged by, the tension in the ships ran high, but by the time darkness began to close in no attack had developed. The Focke-Wulfs had gone elsewhere.

As soon as it was fully dark, King took the ships through two evasive turns to throw off any pursuing U-boats, one of 30 degrees to starboard and, three hours later, 40 degrees to port. Poor visibility during the night led to indifferent station keeping and when dawn broke on the 24th the convoy was in an untidy mess which took all morning to clear up. During this time the *Delane* rejoined and the escort was reinforced by HMS *Berwick*, a formidable 10,000-ton cruiser armed with eight 8-inch and eight 4-inch guns, and the small light cruiser *Dunedin* mounting six 6-inch and three 4-inch. With the arrival of the two newcomers, HMS *Naiad*, her mission completed, broke away and headed back for Scapa Flow.

WS 5A, having survived a thousand miles of the most dangerous waters of the North Atlantic without coming under attack, now steamed on to the south with renewed confidence. In just over two days, when abeam of the Straits of Gibraltar, the convoy would again separate, the fast ships, led by the *Northern Prince*, to attempt the hazardous Mediterranean passage, while the others continued their long run to the Cape and beyond. Meanwhile, it was Christmas Eve and tomorrow was a day for celebration – such as it could be in the circumstances. The odd bottle of whisky would be cracked and long-suffering cooks in their undulating galleys would make a brave face of preparing roast turkey and plum pudding, but the thoughts of the men afloat in Convoy WS 5A would inevitably turn to the homes and families they had left behind.

Chapter Nine

On 18 December 1940, as the first ships of Convoy WS 5A were assembling in the North Channel, the refrigerated steamer *Duquesa* was 700 miles south-west of Freetown and homeward bound from the River Plate. Owned by Houlder Brothers of London, the 8651-ton *Duquesa* carried in her holds 3,500 tons of frozen beef and 15 million eggs – a king's ransom to the belt-tightening citizens of the British Isles. It was a cargo they would never see.

At 1220 that day, as Captain Bearpark and his officers were taking noon sights on the bridge of the *Duquesa*, the *Admiral Scheer* came storming over the horizon. The British cargo liner was unarmed and had a top speed of only 12 knots; the *Scheer* carried a frightening array of 11-inch, 6-inch and 4-inch guns, and had 26 knots at her disposal. It was no contest. Even so, Bearpark declined to surrender, presented his stern to the German ship and made off at all speed.

The *Scheer*'s 11-inch guns had a range of 11 miles and at any time could have stopped the *Duquesa* in her tracks. But the battle-ship's commander, Kapitän-zur-See Theodor Krancke, was playing for higher stakes, holding his fire until his quarry had sent a raider report and received an acknowledgement. Only then did Krancke lob shells across the *Duquesa*'s bows, forcing her to heave-to.

Krancke's object in allowing the British ship to inform the world of her plight was to create a diversion. He hoped to draw attention away from northern waters, where the *Admiral Hipper* had recently emerged from the Denmark Strait and was lying in wait for the Halifax convoys. In this he succeeded. On receipt of the *Duquesa*'s report, the Admiralty acted quickly, ordering the heavy cruisers *Neptune* and *Dorsetshire* out from Freetown to make for the scene of the attack at maximum speed. At the same time the aircraft carrier *Hermes*, the armed merchant cruiser *Pretoria Castle* and the light cruiser *Dragon* were instructed to meet off St. Helena and from there join the search for the *Scheer*. This left the seas to the north clear of heavy units, thereby allowing the *Hipper* to mount her attack on the convoys un-hindered. When the British ships arrived at the *Duquesa*'s last known position, the wily Krancke had gone south with his prize in company. With a German crew on board, the *Duquesa* was taken to a secret anchorage off the coast of Brazil and there acted as a supply ship for German raiders, her precious cargo of beef and eggs proving a valuable morale booster for men on a diet of smoked sausage and pickled sauerkraut. Her coal bunkers empty and her refrigerating machinery no longer working, she was scuttled on 18 February 1941.

As it transpired, Krancke's diversion was wasted, for the North Atlantic decided to live up to its well-earned reputation. When Wilhelm Meisel brought the *Hipper* through the Denmark Strait, he ran straight into a violent storm that pounded the German cruiser so hard that her starboard engine was disabled. A second storm followed on the heels of the first, so that, far from estab-lishing her supremacy on the convoy routes, the *Hipper* found herself engaged in a desperate fight with the elements and hard-pressed to even maintain steerage way. It was an ignominious situation for a purpose-built commerce raider.

Eventually the *Hipper* ended up far to the south of the Halifax–Liverpool track without having sighted a single enemy ship. By this time, although he had been at sea for less than a month, Meisel was seriously concerned for his shrinking fuel reserves. He decided to make for Brest, crossing the Freetown–UK convoy track on the way and hoping to meet up with a large con-voy reported to be bound south. But in view of the atrocious weather conditions still prevailing, this seemed a forlorn hope. And so it would have remained, had it not been for an unexpected twist of fate.

Christmas Eve, 24 December 1940, which for those safe ashore at home was an occasion for muted revelry, turned out to be a nightmare for the men of Convoy WS 5A. A severe SW'ly gale blew up after sunset and raged throughout the night, causing confusion in the slow-moving lines of ships. Rough head seas and poor visibility on a moonless night made a mockery of station keeping, but, somehow, the ships held together. Then, sometime in the early hours of the 25th, the *Empire Trooper*'s past came back to haunt her when one of her engines, damaged by her late German crew, ground to a halt. The liner attempted to hold her position on one engine, but she fell slowly astern and was soon a back-marker for the convoy. A very conspicuous marker she was, too. Tall and wide, she made the perfect target for the *Hipper*'s searching radar. Meisel, suspecting he may have found more than just one big ship sailing alone, decided to shadow her throughout the rest of the night, planning to attack at first light.

The dawn came reluctantly on that Christmas morning, the darkness slowly turning to a grey overcast. But there was some small comfort for Convoy WS 5A, then 650 miles due west of Cape Finisterre. The weather was showing definite signs of moderating. The long, heavy swell raised by the storm was still there, but the wind had lost much of its strength and the sea was reduced to a mere boisterous chop. A dismal mixture of drizzle and mist continued to restrict visibility, but the cloud base appeared to be lifting. As the ships stirred into life and the smoke billowed out from a score of galley funnels, it could almost be said that the spirit of Christmas was in the air.

Trailing well astern of the convoy, both her engines now functioning sweetly, the *Empire Trooper* was making a determined effort to catch up with the other ships. Keeping station on her was the corvette *Clematis*, which had been detached to stand by her during the night. The liner was in good hands, for HMS *Clematis* was commanded by 46-year-old Commander Yorke McCleod Cleeves DSO, DSC, RNR, a remarkable man, ex-Merchant Navy officer, ex-Swansea pilot, who had distinguished himself in the Norwegian campaign.

Immediately ahead of the *Empire Trooper* and her escort was another straggler, the 5874-ton *Arabistan*, owned by Frank C. Strick and Company of London and commanded by Captain Metcalfe. She was far from her usual trading grounds, the warm, benign waters of the Red Sea and Persian Gulf, and was making very heavy weather of it. Some three weeks earlier, conscripted by the necessities of war, she had gingerly negotiated the narrow locks of the near-defunct South Wales port of Penarth and berthed alongside a wharf that had once been a resting place for tall-masted Cape Horners. In these unfamiliar surroundings, the *Arabistan* loaded a cargo of bombs, shells and military stores and equipment, topping off with a large invasion barge – one of the first of its kind – lashed down on deck in two sections. And to complete her contribution to the war in the Middle East, the *Arabistan* also carried a small contingent of New Zealand Maori troops, on route to rejoin their unit after training in Britain.

Seaman Gunner Raymond Buck was standing a lone watch at the *Arabistan*'s 4-inch stern gun when, with the light strengthening, he became aware of a large ship breaking through the mist and rain to starboard. Buck, merchant seaman by trade, gunner by virtue of a few days spent at a naval gunnery school before the war, at first thought the other ship was HMS *Berwick*, a comforting sight on a comfortless morning. Then, as she glided back into the murk, he was swiftly disillusioned. The horizon to starboard was suddenly lit by brilliant yellow flashes, which were followed by the unmistakable and unnerving screech of heavy shells passing overhead. The *Admiral Hipper* had commenced her dawn attack.

For a brief moment Buck was stunned; then he realized that what they had all feared since leaving home was about to happen. He could not handle the 4-inch on his own and he had no communication with the bridge, so he hurled himself down the ladder to the main deck and ran forward to call the rest of the gun's crew, who were still sleeping. Crouching low as he ran, Buck was urged on by the shrapnel whistling and pinging around him.

On the bridge of the *Clematis*, Sub-Lieutenant John Ellyatt had the watch. The corvette being low in the water, her lookouts had failed to spot the *Hipper* when she emerged from the mist and Ellyatt at first took the flash of her guns to be lightning. When shells began to hit the water close to the corvette, he quickly changed his mind and lunged for the alarm bells.

Meisel had caught WS 5A's escort off guard – which was not surprising. The night had been long and punishing; a night spent in an unrelenting struggle to hold the clumsy merchant ships together as they romped and straggled their way through the foul weather. When dawn came at last, the convoy was in chaos, with ships spread all over the ocean. Captain G.L. Warren, commanding officer of HMS *Berwick*, summed it up:

> 'The positions at dawn on 25th December 1940 cannot be given with any exactness. It is, however, known that *Berwick* was further ahead, as she was getting so many reciprocal readings from the convoy on her RDF screen. . . .
>
> 'The position of the *Empire Trooper* is not known, or that of the two remaining corvettes, beyond the fact that the latter were in the rear of the convoy.
>
> The actual composition, formation and disposition of the convoy was not known beyond inspection during daylight on 24th December 1940.'

To a large extent, convoy and escort were out of touch with each other. The *Hipper*'s attack could not have come at a more inopportune time.

The tiny *Clematis*, 900 tons gross and armed with a single 4-inch gun, was the first to join battle with the enemy. As soon as he had assessed the situation, Commander Cleeves, with typical disregard for the odds, immediately turned towards the *Hipper* and charged at full speed, his 4-inch spitting defiance. His signal to the Admiralty, 'AM ENGAGING UNKNOWN ENEMY BATTLESHIP', was as audacious as the man himself. It was an act of incredible bravery, for Cleeves was well aware that one well-aimed salvo from his opponent's big guns would blow the *Clematis* clean out of the water. Sub-Lieutenant John Palmer said later:

> 'I must confess I thought Cleeves was going for a posthumous VC. That was typical of him. He had no hesitation about altering course towards the *Hipper* and opening fire. Undoubtedly, he would have continued to the end – which might have come at any moment.'

As the corvette raced in to attack, with the *Hipper*'s 8-inch shells throwing up tall waterspouts all around her, Commander Yorke

Cleves' main concern was for the protection of the convoy. With the *Clematis* now between the *Hipper* and the merchantmen, he ordered the engine-room to make smoke. The *Clematis*, being an early type of corvette, was not fitted with a smoke generator, but Leading Stoker Harry Penter, in charge of the watch in the boiler-room, improvised by shutting down the air flaps on the furnaces. This produced a huge pall of thick smoke which, lying low on the water, put an impenetrable screen between the *Hipper* and the convoy, which was now scattering. Penter's quick thinking undoubtedly saved many of these ships from certain destruction.

The *Empire Trooper*, the immediate target of Wilhelm Meisel's guns, produced a sudden surge from her faltering engines and ran for the cover of the smoke. It seemed that she might escape unharmed; then, just as she was disappearing from view, a German shell struck below the waterline, blowing a great hole in the liner's hull and killing sixteen men in the troop decks. She took on a heavy list as the water poured into her, but she was in no real danger of sinking.

The *Arabistan*, also running for the cover of Harry Penter's smoke screen, came even nearer to destruction. She received extensive shrapnel damage on deck and one shell scored a direct hit on her forepeak store. A few feet further aft and the shell would have ploughed into her forward hold, which was packed with bombs and shells. The resulting explosion would undoubtedly have vaporized the ship and all on board. But luck was with her that day and her damage was mainly superficial, the only casualty being Seaman Gunner Raymond Buck, who suffered a small shrapnel wound to his foot. It was reported that throughout the action Captain Metcalfe was seen standing calmly in the open wing of the bridge conning his ship through the shell bursts. 'He was ice-cool,' remarked Buck.

Fortunately for the little *Clematis*, all the enemy shells that came her way missed and, apart from being thoroughly doused by the near misses, she was unharmed. Cleves' momentous signal to the Admiralty alerted the convoy's cruiser escort and he had the satisfaction of seeing *Berwick*, *Bonaventure* and *Dunedin* come storming out of the mist and smoke to challenge the *Hipper*. *Bonaventure* was in the lead, and Captain Jack Egerton described the action:

104

'*Bonaventure* turned towards the flashes, but, before sighting the enemy, salvoes of what were probably 4-inch shells were seen straddling the *Empire Trooper*. When sighted, the enemy was thought to be an *Admiral Hipper* class cruiser but at no time, then or later, was she seen clearly enough to be sure. When *Bonaventure* opened fire, at 0812, enemy fire was shifted from *Empire Trooper* onto her but no hits were obtained.

'My policy was to keep nearly end on and thus exploit the advantage of *Bonaventure*'s good firepower forward while presenting a small target to the enemy, while gradually working over to the enemy's starboard quarter, the opposite quarter to the *Berwick*.

'The target was always indistinct, partly due to the mist and partly to the spray flung up at high speeds, and the director layer never had a good aiming mark. Several times when the enemy could be seen from one position he could not be seen from another. In consequence, fire was opened in a series of short bursts using blind ladders as 'shorts' only could be spotted with certainty. *Berwick*'s eight-inch shells were easier to spot than our own though it is not always easy to be sure which was which. The shorts appeared to be in line and it is hoped that the enemy received some at least of the remainder, but no hits could be observed. . . .

'All guns were in action after firing an average of 70 rounds a gun from each of the three fore turrets, which speaks well for the design of this new type of mounting. . . .

'In all *Bonaventure* fired 438 rounds, nearly all as stated above, from the fore turrets, and this confirms the opinion I have always held that it is better for the four turret ships of the Dido class to have three turrets forward and one aft, as in *Bonaventure*, than two and two in *Dido* and *Phoebe*.

'Except for the few salvoes of 4-inch already mentioned and some of the 8-inch later on, when *Berwick* may have been obscured, all misses, the enemy did not fire at *Bonaventure*.

'*Bonaventure* ceased fire at 0836 to avoid undue expenditure of ammunition, and, as the visibility got worse, lost sight of the enemy at 0926. This was reported to *Berwick* and *Bonaventure* was ordered to rejoin the convoy, subsequently taking station on *Berwick* in doing so.'

During the brief but fierce action, the *Hipper* had returned shot for shot with her attackers, but in the poor visibility prevailing she scored only one hit, knocking *Berwick*'s 'X' turret out of the fight and killing its crew of seven Marines. In return, in spite of the great weight of shells thrown at her, the German cruiser received only minor damage and suffered no casualties. However, the odds were stacked against her and Meisel decided to withdraw at speed. In his log he wrote:

'I have decided to break off the operation and to sail to Brest as fast as possible before measures are taken by the enemy, provoked by the attack on the convoy, take effect. If I continued at sea I would have to refuel tomorrow at the latest in order to remain in operation. This has been the task which was set me. I feel the moment has come where the limit of the efficiency of ship and crew is in sight.'

Taking advantage of the poor visibility, Meisel disengaged and, as soon as he was out of sight of the British ships, set course for Brest. His decision was a wise one, for when the news reached the Admiralty of the attack on WS 5A, the Christmas festivities ashore were drowned by the loud clamour of alarm bells. HMS *Naiad*, then 420 miles to the north and making for Scapa Flow, was ordered to return to the convoy, the heavy cruiser *Kenya* was sent south to protect two other convoys in the area, while the battlecruiser *Repulse* and the *Nigeria*, another Colony-class cruiser, were also ordered to sea. In the eventuality that the *Hipper* might attempt to return to Germany via the Denmark Strait, units of the Home Fleet were sent to keep watch in northern waters. In the more likely event that Meisel would head for a French Atlantic port, Coastal Command aircraft began intensive patrols over the Bay of Biscay.

Later that morning, when she was 450 miles to the west of Ushant and driving through heavy rain at 30 knots, the *Hipper* chanced upon a target that was more to Meisel's liking. It was the 6078-ton British steamer *Jumna*, owned by Nourse Line of London, and under the command of Captain N.R. Burgess.

Bound from Liverpool to Calcutta with a cargo of general, the *Jumna* carried a crew of sixty-four and forty-four passengers, the latter being Indian seamen returning home after their ship had been sunk earlier in the year. The *Jumna* had been commodore ship of Convoy OB 260, which had dispersed some hours earlier, and still had on board the commodore, Rear-Admiral H.B. Maltby, and his staff. Maltby, who only seven weeks before had been commodore of the ill-fated *Jervis Bay* convoy HX 84 when it was attacked and savaged by the *Admiral Scheer*, was to be landed at Freetown on the *Jumna*'s way south to the Cape. He would then take passage home as commodore of a northbound convoy.

On sighting the *Jumna*, Meisel challenged her, flashing by lamp, 'DID YOU SEE ANY GERMAN RAIDER?', followed by, 'WHAT SHIP?' The reference to the German raider was evidently designed to mislead Captain Burgess into thinking he was being challenged by a British warship. The subterfuge failed, for, although Burgess flashed back his ship's name, he immediately reversed course and ran away from the *Hipper*.

The *Hipper*'s wireless operators, listening on the international distress frequency 600 metres, heard the *Jumna* begin transmitting. No position was given; they heard only a garbled message, 'SUSPICIOUS VESSELS . . . COMMERCE RAIDER' This was enough for Meisel who, following his painful experience of earlier in the day, was not in the mood to take risks. He ordered his gunners to open fire at will, and at point-blank range the helpless merchantman was soon on fire and stopped. Two torpedoes fired at equally close range sent her to the bottom.

Five minutes after the *Jumna* disappeared beneath the waves, the *Hipper* withdrew at 30 knots. In his report, Meisel said he made no effort to search for survivors, as he believed the British ship's distress call might have been heard and he was concerned to remove his ship from the area as quickly as possible. A wise decision perhaps, but a callous one. As it transpired, no Allied ship or shore station reported hearing the doomed ship's last message, no wreckage was ever found, no survivors, not even a body marked her last resting place. The *Jumna* had gone down, taking with her a total of 111 men, her crew, Rear-Admiral Maltby and his staff, and the forty-four unfortunate Lascar seamen who had survived one sinking only to die in another a few short weeks later. Some time after the *Jumna* failed to arrive in Freetown, she was posted as missing, believed sunk.

Seen in retrospect, the *Admiral Hipper*'s sortie against Convoy WS 5A was at best a half-hearted affair. Meisel had a huge advantage in surprise; it was Christmas Day, when perhaps minds in the convoy were not entirely focused on the right things, the visibility was poor and he had been in contact unseen all night. And his ship was vastly superior to anything in the British escort force. Had he pressed home his attack with determination, Meisel could have caused havoc amongst this large fleet of troopers and supply ships, with disastrous consequences for the British campaign in the Middle East. Confronted initially by a Flower-class corvette armed with one 4-inch and chased off by a barrage of shells from *Bonaventure* and *Berwick*, Kapitän-zur-See Wilhelm Meisel had been found wanting. His ruthless sinking of the *Jumna* served to confirm his inadequacy.

Christmas Day 1940, a day that few who were there would ever forget, ended quietly for Convoy WS 5A. The scattered merchant ships were rounded up, the convoy was reformed and, with the *Arabistan* limping along behind with a hole in her bows, continued on southwards. The sun shone and, for the first time since leaving home waters, the sea was calm. But there were the dead to be buried and any form of celebration, however muted, seemed out of place. The day ended quietly, in the knowledge that the job had been well done. Only one ship, the *Empire Trooper*, had left the convoy. Holed below the waterline, the entire complement of the ex-German liner's troops spent the rest of the day lining the far side to list the ship while a temporary repair was affected. She was then escorted to San Miguel in the Azores by the corvette *Cyclamen*, where she was allowed to make a more permanent repair. There the *Cyclamen* had to leave her while she made a dash for Gibraltar to refuel. The *Empire Trooper*, having put to good use the maximum 72 hours allowed in a neutral port, sailed alone for Gibraltar. Within hours her notoriously un-reliable engines had let her down and she lay drifting in a flat calm sea at the mercy of any passing U-boat. The situation was saved by the return of the *Cyclamen* that night and, with the *Empire Trooper* once more under her own steam, the two ships reached Gibraltar three days later.

There was a sequel to the action when, at 1044 on Boxing Day, HMS *Bonaventure*, which had been detached to assist *Cyclamen* with the *Empire Trooper*, but failed to make contact, sighted the German supply tanker *Baden*. The *Baden*, unaware that the

Hipper had made a run for Brest, was still on station waiting to refuel the cruiser. On being challenged by *Bonaventure*, the *Baden* made off to the west at all speed, but she had no hope of escaping from the 33-knot British cruiser. A warning shot perilously close to her bows was enough to bring her up short, but before abandoning ship her crew set fire to her. Captain Egerton tried to drive the Germans back aboard the tanker by machine-gunning close to the boats, but without success. Egerton reported:

'I prepared to go alongside to carry out salvage operations but it was probable that much damage would have been done and this was given up. A boat was lowered with a boarding party but by the time they got alongside the flames had reached the top of the rope ladder and this idea too was abandoned.

'Salvage might have been possible later in the day as the flames were confined to the midship portion and the vessel appeared to be floating normally. I therefore picked up 8 officers and 31 other survivors, there were no casualties, and proceeded to search for the *Empire Trooper* with the idea of returning to *Baden* before dark to make another attempt at salvage.

'However, on receipt of Senior Officer Force H's 1234/26, *Bonaventure* returned to and sank *Baden* by firing a few rounds into her and finally sinking her with a torpedo.'

When news was received that the *Empire Trooper* had reached the Azores, *Bonaventure* was ordered to proceed Gibraltar at 20 knots to refuel. So, for Captain Jack Egerton and his men, ended a dramatic, action-packed forty-eight hours. There were more dangers ahead, however.

In the early hours of the 27th, a dark, moonless night with rain showers on the horizon, the lookout in the bows of *Bonaventure*, Boy Seaman J.H. McGrath, reported sighting a ship on the cruiser's starboard beam and immediately afterwards a ship on the starboard bow and another right ahead. On the bridge, the officer of the watch, Lieutenant-Commander N.S. Henderson, swept the horizon with his night glasses and, to his horror, saw the dark shapes of slow-moving merchant ships all around him. Steaming south-east at 20 knots, *Bonaventure* had run straight into a northbound convoy.

It was a seaman's worst nightmare realized, for at any moment the speeding cruiser might be run down or go crashing into the hull of an unseen ship crossing her path. Fortunately, Henderson kept his nerve and did the only thing possible under the circumstances, bringing *Bonaventure* round to port under full helm to take up a course parallel with the convoy. *Bonaventure* raced up through the third and fourth columns of the merchantmen and by the time Captain Egerton reached the bridge she was exchanging signals with the convoy's escort HMS *Cathay*. It was then established that the convoy, SL 59, bound from Freetown to the UK, was 100 miles north of its reported position. By the combination of keen eyes and quick thinking aboard *Bonaventure*, what could have been a major disaster was averted.

A few hours after *Bonaventure*'s unexpected meeting with SL 59, the *Admiral Hipper,* having eluded all the Coastal Command aircraft searching for her, entered the French Atlantic port of Brest. There she lay well hidden, for it was not until 4 January 1941 that RAF reconnaissance aircraft discovered her. She then became a priority target for high-level bombers, but despite 175 raids by Coastal Command and Bomber Command over the next three weeks, in which a total of eighty-five tons of bombs were dropped, the heavy cruiser was undamaged.

Chapter Ten

Unlike Kapitän Meisel of the *Hipper*, each time Ernst Krüder sank a ship he made a conscious effort to rescue the survivors, which may well have been commendably humanitarian and in accordance with the unwritten code of the sea, but as the year drew to a close the *Pinguin* was beginning to resemble a floating jail. With the sinking of the *Port Brisbane* on 1 December and the acquisition of another ninety-three survivors, this brought the total of Allied prisoners on board the raider to 405. These men – and eight women – took up a great deal of room in the already overcrowded ship, they must be fed, watered and exercised regularly, and, as they were close to outnumbering the *Pinguin*'s crew, they must be under constant guard.

At this point Krüder's orders from Berlin were quite specific. He was to move south into Antarctic waters and there find and attack the Allied whaling fleet. Obviously, he could not embark upon this adventure encumbered with so many potentially hostile prisoners. He could, of course, abandon them; land them on an uninhabited island and leave them to their fate, but that was not Krüder's way of doing things. He favoured intercepting and capturing a ship in which to send them back to Germany, and that meant a motor ship with sufficient fuel to make the run non-stop. There was, however, very little likelihood of meeting up with such a ship in this area. Most of the Allied merchantmen in the Indian Ocean were coal-burners, requiring at least one refuelling stop on the way north. That left only the *Storstad*. She was a low-consumption motor vessel and, with 10,000 tons of diesel in her cargo tanks, was capable of sailing to the ends of the earth and back without refuelling. Krüder had intended to hold on to the tanker to help with mine-laying when he returned to the Indian Ocean from the south, but the need to get rid of the prisoners was more urgent.

Krüder notified Berlin of his intention to send the *Storstad* home and was instructed to set up a rendezvous with Rogge's *Atlantis*, which was in need of fuel and also had prisoners to get rid of. The three ships met on 8 December in a position far from the shipping lanes, 900 miles to the south-east of Madagascar. Here the *Storstad* transferred 1,670 tons of diesel to the *Atlantis* and in return received another 124 prisoners. The *Pinguin* then topped up her fuel tanks from the *Storstad* and the tanker set off on her 8000-mile voyage to Biscay in the early hours of the morning of the 10th. In command was Leutnant Helmut Hanefeld, a reservist, who had with him a German crew of twenty, all the men Krüder could spare from the *Pinguin*. Hanefeld would be dependent on the *Storstad*'s Norwegian crew to handle the tanker, while his men were left with the seemingly impossible task of guarding the prisoners, who heavily outnumbered them. It promised to be an interesting voyage.

The *Pinguin* had already gone when the *Storstad* sailed. She left the rendezvous early on the afternoon of the 9th, her destination Bouvet Island, a lonely Norwegian outpost some 1,500 miles south-west of Cape Town, where the Allied whaling fleets were believed to be fishing. Neither Krüder nor any of his officers were familiar with these waters, but by a stroke of good luck, when the *Atlantis* captured the Norwegian tanker *Teddy* in the Indian Ocean, a full set of Antarctic charts and sailing directions were found on board, which were duly handed over to Krüder. One of the charts still bore the pencilled courses around Bouvet Island taken by the *Teddy* when she was supply ship to the whaling fleet in the winter of 1939/40. This alone was a priceless addition to Krüder's chart library.

Course was set to pass midway between the Prince Edward Islands and the Crozet Islands, two lonely and uninhabited archipelagoes in the South Indian Ocean, and thence to Bouvet. As the *Pinguin* moved south, accompanied by a close escort of stately albatrosses wheeling and swooping at her stern, so the weather grew progressively colder and less inviting. The caress

112

of the warm breeze and the flying fish leaping at the bow became only a memory, and in their place the keening winds and heaving grey seas of the Roaring Forties. By 15 December, which marked the passing of the *Pinguin*'s sixth month out of Gotenhafen, the air temperature was down to zero; two days later the first iceberg was sighted. They had entered the world of Antarctica.

As the *Pinguin* moved deeper and deeper into this alien sea, the icebergs became larger and more numerous. Navigation, especially in darkness, became increasingly difficult as the ship, reduced to a mere crawl, picked her way between the great tabular ice islands, some of them as much as half a mile long and 150 feet high. On the 19th, when in latitude 60° S, she found herself surrounded by over 100 of these huge bergs, which were accompanied by fields of crackling ice floes. On the floes they saw the first penguins, comical little black and white figures standing shoulder to shoulder to witness the passing of the ship that bore their name. Krüder now judged that he had come far enough south and altered course to the north-west for Bouvet.

On the night of the 23rd, a night as crisp and still as any winter's night in the Baltic, *Pinguin*'s wireless operators picked up faint radio-telephone traffic – ghostly voices speaking in Norwegian. Although they were still 1000 miles from Bouvet, the whaling fleet was there, somewhere over the horizon. Also that night came the news from Berlin that the Führer had awarded Ernst Krüder the *Ritterkreuz* – the coveted Knight's Cross – in recognition of his spectacular success in the Indian and Pacific oceans. Characteristically, Krüder paid little attention to the award and concentrated on the job in hand.

Christmas came and went aboard the *Pinguin* with little celebration. By courtesy of the intercepted British refrigerated ships, there was plenty of good food, and there was the best Bremen export beer, carefully saved for the occasion. In the evening they sang *Stille Nacht* with a great longing for home in their voices, but the day ended as it began, subdued and full of apprehension for what might lie ahead in the New Year. On the 26th, with little wind and a flat calm sea, Krüder found work for idle hands and put an end to the nostalgia by ordering the Heinkel aloft – a practice run for the operation to come. The seaplane was launched without difficulty, but after only two hours in the air it ran out of fuel and was forced to land on the water. Homing in on a radio signal, Krüder steamed at full speed for three hours before the ditched aircraft was reached. An examination of the Heinkel after it was lifted aboard showed that its engine was consuming 40 percent more fuel than normal. The exercise had not been in vain.

With the short festive season over, the weather began to deteriorate and by the 28th the *Pinguin* was feeling her way through the ice under a low overcast and with visibility severely reduced by drizzle. The radio telephone frequencies were now alive with chatter in Norwegian, which was carefully listened to by the *Pinguin*'s Norwegian-speaking wireless operator Pastor. He was able to identify two whale factory ships, the *Ole Wegger* and the *Pelagos*, both of 12,000 tons, each of which had six catchers fishing within a radius of 40 miles. Much of the R/T traffic concerned the expected arrival within the next few days of a supply ship bringing fuel, fresh food and mail for the fleet, from which she would then collect whale oil and blubber.

It was at this point that a daring plan Krüder had been turning over in his mind began to look like a definite possibility. His orders from Berlin were suitably vague, to 'find and attack' the whaling fleet, which left considerable scope for his initiative. From the careless way in which the whalers used their radios, filling the air waves with a constant babble of morse and voice traffic audible to all the world, it was obvious they believed they were safe from attack down here amongst the bergs and ice fields. They appeared to be carrying on exactly as they would have done in times of peace, only concerned with the demanding task of catching and processing as many whales as possible while the season lasted. The ships were unlikely to be armed, and it was Krüder's experience with Norwegian seamen thus far that they had not yet really convinced themselves that this war was any of their business. Many of them would just as soon work for the Germans as for the British. All this being so, then it should be feasible for the heavily-armed *Pinguin* to take them unawares, capture them and send them home as prizes – not just one ship, but the whole fleet. It was an outrageous proposal, full of

114

dangers, not the least being that the Norwegians might use their powerful transmitters to scream for help and bring every British cruiser within reach racing in to give battle.

Pastor kept a close listening watch on the Norwegians throughout that day and learned that the whole fleet was moving westwards to meet the supply ship. They were in poor visibility, with the mother ships continuously transmitting on the D/F frequencies to guide the catchers in on them. During the night Krüder steamed at full speed to the north-west, making a wide arc and taking bearings of the Norwegians at intervals in order to fix their position accurately. Due to the *Pinguin*'s close proximity to the South Magnetic Pole and the resultant sluggish behaviour of her compasses, this was not easy.

The *Pinguin* saw the Old Year out and the New Year in hove-to in a severe north-westerly gale, battling against mountainous seas, blinded by sleet and snow squalls, and with large icebergs close by. She was, as far as could be judged from D/F bearings, some 150 miles north of the factory ship *Pelagos*, whose catchers could be heard complaining bitterly about the bad weather and lack of whales. The *Ole Wegger* was further to the south-west and had found shelter in the lee of an icefield, where her catchers were reporting more success. On the stroke of midnight the Norwegians filled the air waves with hearty New Year's greetings passed between ship and ship. Krüder stayed silent, waiting and listening.

The weather began to improve slowly during the first day of 1941, the wind dropping and the visibility lifting. At the same time the intentions of the Norwegians became clearer. In his war diary Krüder summed up:

'On the basis of observations to date, I judge the situation to be as follows:

1. In the Bouvet area, between 50 degrees East and 20 degrees West, two flotillas of Norwegian catchers are now working.

    a. *Ole Wegger* with seven catchers, Nos 1 to 7 (*Ole Wegger* herself is No.8 for R/T purposes).

    b. *Pelagos* with six catchers, Star 19, 20, 21, 22, 23 and 24, with Star 14 expected to arrive from South Georgia soon.

115

2. Both groups appear to have swept the Bouvet area from east to west. Listening to their talk on R/T, they are moving west. The situation is not good. Weather poor and hardly any whales. Some whales finally discovered between 0 degrees and 5 degrees West.

3. There appears to be no attempt to limit radio traffic. The air is full of chatter in Norwegian which can be heard up to 850 miles off. It is obvious that even though they are at war they feel safe down here.

4. Listening in to busy traffic on R/T reveals that the catchers are employed in a half-moon around the mother ships so as to cover the horizon up to 60 miles around.

5. It is possible that an attack could be made on one of the catchers from astern, but because of the constant radio contact between ships it is most likely that the alarm would be quickly raised. There are so many of them that an attack on one would alert the others.

6. Nevertheless, I hope that a short, quick attack on one would result in an operation against the second group.

7. R/T talk indicates that the supply ship mentioned must be the tanker that takes fuel oil to the ships and takes whale oil away.

8. The best time to attack would be while the supply ship is there and they are all busy with her.

9. It seems that both groups are now busy catching in their allotted zones in the Bouvet area and will stay there. No radio contact with SKL is due before the middle of January, so I decide to shadow the *Pelagos* group and wait to get more news of the supply ship before attacking.'

Continuing to listen in to the Norwegian broadcasts, Krüder learned that the expected supply ship was the *Solglimt*. His well-thumbed copy of Lloyd's Register revealed her to be the ex-Swedish America Line passenger liner *Potsdam*, a ship of 12,246 tons built by Blohm & Voss in Hamburg in 1900. He remembered her well, for she was a regular caller at Bremerhaven in pre-war days. The *Solglimt* was already two weeks overdue at the whaling grounds, a delay which had resulted in the *Pelagos* being low on fuel oil, while the *Ole Wegger*'s whale oil tanks were nearing full capacity.

Krüder also learned of the presence of another Norwegian fleet in the area. The factory ship *Thorshammer* and her catchers were fishing some 500 miles to the south-west. The *Thorshammer* was to be the *Solglimt*'s first call and it was thought she would be alongside the *Ole Wegger* about 13 January. Krüder now moved to a position 100 miles north of the *Ole Wegger* and settled down to wait.

The wait was not a comfortable one. The weather had once again taken a turn for the worse, with high winds, rough seas and blinding snowstorms, described by the Norwegians as the worst weather they had ever experienced. The fleet was scattered and many of the catchers reported losing the whales they had alongside. The weather was equally foul in the *Thorshammer*'s area, and the *Solglimt*, which had at last arrived, was unable to get alongside the factory ship. It was not until the morning of the 10th, by which time the weather had moderated, that the operation proved possible. The *Thorshammer* then contacted the *Ole Wegger*, warning her to be ready to receive the supply ship on the 12th.

Krüder wrote in his log:

'12 January 1941. 0800 hrs: *Solglimt* has passed the most westerly catcher of the *Wegger* fleet some 30 miles to the west of the *Ole Wegger*. Catcher passes message that the cleaning of the *Ole Wegger*'s tanks and pipes will be completed on Monday afternoon. As a result, *Ole Wegger* intends to take her alongside in the morning.

'I will wait some 70 miles north of *Ole Wegger*. Although the two ships will be together at 1000 hrs today, I have decided not to attack, but to wait until the two 12,000 ton ships are alongside each other. They then will be unable to manoeuvre very well and a quick attack will be easier. We have to be careful, for the *Solglimt* may well have been armed for her voyage down the Atlantic. With the ships alongside each other, it would be difficult for the *Solglimt* to use any guns she may have.

'2000 hrs: *Ole Wegger* agrees with *Solglimt* to take her alongside at 0400. I decided to go to the north-west during the night and

117

to take bearings of the ships to plot their various positions. I will start the approach in the morning and come up under the cover of darkness on the side where there are no catchers so as to gain surprise.'

Krüder could not have wished for more suitable weather conditions when, on the afternoon of the 13th, he began his approach to the whaling fleet. The wind was light from the west-north-west, the sea smooth and the visibility 5 to 10 miles between snow showers. The *Solglimt* had reported she was alongside the *Ole Wegger* at 0600 and it was safe to assume that both ships were fully occupied with the business of transferring stores and oil. From his position 70 miles to the north-west Krüder moved slowly south-eastwards, intending to approach the two ships from the west and in full darkness.

At 2315, just one hour into the short Antarctic night, *Pinguin*'s log reads:

'White lights sighted 2 degrees on port bow. A little later, many lights of the two big ships alongside each other and the catchers around them. Shortly after sighting this, there is a snow storm which obliterates everything and stays like that for forty-five minutes.'

After more than a month of careful listening, planning and stalking, Krüder was at last within sight of his goal. The temptation to cover those last few miles at full speed, to storm in and take the ships by force, was very great, but there was more at stake than this. Krüder wanted the whole fleet. With the *Pinguin* completely blacked out, hidden from time to time by whirling snowflakes, her engine beat slow and muffled, and all her guns trained, he moved in stealthily.

Not that there was the slightest chance of the Norwegians becoming aware of the approach of the enemy. Blinded by their own brilliant working lights, with winches clattering loudly and boilers spewing clouds of steam, the whalers were completely oblivious to the world around them.

At 200 yards Krüder stopped engines and allowed the *Pinguin* to glide silently towards the unsuspecting whalers. Two boats carrying armed boarding parties were swung out and ready to lower on the command.

The surprise was complete. At 0020 on 14 January the *Pinguin* suddenly emerged from the darkness, switched on her powerful searchlights and dropped her boats at the run. Anxious to avoid a panic which would send the catchers scattering in all directions, Krüder refrained from firing warning shots, using only his signal lamp to flash the message, 'DO NOT USE WIRELESS AND TELE-PHONE. WE SEND A BOAT.'

The attack was flawlessly executed. *Pinguin*'s big motor cutter, ex-*Morviken*, under the command of Leutnant Erich Warning, ran alongside the *Ole Wegger* and armed men swarmed up her side unopposed. They then split into two parties, one party racing for the *Ole Wegger*'s bridge, the other crossing the factory ship's deck to board the *Solglimt*, again unopposed. The Norwegians, perhaps unable to believe what was happening to them, showed little hostility towards the Germans, but their annoyance at this unwarranted interruption of their vital work was obvious. Quickly, while they were still disorientated, Warning's men herded them into the accommodation at gunpoint. Meanwhile, Warning confronted the masters of the two ships, Captain Evensen of the *Ole Wegger* and Captain Andersen of the *Solglimt*, and advised them that their ships were now in the hands of the German Navy. He told them to remain calm and to order their men to carry on with their work, for which they would be paid in full by the Reich. Failure to cooperate would result in their ships being sunk. For Evensen and Andersen there was no argument to be made. They accepted the first option without hesitation.

At 0045, twenty-five minutes after the start of the operation, a lamp flashed out from the *Ole Wegger*'s bridge. The message to Krüder was short and explicit. It read: 'SHIPS IN OUR HANDS'. A few minutes later Warning signalled details of his incredible haul:

'1.   *Ole Wegger*, Norwegian, 12,201 tons with 7000 tons whale oil and 5,500 tons fuel. Crew about 190 men, provisions for ten weeks. Speed 10 knots with daily consumption of 45 tons. Unarmed. Left Rio de Janeiro in November 1940.

'2.   *Solglimt*, Norwegian, 12,246 tons, 4000 tons whale oil and 4000 tons fuel oil, crew sixty men, but space for nearly 300 more, provisions for ten weeks. Unarmed, but mounting for AA gun, which was put on in Montevideo. Bound from Montevideo to Montevideo.'

The discovery of the gun mounting led Warning to look for the gun. In one of the *Solglimt*'s holds, amongst the boxes of spares and drums of oil, he found two 10.5 cm guns with 300 rounds of ammunition for each gun. A search of the *Ole Wegger*'s holds revealed a similar gun and ammunition. The Norwegians had either been too busy to mount these guns or, so sure were they of their invulnerability, that they considered them unnecessary.

Leutnant Hans-Karl Hemmer, who commanded the second cutter with orders to round up the whale catchers, pulled off an equally brilliant coup. Hemmer, who spoke no Norwegian and very little English, solved the problem of communication by hanging a card around his neck which proclaimed in large letters: I AM ENSIGN HEMMER, OFFICER OF THE GERMAN NAVY. YOUR BOAT IS CAPTURED. DO NOT OFFER RESISTANCE, LET YOUR CREW STAND TO ATTENTION.

Hemmer later said of the operation: 'It was a black night, misty with visibility 1000 yards. We motored up to the first boat, naturally the slowest one. I rushed on board and up the ladder to the captain's room, pulled my pistol and flashlight, and was met by the sight of a man sleeping in his woolly underwear and snoring in a fug you could cut. I shook the man by the shoulders and rasped out my ditty in a broken voice. The result was staggering. He grunted and turned over. That nearly disarmed me. Just imagine how surprised that captain should have been at suddenly seeing a German officer (especially one with a cardboard sign hung around his neck) fumbling about by his bunk 10,000 miles down in the Antarctic.'

In this highly unorthodox but effective manner, Hemmer and his party of eighteen men secured four of the 300-ton catchers. Three others got away. Unfortunately the *Pinguin* was unable to go in pursuit of the runaways, for at this most inopportune moment she had suffered a cracked cylinder head in one of her engines. However, Krüder was well satisfied with the night's work which, without a shot being fired, had netted him two

12,000-ton mother ships and four catchers, not to mention 11,000 tons of whale oil.

And Krüder had not yet finished. There was still the other half of the fleet, the factory ship *Pelagos* and her seven catchers, believed to be working some 220 miles to the east. If they were to be gathered home, this must be done swiftly. It required only one of the *Ole Wegger*'s escaped catchers to raise the alarm and the *Pelagos* and her brood would scatter to the four winds. Given the prevailing poor visibility, if they kept radio silence, Krüder would have little hope of finding them.

The *Pinguin*, still limping along on one engine, left the scene of her conquest at 0440 on the 15th. Krüder left with some misgivings for the safety of the prize crews he left behind. The Norwegians outnumbered them by twenty to one and, although Warning and his men were well armed, they might be overwhelmed at any time by sheer weight of numbers. Not that he need have been concerned. The whalers were so inured to the business of catching and processing as many whales as possible while the season lasted that they carried on working as normal.

It was full daylight when the *Pinguin* set off and, in order to confuse any watching Norwegians, Krüder steered north until he was out of their sight. He then altered to the east and, when, at 0800, engine repairs were completed, steamed at full speed, homing in on radio traffic between the *Pelagos* and her catchers. Unusually, the visibility was excellent. Later that day the *Pelagos* could be heard calling the *Ole Wegger* and *Solglimt*, but received no reply. At 2000 she gave up trying to make contact, presumably assuming – or so Krüder hoped – that the other ships were too busy to answer.

Two hours later the strength of the radio transmissions indicated that the *Pinguin* was very near to the *Pelagos* fleet. Then, at 2209, as the raider was negotiating her way around an ice field with the darkness closing in on her, a single white light was seen ahead. Ten minutes later she passed what Krüder assumed to be the most westerly of the *Pelagos*' catchers. The boat was hove-to with a whale alongside, but, although the *Pinguin* passed only 3 to 4 miles off, there was no reaction from the Norwegian, indicating that her crew must have been asleep.

Another forty-five minutes passed, with the *Pinguin* racing

121

through the night at 16 knots, then she saw a soft glow on the horizon ahead, which became a cluster of working lights. Soon it could be discerned that the lights came from one large ship with five smaller ones clustered around her. They had found the *Pelagos*.

Although the darkness was complete, the horizon was clear and Krüder was concerned that his approach would be detected; then, as if on cue, a light mist began to form. This, combined with the clouds of steam billowing from the factory ship's boilers, allowed the *Pinguin* to maintain full speed until Krüder brought her up short within 200 yards of the *Pelagos*. There she lay undetected for an hour while Krüder assessed the situation. Then, on the stroke of midnight, he switched on his searchlights, flashed a signal to the *Pelagos* ordering her not to use her radio and sent his boats away.

The boarding was a carbon copy of the assault on the other factory ships twenty-four hours earlier. The crew of the *Pelagos* offered no resistance, nor did those aboard the catcher that arrived alongside her at the same time as the *Pinguin*. Once in the hands of a prize crew, this catcher was sent to round up the others. Before the night was out Krüder had added to his list of prizes the 12,083-ton *Pelagos*, which had on board 9,500 tons of whale oil, 800 tons of fuel oil and a crew of 210, and seven catchers, all sturdy 300-tonners.

Leaving the *Pelagos* and her catchers in the hands of prize crews, Krüder then returned to the west to link up with the *Ole Wegger* fleet which, led by Erich Warning, was steaming towards him. Meanwhile the weather had closed in again. Thick fog and snow showers reduced the visibility to nil and the ships were navigating blind, their only guide being radio bearings taken of each other. Eventually, with improved visibility, a rendezvous was made at 1030 on the 16th, and the *Pinguin* led them back to the *Pelagos*, reaching her nine hours later.

And so ended a brilliant cutting-out operation, the like of which had not been seen since the days of Nelson. Single-handedly, and without firing a shot, the *Pinguin* had rounded up, in one day, 39,847 tons of valuable shipping and was in possession of 20,500 tons of whale oil worth over a million pounds sterling. But this could not have been achieved without the seemingly willing cooperation of the Norwegians. Doctor Hasselmann, one of the *Pinguin*'s two surgeons, wrote of the *Pelagos* action: 'Once the Norwegians got used to the idea, everything went as though we were not there at all. They carried on their work as usual, and their attitude towards us, if not friendly, then at least not actively hostile. They took very little notice of us at all, and they made no attempt to turn the tables on us, which they certainly could have done with a well-planned *coup de main*, for in the absence of the *Pinguin* there were very few German seamen left behind as guards. I think the explanation of this passivity is that they believed a German warship to be not far away.'

Chapter Eleven

On 30 January 1941 dawn broke with its usual dramatic suddenness over Sierra Leone, quickly chasing away the shadows cast
by the mountains overlooking the harbour of Freetown. Down
on the water the morning mist thickened momentarily, muffling
the clank of windlasses and the rattle of anchor chains that
greeted the new day. Convoy SLS 64 was about to set sail for
home.

Although the sun was not yet above the horizon, the heat was
already oppressive, signalling another sweltering day in this fetid
land of mangrove swamps and rain forests. Known to Europeans
around the world as 'the white man's grave', Sierra Leone, first
settled by freed slaves from Jamaica and Nova Scotia in the late
18th century, and asleep ever since, had suddenly moved into the
front line of the war following the closure of the Mediterranean
to Allied shipping in the summer of 1940. Overnight, Freetown's
deep-water harbour, capable of holding up to 150 ships at
anchor, had become one of the most important convoy assembly
points in the world. Ships coming round the Cape from the East,
from South America, and from West African ports all con-
gregated at Freetown to await a safe passage home. But with an
annual rainfall of 180 inches, temperatures soaring into the
nineties in the heat of the day, and plagued by every disease
known to man, few who were forced to endure the charms of the
port were sorry to leave. Not least the men who manned the ships
of Convoy SLS 64. The collective sigh of relief that went up
when the anchors came home might well have been audible far
out to sea.

Even by the standards of 1941, SLS 64 was a Cinderella of a convoy. Consisting of twenty-one merchant ships, mainly old coal-burning tramps, many of whom would be barely able to maintain the designated convoy speed of 8 knots, they carried between them some 120,000 tons of cargo for British ports. Ahead of them lay 3000 miles of extremely hostile ocean, an ocean at this time of the year torn by violent storms, and in its upper reaches infested by marauding U-boats, while overhead Focke-Wulfs, sagging under the weight of their bomb load, patrolled the leaden skies in search of soft targets. And, it now seemed, for much of this long passage SLS 64 was to brave these hazards without a single escort.

At the convoy conference on the previous evening aboard the *Edinburgh Castle*, an ex-First World War armed merchant cruiser acting as the Royal Navy's base ship, the news had been broken by the Senior Naval Officer. It was customary for one of the seven armed merchant cruisers making up the Freetown Escort Force to accompany a north-bound convoy until it was abreast the Straits of Gibraltar, where it would be met by destroyers of North Atlantic Command, and later by destroyers of Western Approaches Command. Regrettably, the SNO explained, the Freetown Escort Force was presently stretched beyond its limits and SLS 64 must go it alone – at least until a rendezvous was made off the Azores with the Gibraltar – UK convoy HG 53. There was, however, little cause for concern, the SNO hastened to assure the merchant captains and senior officers present. Admiralty reports indicated that Dönitz had moved at least thirty of his U-boats into the Mediterranean, leaving only a token force in the North Atlantic. Of the German capital ships, the *Scharnhorst* and *Gneisenau* were believed to be still in dry dock in Kiel, the *Admiral Hipper* was still in Brest licking her wounds following her abortive strike on WS 5A, while the *Admiral Scheer* was in the South Atlantic heading for the Indian Ocean. This, or so the theory was, left the seas clear for SLS 64 to sail northwards unmolested.

Appointed Commodore ship for SLS 64 was the 4876-ton *Warlaby*, a 14-year-old coal-burning steamer owned by Ropner's of Hartlepool, the archetypal British tramp homeward bound from Alexandria with 7000 tons of cotton seed. Having a top speed of 11 knots, the *Warlaby* was one of the faster ships of the convoy, which was possibly her only qualification to be leader of the pack.

As senior ship, the *Warlaby* would have been expected to carry an experienced convoy commodore, usually a retired naval officer of flag rank, and a staff of half a dozen Royal Navy signallers. But such was the parlous state of Britain's fleet in 1941 that the mantle of Commodore fell on the shoulders of the *Warlaby*'s master, Captain Septimus Murray. With the help of two Royal Navy signallers and a thick folio of Admiralty instructions, much of which he would never find the time to read, Murray was expected to lead and hold together a motley pack of tramps without even as much as an armed trawler in attendance. His confidence was not bolstered when he learned that, following the convoy conference, one of the masters had called at a local watering hole for a drink or two on the way back to his ship and left his briefcase in the bar. The briefcase, containing full details of the convoy's makeup and movements, disappeared; stolen by a common thief, perhaps, but Murray feared its contents might already be on their way to Berlin via Dakar.

As the sun came up over the Loma Mountains to the east the *Warlaby* led the way out of the anchorage, closely followed by the *Nailsea Lass*, ten months out from home and carrying jute from India. Then came the Glasgow-registered *Lornaston* sagging under a full cargo of iron ore, the 4542-ton *Shrewsbury* loaded with wheat and linseed, the *Blairatholl* with mineral concentrates, and so on; twenty-one ships, fourteen British, three Norwegians and four Greeks. One by one they brought home their anchors and manoeuvred into line. Bringing up the rear was Kaye, Son & Company's *Margot*, commanded by Captain Ivor Price, and carrying a cargo of cotton and cotton seed. Price had been designated Vice-Commodore and authorized to take over from Murray, should anything happen to the *Warlaby*.

The heavily-laden merchantmen moved slowly down the long reach of Freetown harbour, passing close to the 26,000-ton battle-cruiser HMS *Renown*, moored in the outer anchorage. With her grey-painted hull spotless and her white canvas awnings stretched taut, the big warship offered a stark contrast to the rust-streaked tramps, their salt-caked funnels belching black smoke. Inevitably, the rumour flew around the convoy that the *Renown* was also going north and would cover them on the passage home with her 15-inch guns. It was, of course, only a rumour. Anything as mundane as convoy escort duty did not figure in HMS *Renown*'s plans. She was on station at Freetown to protect the South Atlantic trade routes, ready to put to sea should any of the German Navy's capital ships threaten.

Working up to 7 knots, the *Warlaby* led the way past Cape Sierra Leone, its red and white painted lighthouse flanked by clumps of tall coconut palms, past Carpenter Rock with its skeletal remains of an Elder Dempster ship that had cut one corner too many, and around onto a westerly course for the Fairway Buoy. Once past the buoy and feeling the long swells of the open Atlantic, the ships began the laborious process of forming up into six columns abreast for the voyage home. Captain Murray's orders to the other masters were brief and to the point: 'Ships to be 2 cables apart, stem to stem, columns to be 3 cables apart by day and 5 cables by night. Convoy speed 8 knots. Keep closed up'. In the absence of an escort, there was little else he could say. The Greeks and Norwegians were unarmed, while the British ships mounted 1914–18 vintage guns manned by men more used to splicing ropes or firing furnaces. Convoy speed was set at 8 knots, a speed which all ships had declared they could comfortably maintain. But Murray knew well that there were some amongst the the ruddy-faced, pipe-smoking individuals who had attended the conference aboard the *Edinburgh Castle* who were supreme optimists. In more ways than one, this promised to be a voyage to sort the wheat out from the chaff.

Twelve hours later the convoy was off the coast of French Guinea and, having adjusted to the peculiarities of its various members, was making orderly progress in six columns abreast. Column 1 was led by the *Margot* (vice-commodore); Column 2 by the *Shrewsbury*, Captain A. Armstrong; Column 3 by the *Warlaby*; Column 4 by the *Westbury*, Captain William Embleton; Column 5 by the *Borgestad*, Captain Lars Grotness; and Column 6 by the *Empire Energy*, an ex-Italian ship under the control of the Ministry of Shipping. It was a dark, sultry night, with the smell of woodsmoke and rotting vegetation coming off the land. The sea was calm, mirrorlike, the darkened ships gliding across it betrayed only by the phosphorescence of their wakes. In less fraught times the balmy night would have been enjoyed by those keeping watch above decks, but tonight nerves were on edge. Men spoke in whispers, and from time to time the long frothing trail left by a frolicking porpoise set up the cry of 'Torpedo!' Each ship of the convoy was preoccupied with its own survival, and no one saw the *Nailsea Lass* go.

The *Nailsea Lass*, a 1917-built steamer of 4289 tons owned by Evans Reid, a company formed in the early 1930s to manage ships of Cardiff shipowners ruined by the depression years, was stationed immediately astern of the *Warlaby*. Commanded by 38-year-old Captain Thomas Bradford, she was bound from India to Liverpool with 6,200 tons of jute and other produce. In the lean days before the war the *Nailsea Lass*, along with many of her kind, had worked the cross-trades of the world with little or no time for maintenance, and in 1941 was a tired old ship unlikely to make 8 knots even with a fair wind. After two months in the fecund waters of the Indian coast, her bottom was heavily fouled with weed and barnacles, and, although her engineers did their best to coax a few extra revs out of their elderly machinery, she could not maintain convoy speed. She fell further and further astern until, by midnight, she had lost contact with SLS 64 altogether. Tom Bradford was forced to accept that he must continue the voyage alone. This he did philosophically, consoling himself with the knowledge that the convoy had not offered much in the way of protection, other than that found in numbers. At least he would from now on be free to make his own decisions. The first of these came in the early hours of the next morning.

At 0400 on the 31st Chief Officer Alfred Hodder, who had just taken over the watch on the bridge of the *Nailsea Lass*, heard a report from the oncoming helmsman that he had found the deck in the region of No.3 hatch 'very hot' as he passed the hatch on the way to the bridge. Mindful of the tendency of jute cargoes to spontaneous combustion, Hodder immediately informed Captain Bradford. No.3 hatch covers were taken off and it was seen that bags of coconut shell charcoal stowed in the tween deck were glowing red-hot. Bradford's first action was to stop the ship to decrease the draught, then the hoses were run out, but it was well

128

into mid-morning before the fire was brought under control and finally extinguished. By this time any chance the *Nailsea Lass* might have had of catching up with the convoy had gone.

And as SLS 64, now reduced to twenty ships sailing in mutual support, made its way slowly to the north with the *Nailsea Lass* limping along behind out of sight, German naval forces were gathering in its path.

Behind the breakwaters of Brest, the *Admiral Hipper* had steam up with orders to put to sea on 1 February. Early that morning, right on schedule, the now familiar RAF reconnaissance aircraft flew over and reported back to the Admiralty that the German cruiser was still at her berth. Meisel waited until the plane was out of sight and then slipped out of harbour. His instructions from Admiral Raeder were make full speed to a position 1000 miles west of Cape Finisterre, refuel from a waiting tanker and then remain on station to await developments.

Deep in the Bay of Biscay, at Mérignac airfield near Bordeaux, Focke-Wulf Kondors of No.1 Gruppe/Kampfgeschwader 40 (No.1 Squadron/40th Bomber Group) were warming up on the tarmac, also awaiting orders. Since early January, when Dönitz and Raeder, taking advantage of the absence of Reichsmarschall Goering on one of his frequent hunting trips, had put their case to Hitler, 1/KG 40 had been assigned to cooperate with the U-boats in locating Allied convoys. The role of the four-engined Kondors, which had a range of 2000 miles, was to track down convoys, attack where possible and at the same time to home in the nearest U-boats. Previous to this, the Kondors, which moved to Mérignac in August 1940, had had considerable success on their own, accounting for eighty-five ships of 363,000 tons. Their initial attempts at cooperation with the U-boats had so far proved fruitless, the U-boats always failing to make contact with any reported convoys.

Some 800 miles to the south-west, *U-37*, commanded by Korvetten-Kapitän Nicolai Clausen, was trawling her net between the coast of Morocco and Madeira. Sailing from Lorient in the previous November with orders to make for Freetown, Clausen, who was on his first voyage in command, had sailed through empty seas on his way south. It was not until he was off Cape Juby, in the channel between the Canaries and the African mainland, that he had his first success – if it could be so called – sinking by gunfire the 223-ton Spanish sailing vessel *San Carlos* on 16 December. The *San Carlos* was an innocent neutral loaded with barrels of salt fish and demi-johns of wine, which could by no stretch of the imagination be linked to the Allied war effort and was hardly worth the price of the shells expended on her. At best, she provided an opportunity for Clausen to exercise his 88mm gun's crew.

Nicolai Clausen's run of poor luck continued; the deep-loaded merchantmen he was seeking were, in fact, all passing well to the west of the Canaries, a state of affairs German Intelligence had failed to bring to his notice. On the 19th it did seem that Clausen's luck had at last turned when he sighted and sank, firstly an enemy submarine, and a few hours later a medium-sized tanker. Much to his dismay, these were later identified as the 1379-ton ocean-going submarine *Sfax*, and her fleet tanker, the 2785-ton *Rhône*, both under the Vichy French flag. This was a disastrous opening for Clausen's first command and he decided to return to the north to seek better fortune off the Straits of Gibraltar.

On 6 February, seven days out of Freetown, still without escort and, miraculously still unmolested, SLS 64 was some 270 miles south-west of the Canary Islands and only four days steaming away from her rendezvous with Convoy HG 53. Two more ships had fallen out on the way, the *Empire Energy* and the *Dartford* on 1 February, both with engine trouble. Now, in strong North-East Trades encountered north of the Cape Verde Islands, it was the turn of the *Gairsoppa*.

The 5237-ton *Gairsoppa*, a 22-year-old coal burner of the British India Steam Navigation Company under the command of Captain Gerald Hyland, was heavily loaded with pig iron from India, and also had on board silver ingots worth £600,000 – about £14 million in today's money. Battling against strong head winds and seas, her coal consumption rocketed and she was soon in danger of emptying her bunkers. The situation became so serious that Hyland calculated even to reach the nearest UK port he would have to reduce speed to 5 knots. And so, at dusk on 6 February, having informed the Commodore, the *Gairsoppa* fell out of the convoy and prepared to make her own way home. Bearing in mind he had a fortune in silver bullion in his charge, this was not a comfortable decision for Captain Hyland to take.

SLS 64, reduced to seventeen ships, pressed on to the north. Meanwhile, on the afternoon of the 6th, Convoy HG 53 sailed from Gibraltar. HG 53 was made up of sixteen merchantmen, fifteen British and one Norwegian. The majority of them were short-sea Mediterranean traders, the smallest a mere 1,236 tons, and the largest 2,824 tons. The Commodore ship was the 2471-ton *Dagmar 1*, an ex-Danish ship sailing under the Red Ensign and commanded by Captain A.D. Holborn. On board were Commodore O.H. Dawson, RN, and his signals staff. Initially, escort for HG 53 was provided by the sloop HMS *Deptford*, which would later be reinforced by destroyers of Western Approaches Command.

Steaming in six columns abreast, HG 53 cleared the Straits of Gibraltar and steered due west, under orders to strike deep into the Atlantic before turning north. While this may have been a wise precaution in view of the somewhat questionable neutrality of Spain and Portugal, it was contrary to what these small ships were accustomed to. Their normal practice was to hug the coast, where the weather was usually kinder. Out in the open Atlantic they ran into strong westerly winds and were soon labouring heavily as they rode the Atlantic rollers. Progress was painfully slow and three days after sailing they had made good only 400 miles, at an average speed of 5½ knots. However, by then the weather had at last begun to moderate, the gales giving way to a light SW'ly, with dull overcast, but good visibility.

Dawn on 9 February was two hours away and reluctant to come. The moon had set and the darkness was intense and foreboding, but the men in the merchant ships were in good heart as they went through the routine of changing the watches. They were not aware that they were being followed.

Nicolai Clausen had sighted the smoke of HG 53 on the horizon at sunset on the 8th and had spent the night stalking the convoy. While on the surface, he sent a sighting report to the Flag-Officer U-boats, who in turn alerted 1/KG 40 at Mérignac. *U-37* was then ordered to shadow the convoy, reporting back at intervals, and to attack as soon as the opportunity presented itself.

That opportunity came at 0430 on the 9th, by which time *U-37* had overtaken HG 53, and was lying submerged to port of the convoy. Carefully, Clausen laid his sights and at 0437 fired a fan of three torpedoes. One of these hit the *Courland*, lead ship of the port column, the second raced through the lines of ships to slam into the hull of the *Estrellano*, steaming at the head of column 5. The third torpedo missed completely.

The 1324-ton *Courland*, owned by the Currie Line of Edinburgh and commanded by Captain Smith, was hit on the port side in the vicinity of the engine-room and went down quickly, taking three of her crew of twenty-nine with her. Fortunately for the survivors, another of Currie's ships, the 1473-ton *Brandenburg*, commanded by Captain Henderson, was close at hand. Regardless of the danger to his own ship, Henderson dropped back and scooped the *Courland*'s men out of the water.

The *Estrellano*, a 1983-ton Mediterranean trader owned by the Ellerman & Papayanni Line of Liverpool, and commanded by Captain F. Bird, came to a sudden halt when Clausen's torpedo found its mark. The blast blew a great hole in her hull in way of No.4 hold and reduced much of the port side of the super-structure to a tangled mass of metal. As the sea poured into her breached hull, the ship took a heavy list to port. Sending a brace of distress rockets soaring into the night sky to warn the other ships, Captain Bird ordered his crew to abandon ship without delay. This was not easy, for the port lifeboat had been wrecked by the blast and, as the ship was listing to port, great difficulty was experienced in swinging out the starboard boat. Brute force born out of desperation got the boat out and the men were boarding when the *Estrellano* suddenly went down by the stern. She had remained afloat for only two minutes after being torpedoed.

The crowded lifeboat, still hooked onto its davits, went down with the ship, capsizing when it hit the water. The occupants were thrown into the sea to join the others who had jumped from the ship's rail. Their ordeal, frightening though it may have been, was not a long one. HMS *Deptford*, alerted by the bursting rockets, was quickly on the scene, hauling Captain Bird and twenty-one of his crew from the wreckage-strewn water. Five others were missing, never to be found, while one of the rescued, the young cabin boy McIntyre, died on board the sloop from his injuries.

Immediately after the torpedoing of the *Estrellano*, Commodore Dawson signalled an emergency turn of 40 degrees to starboard, and the convoy swung sharply away from the danger. *U-37* followed them around and crossed astern of the ships. Half an hour later Clausen fired a single torpedo from his stern tube, which narrowly missed the Commodore's ship *Dagmar 1*. Once again the darkness was rent by rockets bursting overhead. The *Deptford* raced in to drop a pattern of sixteen depth charges, but by this time Clausen had gone deep and was stealthily withdrawing out of range.

Sunday 9 February dawned fine and clear, with a moderate westerly breeze stirring up tumbling white horses on a wintery blue sea. Barely two hours had passed since the brutal savaging of the convoy by *U-37*, a nightmare in which two ships had gone and nine men had died in the space of a few minutes. But the world could not stand still and already the other ships had closed ranks and were pressing on, with the *Deptford* zigzagged astern of them probing underwater with her Asdics.

Meanwhile, 800 miles to the north-east at Bordeaux-Mérignac, six Kondors of 1/KG 40, led by Hauptmann Fritz Fleigel, were racing down the runway to lift off, tails to the rising sun. Admiral Dönitz, who had just returned from Paris, was about to see his theories on U-boat/aircraft cooperation put to the test. In this case it was not quite as he had intended, for *U-37* was the spotter, while the Kondors were being homed in on the convoy, and not vice-versa.

It was two hours into the afternoon before Fleigel's Kondors sighted the fourteen ships of HG 53 some 300 miles west of Cape St Vincent. The convoy was on a course of 285° making 7½ knots, with the wind SW'ly force 3, the sky clear and the visibility good. Conditions were ideal for an attack on the slow-moving ships, but the heavily-laden bombers were near the edge of their operational range and any attack they made would need to be quick and decisive.

Dropping down low over the water, Fleigel came up on the convoy from astern, catching the ships completely unawares. No lookout turned to scan the horizon astern, no one heard the muted roar of the powerful BMW engines. U-boats, surface ships,

133

they were looking for, but, as it was believed no German aircraft could reach this far south, no one was watching the skies.

Captain A.D. Holburn, commanding the *Dagmar 1*, described the attack in his report to the Admiralty:

'We were steering a course of 285 degrees, the weather at the time being clear with good visibility; there was a moderate swell and the wind SSW 3. The aircraft approached on our starboard quarter and each machine concentrated on a column of the convoy, flying from astern. The planes approached very low – at about 150 feet. We did not hear the planes approaching and they were almost over the convoy before we realized their presence. I immediately gave the order for action stations and in not more than a minute we opened fire on the enemy plane which was attacking our column. We got away two full bursts, one with our Bren gun and the other with our Hotchkiss. I am sure that we hit the plane. I could see the tracer bullets going into the machine, but they seemed to have no effect at all. There were three ships astern of us, so these must have had even less time to man their guns and open fire.

'The aeroplane attacking my column of the convoy did not attempt to drop any bombs on the *Britannic*, the ship astern of me, but flew on and released three bombs, one which hit my ship and two which were near misses. It seemed to me that two bombs were released together and one just a second after. One bomb hit the boat deck above the engine-room, on top of the accommodation on the starboard side. The boat deck was completely demolished and also the deck below; the ship's side was opened right up, down to the waterline. The engine-room was put out of action; the boilers were smashed and the steam pipes were adrift. The near misses were very close to the ship's side, but I do not think they did any damage, although a column of water about 30 feet in height was thrown up.'

With his ship crippled and possibly sinking, Holburn had no alternative but to abandon. The *Dagmar 1* sank some hours later.

The 2490-ton *Britannic*, one of the larger ships in HG 53, and down to her marks with iron ore, did in fact suffer an even more devastating attack, as Captain R. Jennings later wrote:

'One of them approached our stern and as she did we fired with both Hotchkiss guns. He flew directly over the ship from stern to stem at 100 feet, dropping a salvo of two bombs which fell on No.3 hold, slightly to starboard; both bombs were fairly small and were released together. These bombs exploded and wrecked the Chief Engineer's cabin, killing him instantly, and the hatch covers, beams and derricks of No.3 hold were blown away. The planes flew straight over the convoy, flew ahead and made a wide sweep to starboard. They returned at about 1505 and made a second low-level attack on the convoy in the same way as before, flying from stern to stem over the ships. A single plane approached us, flew directly over the ship and dropped a salvo of two bombs; the first bomb went right through the starboard lifeboat, and the second one fell just off the starboard beam, exploding in the water close to the ship's side. This explosion split the starboard plates, cracked the forward bulkhead and the ship rapidly made water. We fired the Hotchkiss guns this time also and I saw the tracer bullets going into the fuselage of the plane; our fire was definitely in line with the aircraft, but I do not know if it was damaged. At both attacks the enemy raked the ship with machine-gun fire.

'The concrete bridge protection collapsed with the second explosion, also the wheelhouse and the wireless room. I could see that the ship was not going to last very long and I gave the order to abandon. We pulled away from the ship in the port lifeboats at about 1530; as we did I noticed that the shell plating on the port side was also blown away. We stood by the ship and watched her sinking rapidly, until she finally disappeared at 1600.'

Glen & Company's 1759-ton *Jura*, carrying a cargo of iron ore from Huelva to Aberdeen, was next. She was hit by two bombs, one of which went down her funnel and blew the heart out of the little ship. The *Iceland*, yet another of Currie Line's ships, commanded by Captain A.W. Cavaye, which had so far escaped the attentions of the Focke-Wulfs, went to her aid. Captain Cavaye described the end of the *Jura*:

'As I steamed towards the *Jura* I could see that the lifeboat on the side of the ship which was blown away had gone, but when passing round the stern I saw 17 men in the remaining boat. I presumed these to be the majority of this ship's personnel, as she was not much bigger than the *Iceland* and her crew probably numbered about 25. The *Jura* was loaded with iron ore, which caused her to sink rapidly, so I blew my whistle to hurry the men in letting go the painter, but they were about a second too late in doing so, and as the ship sank the boat was dragged under, all the men being thrown into the sea. As far as I can remember, only 9 survivors were picked up out of the original 17 in this boat; the Chief Officer died whilst in this boat. He was riddled with machine-gun bullets from the aircraft.'

In all, seventeen of the *Jura*'s crew of twenty-six perished in the attack. Her sister ship, the 1514-ton *Varna* was more fortunate. The *Varna*, under the command of Captain L. Saul, and bound for South Wales with a cargo of pit props, received serious damage, but fought back fiercely when a Focke-Wulf swooped on her from astern. Captain Saul reported:

'The Chief Officer, who was in the starboard pill box, fired a full belt at point blank range; deponent [Saul], who was in the port pill box, got away a few rounds when the plane dropped a bomb which secured a direct hit in way of the foremast on the starboard side. The force of the explosion shattered the pill boxes, the bridge, the cement protection on the wheelhouse, and blew the deck cargo of pit wood in the vicinity of the explosion all over the vessel. The plane machine-gunned and cannon-shelled the vessel from his forward and after guns, and the Chief Officer was wounded by shrapnel which passed through the cement pill box. There was a five-foot tear in the forecastle head deck and the starboard bulwarks forward were blown out. An area of about 200 square feet of the fore deck was badly set down, with all the plate landings opened up.'

In spite of her extensive damage, the *Varna* remained afloat and under way. Before the Focke-Wulfs climbed away and headed north, they claimed one last victim, hitting the small Norwegian-flag ship *Tjedo* with two bombs. She was abandoned by her crew and sank as they pulled away in the boats.

Once again, now down to ten ships, HG 53 closed up the gaps and continued to steam westwards, but Admiral Dönitz had not yet finished with this ill-fated convoy.

Nicolai Clausen, who had watched the mauling of HG 53 by the Focke-Wulfs from a safe distance, shadowed the convoy throughout that night and at daybreak on the 10th *U-37* was once more in a favourable position to attack. At 0630 Clausen fired two torpedoes, both of which struck the *Brandenburg*. The 31-year-old ship, deep-laden with iron ore, broke her back and sank in seconds, taking with her Captain Henderson, his crew of twenty-two and, cruelly, the twenty-seven survivors of the *Courland*, picked up only 24 hours earlier.

As the sun came up that day the remaining ships of HG 53 wheeled slowly to starboard and settled down on a northerly course for home waters, 1000 miles away. Already they had paid a heavy price, seven ships and seventy-six men lost. What other horrors lay ahead of them no one dared to contemplate.

Chapter Twelve

For one ship, at least, the saga of Convoy HG 53 did not end there. Scenting the opportunity to score a major sea victory, Admiral Raeder now called in the *Hipper*, then still on station 1000 miles west of Finisterre. His orders to Meisel were to complete the destruction of HG 53 at his leisure, a simple enough task, or so it would seem. Meisel, by then weary of keeping a fruitless and uncomfortable vigil in the path of the Atlantic storms, needed no encouragement. Establishing radio contact with Clausen in *U-37*, who had continued to shadow the convoy, he steamed south-eastwards at full speed. Intelligence reports coming in from Berlin advised Meisel that the field was clear for the *Hipper* to do her work. The only credible opposition, Admiral Somerville's Force H, based on Gibraltar, had moved into the Mediterranean and was busy bombarding the Italian port of Genoa.

Meisel held all the aces in his hand, but, as he found to his cost, the Atlantic is very wide and the ships sailing upon it infinitesimally small. The *Hipper* completely missed the battered remains of HG 53 as it steamed north, but she did fall in with an unfortunate straggler from the convoy.

The *Iceland*, bound from Seville to the UK with 12,000 cases of oranges, had come unscathed through the attacks on HG 53, but she now ran into trouble of another kind. Built in 1914, she successfully ran the gauntlet of the U-boats in the First World War, but she had been hard used in all her long years of service at sea. Her age was beginning to tell. On the afternoon of the 10th, perhaps as a result of the violent alterations of course she had made during the air attacks, one of the chains connecting her steering engine to the rudder quadrant suddenly parted. Unable to steer, Captain Cavaye had no alternative but to heave-to and drop out of the convoy. For the next three and a half hours the *Iceland*'s engineers worked to replace the broken link in the chain, while the little ship, alone and vulnerable, rolled beam-on to the Atlantic swell. By the time the repair was completed, darkness had fallen, and only then, under the cover of night, did Cavaye feel relatively safe. He was also aware that there was now little hope of the *Iceland* rejoining the convoy. The other ships, urged on by the terrible events of the past twenty-four hours, were hurrying north at all possible speed. Cavaye followed in their wake, but the best the *Iceland*'s engineers were able to coax from her tired old engine was a reluctant 9 knots.

The *Iceland* steamed on through the night with extra lookouts posted and her guns, a 12-pounder and two Lewis guns, manned at all times. Cavaye blessed the fickle Atlantic weather when, shortly after noon on the 11th, heavy rain set in. The visibility was severely reduced, affording the lone ship a temporary cloak of invisibility. But it was only temporary. At 1530 precisely the rain suddenly stopped and, as if a curtain had been drawn back, the horizon was revealed. Having swept from port to starboard with his binoculars, Cavaye glanced astern and was surprised to see a large warship 4 miles off the *Iceland*'s starboard quarter and approaching at high speed. He wrote in his report:

'At first I could not decide what she was, but in a few minutes, as she approached our starboard beam, I could see it was the German cruiser *Admiral Hipper*. We were then in latitude 37 N and about 500 miles from the Portugeuse coast, steering N by W (approx) at 9 knots. The sea was very rough with a SW wind force 5/6 moderating. The weather was overcast with poor visibility. As far as I remember a single shot was fired first, simultaneously with the signal "Do not use your wireless. Abandon ship. I am going to sink her." This first shot passed over the ship, but as this signal was flying at the time, I think it was meant to miss. The *Admiral Hipper* was equipped with 11-inch guns and could steam at 35 knots (Cavaye over-estimated his enemy), so I decided that resistance was futile, especially as she was very close off our starboard beam. Before we had a chance to get into our two lifeboats, another shot

139

was fired, which I think was intended to make us hurry. No sooner were we in the boats than very heavy shellfire commenced and in a few seconds the ship was ablaze from stem to stern. My ship took an hour to sink, and they had to fire a torpedo into her to finish her off.'

And so the little *Iceland* came to the end of her long and honourable career. On fire, and with her hull blasted open to the sea, she went down with dignity. Her lifeboats, after battling their way through the rough seas, reached the *Hipper* and went alongside. Cold, wet and demoralized, Captain Cavaye and his crew of twenty-two climbed aboard and into captivity.

Of their reception on board the *Hipper*, Cavaye had to say:

'After boarding we were immediately taken below, two officers being turned out of their cabin in order to accommodate the Chief Officer and myself, the rest of the crew being taken to accommodation aft. We were treated very well on this warship, I think the average German naval man has a feeling of comradeship towards other sailors.'

The attack on Convoy HG 53 was later claimed by Admiral Dönitz to be the only combined U-boat, air and surface operation ever to take place in the Atlantic. In view of the *Hipper*'s minimal participation, this claim must be viewed with some scepticism.

German Radio Intelligence had by now detected the presence of Convoy SLS 64, then 150 miles to the south-west, and steaming on a northerly course at 7 knots. The convoy was still without escort. Dönitz then ordered Meisel to abandon the search for HG 53 and to proceed south at full speed to intercept SLS 64.

Incredible though it may now seem, at this time SLS 64 was completely unaware of the attacks on HG 53 by *U-37*, the Focke-Wulfs and the *Hipper*. Not one of the nine ships so cruelly and quickly despatched succeeded in sending an SOS either by W/T or R/T – or, if they did, their calls for help were lost in the ether. None of the ships in SLS 64, all of which were keeping continuous radio watch, reported hearing a distress. And so the convoy steamed on in ignorance of the danger abroad, its only concern a steadily falling barometer.

At noon on the 11th the convoy was midway between Madeira and the Azores and making a course of 008 degrees at 7 knots. The *Warlaby* had dropped astern with an engine problem, and in her absence the Vice-Commodore, Captain Ivor Price in the *Margot*, had temporarily taken charge. He was on the bridge when a large ocean liner was sighted overtaking the convoy on its port quarter. Price identified her as an ex-Union Castle liner of the Cape run, but now carrying 6-inch guns and obviously an AMC. The word went round the convoy that this was the escort they had been waiting for, but when the *Margot* challenged her by flag and lamp, the other ship did not answer. Sensing danger, Price, a shrewd North Walian, called for an emergency turn of 40 degrees to starboard and, as one by one the ships sheered away from the stranger, she followed them around and closed to within 3 miles, still refusing to identify herself. Alarm bells rang, guns' crews closed up, and for the next forty-five minutes the convoy and the unidentified armed liner sailed on parallel courses, but not communicating. It was a tense situation that might easily have ended in a shoot-out, needing only one of the largely inexperienced merchant ships' guns' crews to open fire. The situation was defused when the stranger suddenly made off to the west at speed. Her identity was never established, but Ivor Price was adamant that she was ex-Union Castle. It is known that the *Caernarvon Castle* and *Pretoria Castle*, both AMCs, were in the area at the time, so Price was probably right.

After the excitement of the afternoon the convoy slowly settled down again, although the *Warlaby* did not return to her position at the head of Column 3 until late that evening. An hour later Second Officer G.E. Turner of the *Oswestry Grange* and Third Officer D. McLean of the *Blairatholl* both heard the drone of an aircraft flying overhead. Neither officer thought this incident worth reporting to the Commodore at the time, which was regrettable. The sky was clear, the moon full and the visibility good, and it is probable that the convoy had been spotted by a low-flying Focke-Wulf from 1/KG 40, searching on orders from Admiral Dönitz.

The weather deteriorated rapidly overnight and by the early hours of the 12th it was blowing hard from the west-north-west, with a rough sea and heavy swell running on the beam. If any progress was to be made, a northerly course must be held, and the deep-laden ships , beam-on to the weather, suffered badly. Rolling drunkenly and down to 6 knots, barely steerage way, they struggled hard to maintain some semblance of order in their ranks. The West Hartlepool tramp *Ainderby* and the Greek-flag *Polyktor*, another First World War veteran, were already straggling astern.

The rendezvous with HG 53 was scheduled for 0700 that morning and at the first hint of dawn the murky horizon was being eagerly searched by dozens of pairs of binoculars. First Radio Officer John Cave was on the bridge of the *Margot*:

'I was on the bridge with the Mate on the 4 to 8 watch. The radio officers used to do quite a lot of bridge signalling. I had "AM", the flag signal for "Welcome", bent on the halyard ready, and all I had to do was to pull the halyard to break it out.

'Promptly, at the expected time of 7 o'clock, the Mate shouted that he could make out one of the escorts. It was fortunate for us that the Commodore carried a Naval signalling crew, and beat us to it, for I can still see the forward guns of that "escort" turning towards the convoy.'

The *Margot* being the leading ship of the port column, Cave and her chief officer, D.J. Morris, were first to sight the *Hipper*. Maintaining the element of surprise, Wilhelm Meisel had brought the cruiser in from the dark side of the horizon, aiming to pass ahead of the convoy from west to east. He opened fire as soon as the slow-moving merchantmen came into sight. His first shells were aimed at the *Shrewsbury*, lead ship of Column 2. The *Shrewsbury*, owned by the Alexander Shipping Company, a subsidiary of Houlder Brothers, was nearing the end of a long voyage from the River Plate. Third Officer C.D. Simms was off watch:

'I was in bed at the time and when I came out of my room I saw the cruiser about four points on our starboard bow firing at us, at a distance of 3000–4000 yards. She was firing with her main armament forward, but I do not know if she was using her after guns. There were twin guns in the turret, working independently. She seemed to be firing in threes at five or six minute intervals. The cruiser was sailing up and down at a speed of about 12 knots. It had a monoplane aft. Her funnel was streamlined with the fore end built up to protect the bridge from smoke. The Gunner and Chief Engineer were on deck at the time and at first they thought it was one of our own ships as we were expecting to rendezvous.

'The first shot from the enemy cruiser hit us, smashing our funnel and port lifeboat. When I got on deck they were lowering the starboard jolly boat. The forward raft was got away and I was sent to get a raft over from the gun platform. This I did and called for anybody to come and get on it, and the 3rd Engineer, 4th Engineer and an Army gunner got away from the ship on this raft.'

The *Hipper*'s gunners made short work of the *Shrewsbury*, pounding the 4,500-ton ship ruthlessly. She received six direct hits in quick succession, some below the waterline, and was finished off with a torpedo, which broke her back and sent her to the bottom. Twenty of the *Shrewsbury*'s crew of thirty-nine lost their lives, eighteen of them in the only lifeboat to get away, callously blown out of the water as it pulled away from the sinking ship. Simms was among the lucky survivors, spending thirty-six hours adrift on the raft before being picked up by the Royal Navy.

Having despatched the *Shrewsbury* and most of her crew, Meisel then turned his guns on the *Warlaby*. Caught broadside on as she sheered away from her attacker, the *Warlaby* took the full weight of a salvo of eight shells. This brought down her foremast, demolished her bridge, her funnel and engine-rooom casing. All her lifeboats were shot away and a number of fires started. Chief Officer J.G. Evans had the watch on the bridge of the Commodore's ship:

'... the lookout reported a naval craft approaching from the westward. I was on the bridge on watch and at once called the Master. He came on the bridge with the Yeoman of Signals who tried to make out the nationality of the ship but it was too dark to recognize the ensign she was flying. She came steaming on ahead of the second column, then, without warning or signal to heave to, she opened fire. My captain, being the Commodore, immediately hoisted a signal for the convoy to disperse but the enemy shot it down at once. The enemy continued to shell us unmercifully. The

Captain ordered me to go down to the W/T Operator and get him to send a message as quickly as possible. I did so, then returned to the bridge. Then I went amidships where most of the crew had gathered, and we put a raft overboard. Two men jumped over and got on to it, but no one else would leave. I told them they would have to jump as by now all the boats had been shattered and it was impossible for the ship to last much longer. The men still refused to jump; we had to keep dodging the shells as, whenever the enemy saw a cluster of men, they fired in that direction, pumping away with pom-pom and everything they had. I put another raft over the side large enough for twenty men, but again they refused to jump, then I put a net over for twelve men. The shelling had caused a fire in No.2 hold and No.4 hold, the ship took a heavy list to port and turned right round. Soon after this, as the ship started to roll over, I saw the Captain still on the bridge with the 2nd Mate, then a shell struck the bridge and that was the last I saw of both of them.

'At 0830 the ship went down, throwing the crew into the water; I was the last to leave the ship. Some of the men got away on rafts, the rest were swimming about amongst the wreckage, but I do not know how many were still alive after the shelling, and I could not recognize anyone in that light. I managed to cling on to a piece of wreckage, then the raider steamed slowly through the struggling groups of survivors and passed near me, but no attempt was made to rescue anyone.'

After three hours in the water, Evans came across an empty liferaft and clambered aboard. He was rescued in the afternoon of the next day by the ocean boarding vessel HMS *Camito*, which had come out from Gibraltar. Only two other men survived the sinking of the *Warlaby*, her cook, G.R. Thomas, and Able Seaman C.W. Brown. Captain Murray, eight of his officers and twenty-seven ratings perished.

Murray's last signal to the convoy, "T-4" hoisted at the yardarm, was an order to scatter and run to the south. Most ships followed the *Warlaby*'s example and turned to starboard under full helm, but some could not escape the devastating fury of the *Hipper*'s 8-inch guns. At the head of Column 4, the 4712-ton *Westbury*, out of the same Houlder Brothers' stable as the *Shrewsbury*, was hit repeatedly and set on fire as she sheered away from the danger. A torpedo finished her off and she sank with the loss of five men, including Captain William Embleton, his chief officer Ambrose Turner, and Third Officer David Evans. Meisel then concentrated his fire on the Greek ship *Perseus* as she offered her port side to the raider, scoring four hits on her poop and her bridge. She caught fire and was sunk by a torpedo. Captain Athanasios Costaropoulos and fifteen of his crew of thirty-six lost their lives.

Little is known of the fate of McCowan & Gross' 4896-ton *Derrynane* and the Norwegian motor vessel *Borgestad*, other than they both opened fire on the *Hipper* and paid the price of their defiance. The *Derrynane*, carrying a cargo of 8,219 tons of iron ore, was said to have exploded when she was hit by shell-fire and went down in a few minutes. Her crew of thirty-six were all lost. No one saw the *Borgestad* go and no trace was ever found of her or her crew of thirty-one, which included the only woman sailing in SLS 64, 20-year-old stewardess Norma Nergärd.

Two other ships had narrow escapes as they attempted to flee from the *Hipper*'s guns. The *Volturno* and the *Lornaston*, rear ships of Columns 1 and 3 respectively, were both hit, the *Volturno* sustaining heavy damage on deck. The *Volturno* fired back and claimed to have scored a hit on the German cruiser before her 4-inch jammed.

Before she withdrew, the *Hipper* damaged the *Ainderby*, straggling astern, and sank the *Oswestry Grange* with her cargo of frozen beef from the Argentine. The latter was destroyed by a fusillade of shells, which continued while her crew were abandoning ship. Captain Edgar Stone, Fourth Engineer Sydney Burton and three ratings were drowned when their lifeboat capsized.

The *Hipper* had taken SLS 64 completely unawares. The sudden shock of her appearance when they were expecting to meet friendly ships, and the ferocity of her attack, caused considerable panic amongst the unescorted merchantmen. Some ships were abandoned without good cause, among them Denholm Line's 3419-ton *Clunepark*.

Captain William Masson, who was on the bridge of the *Clunepark* when the *Hipper* opened fire, immediately ordered the helm put hard to starboard. He then steadied the ship on a southerly course and some minutes later, although the *Clunepark* had not been hit, he stopped her and ordered the crew to take to the boats. Masson then left the bridge and, accompanied by Chief Officer John McCreadie, supervised the lowering of the lifeboats, a difficult operation with the ship rolling heavily beam on to the swell. It was while Captain Masson was absent from the bridge that the confusion arose. Second Officer Victor Smith, who had been asleep when the attack started, later reported:

'I came out on deck in pyjamas and on the port beam saw the raider firing a broadside. I returned to my cabin, dressed quickly, and made my way by the starboard side to the bridge, went into the chartroom and collected the books and papers and placed them in the weighted bag which was then placed on the bridge in preparation for being dumped. Nobody was on the bridge at this time. Looking aft, I observed the ship's starboard boat approximately half a mile astern with one raft alongside. The engine-room telegraph was at stop. I put the engine-room telegraph to full ahead and at this moment the Chief Officer came up onto the bridge. Previous to this, I met the Chief Officer on the midship deck. I asked him if the ship had been hit, he said no. I then mentioned that the ship was not supposed to be abandoned until the vessel was in a sinking condition. As far as I can remember, I said, "I will take the wheel, let me know when the raider is astern." The helm was put hard to starboard and a course W by S was steered from the compass. Subsequently, under orders from the Chief Officer, the helm was altered to keep the raider astern. Nothing more was seen by me of the boats. I do not know of any steps taken to recover the boats. It was my duty to be in charge of the lowering of the starboard boat, but as I had not heard the abandon ship order I did not go to my boat station. I think I left the bridge at 0730 ship's time. The Master was then in charge.'

Why Second Officer Smith took it upon himself to put the *Clunepark*'s engine to full ahead when he found the bridge deserted is an unsolved mystery. The most likely explanation is that, having been rudely awakened only three hours after coming off watch, he was disorientated and decided to take action to save the ship from the raider by putting her stern-on. Unfortunately, three lifeboats and a raft were tied up alongside and when the ship surged ahead their ropes parted and they drifted astern.

146

When some sort of order had been restored aboard the *Clunepark*, Captain Masson did go back to look for his boats, but was unable to find them. Two men on the raft were later picked up by the *Blairatholl*, but the launching crews of the lifeboats, eight men, among them the ship's two young apprentices, were not seen again.

Commenting on the sad fiasco, Dan Hortop, a seaman in the *Clunepark*, said: 'What was in his (Captain Masson) thoughts that early morning of 12 February 1941 we shall never know. Maybe the sight of those ships being shelled, with their crews having no chance of lowering boats, decided him to order "abandon ship". Whether the other officers had different ideas we didn't know, yet we sensed something was amiss, and most of the crew stayed on board.'

Among those who kept a cool head in this confused and frightening situation was John Cave, senior radio officer of the *Margot*. He wrote in his report:

'Without realizing, I found myself in the radio room reading a scrap of paper on which was our last four-hourly position. If we had been sailing independently the first thing would have been to transmit a special raider message on the distress frequency and include this position. As it was, this was left to the Commodore, but he had been the first to go, identified from his flag hoists. I put on the headphones and listened. Several ships were using their radio and it was very conflicting. Suddenly, an idea flashed into my mind.

'I started up the old spark transmitter and, using our international call sign, sent a raider (RRRR) message, giving our position and description of the attack. Pausing to listen for any acknowledgement, which did not come, I used the collective naval call sign (GBZZ), usually reserved for those seeking assistance when attacked by pirates in the China seas, and "answered" a mythical warship, using operator's slang abbreviations and finishing with, of all things, "good morning, see you soon". What the operator on the Von *Hipper* said, did or thought is questionable, but from then on the situation changed for the better, and the shelling seemed to stop.

I knew our own 4.7 gun had been firing while I was sending the fictitious message, and getting no answer from the bridge voice-pipe, I went to tell the "Old Man" what I'd done and that the codes and other confidential books had been dumped. Everything seemed at a standstill. All around us was smoke, and then I noticed the crew were already in two lifeboats, and were apparently standing by for the "Old Man" and myself. I found him in the chartroom ramming the local chart down his lifejacket. "Go down to my room, Sparks," he said, "and get out two glasses." He followed me down the ladder, and by the time I'd put the glasses on the table he was already pouring out two full tumblers of whisky. I didn't even feel it go down, but well remember the pair of us hanging on to the rope ladder until the opportunity came to jump onto a thwart as the boat came alongside, bucking madly in the high swell.

'Every now and then we would hear loud thumps, and we all joined in sympathy for the lads of those ships that were being slowly and methodically finished off by the *Hipper*. It was some time before anybody realized that the large watertight biscuit container slung under one of the thwarts was the culprit as it responded in drum-like thuds to the motion of the boat.

'After a while, hearing no other noises, the Captain told everybody to keep a sharp lookout for that second or two while the boat was at the crest of the wave. As we came up the *Margot* was still plainly in sight, and before we went down into the trough of the wave another lifeboat was spotted. The "Old Man" stood up and had a good look at it the next time as we rose on the swell. "She's from the *Volturno*," he shouted, and then to those on the oars, "Row, you buggers! If he gets there first he'll claim salvage." We went down into the trough, and without further ado he brought the helm hard over and we headed back to our ship.'

The *Hipper*'s action against SLS 64 lasted no more than thirty minutes, during which time, with guns and torpedoes, she sank seven ships, the *Warlaby*, *Shrewsbury*, *Westbury*, *Perseus*, *Borgestad*, *Derrynane* and *Oswestry Grange*, a total of 32,806 tons of shipping. With these ships went 50,000 tons of valuable cargo and 146 irreplaceable men and one woman. Meisel's shells also damaged the *Lornaston*, *Volturno* and *Ainderby* and, of course, caused complete confusion in the convoy, ships scattering to all points of the compass. Four ships, the *Clunepark*, *Margot*, *Volturno* and *Anna Mazaraki*, were abandoned by their crews and later reboarded, the contention being that by taking to the boats the raider would think they were hit and sinking. The ruse worked in as much as these ships survived, but most of them lost their lifeboats when they could not be hoisted in the swell, and, in the case of the *Clunepark*, eight men lost their lives.

And yet, having had the astonishing good fortune to waylay a slow-moving convoy, completely unescorted and far removed from possible outside intervention, Meisel made no attempt to destroy SLS 64 down to the last ship, which he could so easily have done. To this day John Cave is convinced that his pretence of radio contact with a nearby Royal Navy ship had been heard by the *Hipper*'s wireless operators and may have convinced Meisel that it was time for him to go. Certainly, it was very soon after Cave's fictitious conversation with the Navy that the *Hipper* abandoned the attack and made off to the north-east at full speed.

There is some evidence, particularly in the case of the *Warlaby* and *Shrewsbury*, that Meisel made deliberate efforts to kill survivors as they were abandoning ship. This may or may not have been true, but he certainly made no attempt to rescue any of those men he had so suddenly condemned to the water. After the attack Meisel made the claim to Captain Cavaye, prisoner aboard the *Hipper*, that he could easily have sunk all the ships in the convoy, but left three to pick up the survivors.

With the *Warlaby* sunk and Captain Murray lost, Captain Ivor Price of the *Margot* now found himself in charge of what was left of Convoy SLS 64. Those ships remaining were very widely scattered and Price was able to gather together only the *Volturno*, *Clunepark*, *Blairatholl*, *Anna Marazaki* and *Polyktor*. The *Blairatholl* reported she had on board eighty-six survivors from the *Warlaby*, *Shrewsbury*, *Oswestry Grange* and *Westbury*, while the *Polyktor* had picked up twenty-one men from the boats of the *Perseus*. Of the other ships believed to have escaped the *Hipper*'s guns, the *Ainderby*, *Lornaston*, *Empire Energy*, *Varangberg*, *Bur* and *Kalliopi*, there was no sign. Price assumed they must have lost confidence in the convoy and elected to make their own way to the north, a decision he would have held against none of them in view of the events of the past few hours.

Before leaving the area, Price carried out a search for survivors, taking the six ships in line abreast back along the track of the convoy. After three hours, having sighted nothing but floating wreckage, Price conferred with the masters of the other ships. The consensus was that, as some ships had lost their lifeboats, the *Volturno* was in urgent need of repairs and there were survivors to land, they should make for the nearest friendly port. The choice was between Funchal, Madeira and Ponta Delgada in the Azores, both of which, although ostensibly neutral, would offer them temporary shelter. The vote was for Funchal and, steaming in line astern with the *Margot* in the lead, course was set for Madeira.

A signal decrypted by Bletchley Park reported the *Hipper* had reached Brest on the 14th low on fuel, with propellor trouble, and having used half her main armament ammunition and twelve torpedoes. A German High Command communique was issued on the same day making the following claim:

'German warships operating in the Atlantic have attacked a large enemy convoy in continuation of their annihilating blows by U-boat and long-distance bomber off the west coast of Portugal during the last few days. They sank 13 armed enemy merchant ships, including several large liners laden with war material for England. The convoy was completely dispersed by the attack.'

Next day the High Command increased Meisel's score to fourteen ships, claiming a total of 82,000 tons sunk.

150

Chapter Thirteen

The *Admiral Hipper* had retired from commerce raiding with precious few honours to her name. Her poor relative, the ex-merchantman *Pinguin*, on the other hand, continued to enhance her reputation. Fresh from rounding up the entire Norwegian Antarctic whaling fleet, she was preparing to return to the Indian Ocean.

On 19 January news reached the Senior Naval Officer in the Falkland Islands that the *Ole Wegger*, the *Solglimt* and a number of catchers had been sunk by a German raider off Bouvet Island. The only large unit of the Royal Navy in the area, the armed merchant cruiser *Queen of Bermuda*, was immediately ordered south to search for the raider. On the 22nd she reached South Georgia, where she learned the full extent of Ernst Krüder's audacious coup. It was far worse than had at first been thought. The Norwegian ships had not been sunk by the *Pinguin*, but captured. Three large vessels, eleven catchers, 150,000 barrels of hard-won whale oil, some 6000 tons of good quality fuel oil, a huge amount of food and fresh water, and 700 men had been rounded up and spirited away. This was a disaster of major proportions.

In South Georgia local opinion was that the Norwegian ships would be taken into the South Indian Ocean, where the whale oil would almost certainly be transferred to Japanese ships. The ships themselves would then either be sunk or handed over to become part of the Japanese whaling fleet. On the strength of this intelligence, the *Queen of Bermuda* searched south and east, probing right down to the Antarctic Circle, but found nothing.

On orders from the Admiralty, the AMC was then reduced to destroying all whaling installations in the outlying islands, so that nothing more should fall into the enemy's hands.

In fact, Ernst Krüder had no plans to hand over his prizes to the Japanese – or anyone else, for that matter. The whale oil, convertible into margarine and glycerine for explosives, was sorely needed at home in Germany; as to the big ships, they would be worth holding on to until after the war, while the catchers might make ideal escorts for the U-boats. It was Krüder's intention to send the whole fleet home. Whilst he was well aware that the voyage they must embark upon was long and perilous, being mainly through Allied dominated waters, he had confidence in his prize crews, even though they would be heavily outnumbered by the Norwegians in the ships. Only four men could be spared for each catcher to supervise a Norwegian crew of twelve.

The captured ships, *Ole Wegger*, *Solglimt*, *Pelagos* and the eleven catchers, were first taken to an isolated location 200 miles north-west of Tristan da Cunha, where they kept a rendezvous with the tanker *Nordmark* to refuel and reprovision. The *Pelagos*, under the command of Oberleutnant Küster, sailed for Bordeaux on 25 January, to be followed later that day by the *Solglimt*, commanded by Leutnant Bach. Each would take different routes to Biscay.

The *Ole Wegger* and the catchers required more preparation, and it was not until 20 February that this fleet, the factory ship and ten catchers, was ready to sail. Led by the *Ole Wegger*, under the command of Leutnant Blaue, the ships left at spaced intervals during the night. A further rendezvous was arranged in the North Atlantic, where the catchers were refuelled by the tanker *Spichen* between 5 and 7 March. Thus far, the voyage had been without incident and for most of the ships under Leutnant Blaue's command it would continue so. Only two of the catchers, *Star XIX* and *Star XXIV*, who were sailing in company, were unfortunate enough to fall foul of the Royal Navy. On 13 March, abeam of the Straits of Gibraltar, they were intercepted by the sloop HMS *Scarborough*, which was on the lookout for blockade runners. *Star XXIV* was first to be stopped and, as she appeared to be legitimate, was passed by the *Scarborough*'s boarding party and told to go on her way. Both catchers might have escaped had not the *Star XIX*'s German crew panicked and scuttled their ship when *Scarborough*'s boat approached her. The game was up and *Star XXIV* had no option but to follow her sister's example.

The bigger ships, the *Pelagos*, *Solglimt* and *Ole Wegger*, with their valuable cargoes, evaded detection and reached Bordeaux between 11 and 20 March. They did not go to sea again under the German flag, but their loss was a severe blow to the Allies, not least to Lloyd's of London, with whom they were each insured for in excess of £300,000. The eight whale catchers that survived the voyage north were all put to good use as submarine hunters and minesweepers.

The remaining catcher, the newest and best of the fleet, the 354-ton *Pol IX*, Krüder had held back to act as *Pinguin*'s scout. She was renamed *Adjutant* and manned with a full German crew under Leutnant Hans-Karl Hemmer. A rendezvous was then arranged with the supply ship *Alstertor*, which had arrived from Germany on 18 February, and the three ships headed east for Kerguelen Island.

Kerguelen, where the *Pinguin* and her auxiliaries arrived on 12 March, is as secure a hiding place to be found anywhere on the face of the great oceans. Lying deep in the South Indian Ocean, 3,300 miles south-east of the Cape of Good Hope, Kerguelen, aptly named Desolation Island by the French navigator Yves de Kerguélen-Trémarec, who discovered it in 1772, is the largest in an archipelago of some 300 islands and rocks. Mountainous, with brooding glaciers and dark peat bogs, it is a grey, uninviting place, uninhabited in the 1940s, but having a good natural harbour on its north side. Here Krüder anchored his small fleet, safely hidden from seawards in the unlikely event that the Royal Navy might come searching for him. Over the following two weeks the crews of the three ships worked long hours preparing the *Pinguin* and the *Adjutant* for their coming operations in the Indian Ocean. The raider's engines and deck gear were overhauled, she was painted round and took stores from the *Alstertor*, including a new Heinkel 59 reconnaissance aircraft. At the same time the *Adjutant* was fitted out as a mine-layer and took on board forty of the *Pinguin*'s remaining mines. This left the raider with 130 mines on board.

Her mission accomplished, the *Alstertor* was released to find her own way home and on 25 March the *Pinguin*, now disguised as Wilhelmsen Line's *Tamerlane* and flying the Norwegian flag, sailed from Kerguelen in company with the *Adjutant*. Krüder's orders were to rendezvous with the tanker *Ketty Brovig*, a Norwegian ship taken as a prize by the *Atlantis*, at the Saya de Malha Bank, a coral patch off Mauritius. The *Ketty Brovig* was to oil the *Pinguin* and *Adjutant*, and then join Krüder as a supply tanker and auxiliary minelayer. The three ships were then to steam north in company to lay mines off the west coast of India in the approaches to Karachi and Bombay.

The *Pinguin* and *Adjutant* reached longitude 75 degrees East on 1 April and then steered due north along the meridian. Early on the morning of the 2nd they met up with the tanker *Ole Jacob* in 25 degrees South, near the rendezvous point codenamed *Herman*. The *Ole Jacob*, another of the *Atlantis'* prizes, reported to Krüder that she had also arranged to meet with the *Ketty Brovig*, but had been unable to find her. This was an ominous development and, after topping up his fuel tanks from the *Ole Jacob*, Krüder hurried north, his fears for the *Ketty Brovig* growing. Arriving at the Saya de Malha Bank five days later, he found the horizon empty. The *Pinguin*'s aircraft made a number of flights, but failed to locate the tanker. By 12 April, having found no trace of the *Ketty Brovig*, Krüder concluded that the ex-Norwegian had either been sunk or captured by the enemy. He was not far wrong.

At the end of February 1941 the 8000-ton North-German Lloyd steamer *Coburg* was sheltering in the Italian-controlled Red Sea port of Massawa, awaiting the opportunity to make a dash for home. British troops had by this time overrun Italian Somaliland and were advancing into Eritrea. On 5 March, with Massawa threatened, the *Coburg* put to sea. Soon after sailing, she received orders to rendezvous with the *Ketty Brovig* off the Saya de Malha Bank to refuel and reprovision before beginning the long voyage to Europe. Unfortunately for both German ships, the *Coburg*'s orders were transmitted using an Italian code the Royal Navy had been reading for some time. They were both subsequently intercepted at the rendezvous by the cruisers HMAS *Canberra* and HMNZS *Leander*, and were scuttled by their own crews to avoid capture.

154

Having spent more time off Saya de Malha than he thought was wise, Krüder accepted that the *Ketty Brovig* must be lost and moved north with the *Adjutant* to resume his campaign against Allied shipping. Conscious that, as a result of the activities of the *Pinguin* and her fellow raiders, British warships might be out in force in the Indian Ocean, he proceeded with caution. Arriving at the northern end of the Mozambique Channel, he began to search along the track taken by ships homeward bound from India and Ceylon, sweeping north-eastwards by day and south-westwards by night. The South-West Monsoon had not set in and the skies were clear and visibility excellent. With the *Adjutant* steaming on a parallel course and the aircraft overhead by day, a very wide area was covered.

But it was all in vain. After six days of monotonous patrolling, during which the Heinkel made no fewer than thirty-five flights and, sighting no more than the odd Arab dhow, Krüder decided to move east, deeper into the Indian Ocean. On the morning of 24 April, when 360 miles north-east of the Seychelle Islands, his patience was at last rewarded. At 0800 the *Adjutant*, out of sight of the *Pinguin*, found herself on a collision course with a ship heading west-south-west for the Mozambique Channel. Leutnant Hemmer at once hauled around onto a parallel course, keeping his distance from the stranger, so that only her funnel and mast were visible above the horizon. Using his short-range Hagenuk radio, he informed Krüder that he was shadowing a 6000–8000-ton freighter, almost certainly British.

She was, in fact, the 6828-ton *Empire Light*, a wartime-built ship owned by the Ministry of Shipping and managed by the British India Steam Navigation Company, on passage from Madras to Durban and the UK with a cargo of produce from the Indian coast. She had sighted the *Adjutant* early on in the morning, but assumed from her size and unusual build to be a small British warship or auxiliary on patrol. When the *Adjutant* turned away and dropped below the visible horizon, it was thought she had gone on her way. The *Empire Light* held her course and speed, completely unaware that she was in danger.

When Krüder received Hemmer's sighting report, he immediately recalled the Heinkel, which had been in the air since first light. The weather was fair, but there was a long swell running and, although the seaplane landed safely on the water, it was well into the afternoon before it was lifted aboard. The *Pinguin* then set off at full speed for the position given by the *Adjutant*.

Hemmer was still stalking the unidentified ship alone when darkness closed in at around 1900, the *Pinguin* having not yet appeared on the scene. Under the cover of the night, Hemmer moved closer to his quarry, fearful that she might escape. At 2300, with the *Pinguin* still not in sight, he became concerned that the raider would steam past him in the darkness and broke radio silence to request the other ship's position. Krüder replied that he was some 10 miles astern and anticipated it would take him another three hours to catch up. From then on Hemmer showed a small light from the *Adjutant*'s stern at short intervals.

It was 0200 on the 25th before a dark shadow seen astern announced the arrival of the *Pinguin*. She came up at full speed, overtaking the *Adjutant* like a ghost of the night, only the bright phosphorescence of her bow wave and the steady beat of her engines betraying her presence.

At 0515, with just sufficient light from the coming dawn to reveal the outline of the *Empire Light*, Krüder opened fire, taking the British ship completely by surprise. The *Pinguin*'s gunners, as always, were superbly accurate, shooting away the *Empire Light*'s topmasts and wireless aerials with their first salvo. A second salvo brought down the steamer's funnel and knocked out her steering gear. Soon she lay helpless, awaiting a boarding party. Within the hour her 70-man crew were prisoners aboard the *Pinguin*. When she had been stripped of anything useful, including her code books, which had not been dumped in the confusion of the sudden attack, the British ship was sunk by scuttling charges. It had been a copybook operation; no lives lost, no SOS sent out.

Although the sinking of the *Empire Light* eased some of Krüder's frustration, he had yet to find the tanker required to ensure the success of his future plans. He still needed another auxiliary minelayer. Delaying only to see the scuttled ship slip below the waves, he steamed north towards the Arabian Sea and the track taken by tankers in and out of the Persian Gulf.

For two days the *Pinguin* and *Adjutant* trawled their net northwards, the two ships some 50 miles apart and the Heinkel aloft whenever possible, but the horizon remained stubbornly empty as they crossed the Equator. Krüder was beginning to believe the British had confined all their ships to port when, on the afternoon of the 27th, three ships hove in sight at the same time, two southbound and one northbound. None of them was the tanker he was seeking, but it was his business to sink enemy ships and, while he could not hope to deal with all three, he would add at least one to his score. He chose the largest of the trio, the northbound ship, then steering a course of about 070 degrees, and most probably making for Colombo.

Krüder had chosen wisely. His prey was the 7266-ton *Clan Buchanan*, one of the elite in the Indian Ocean trade. She belonged to Cayzer Irvine of London and Glasgow, the world's largest cargo liner company, and known, through its distinguished service in the First World War, as the 'Scottish Navy'. Built in Cayzer Irvine's own shipyard at Greenock in 1938, the *Clan Buchanan* was a first class ship, capable of handling all cargoes, including heavy lifts. Her triple expansion steam engines, supplemented by a low pressure turbine, gave her a top speed of 17½ knots, a speed few cargo ships of her day could hope to match. Commanded by Captain D. Davenport-Jones, RNR, she carried a crew of twenty-five British officers and ninety-six Lascar ratings. This was a traditional Clan Line mix dictated by the company's long-established trading links with India. She also had on board two DEMS gunners, supplied by the Royal Navy, who led the guns' crews, made up of ship's officers, most of whom will have attended a short gunnery course in the UK. Her armament consisted of a 4.7-inch, a 12-pounder and two .303 Hotchkiss machine-guns.

The *Clan Buchanan* sailed from Liverpool at the end of March 1941, loaded with 6000 tons of military stores and equipment for the British Army in India, which was then preparing to meet the threat of Japanese aggression. On her 7000-mile-long passage down the Atlantic and around the Cape she sailed alone, running the gauntlet of the U-boats and Focke-Wulfs in the north and surface raiders in the south, who were then sinking ships at the rate of twenty a week. Steaming at maximum speed, the *Clan Buchanan* came through unscathed, reaching Durban on 18 April. Here she took on bunkers, fresh water and provisions,

157

and a quantity of Army mail, sailing again on the 19th.

At this stage of the war no U-boats had yet appeared in the Indian Ocean and the *Clan Buchanan* was routed through the Mozambique Channel, the shortest route to India. Davenport-Jones had been warned of the possibility of at least two German surface raiders being at large, but their immediate whereabouts was very much a matter of conjecture. As it transpired, using her superior turn of speed, the *Clan Buchanan* made a fast and un-opposed passage through the Channel, running clear of the Comoro Islands on 23 April.

Two days later, on the morning of the 25th, while less than a day's steaming over the horizon to the east the *Empire Light* was going down under the *Pinguin*'s guns, the *Clan Buchanan* was abeam of the Seychelles. She carried three radio officers, who were keeping a listening watch around the clock, but owing to the deadly accuracy of Krüder's gunners, she heard nothing of the *Empire Light*'s fate. Steering a north-easterly course, Davenport-Jones intended to pass between the Laccadive and Maldive Islands using the Eight Degree Channel. Having steamed 9000 miles without coming to harm, and now moving into the sphere of the Royal Navy's East Indies Fleet, based in Ceylon, he might have been forgiven for a degree of complacency. He did not drop his guard completely, but he felt that at long last it was safe to relax his vigilance.

When Krüder sighted the *Clan Buchanan*, he followed his well-tried standard procedure, keeping his distance and steaming on a parallel course just below the horizon. At midnight he altered onto a converging course to intercept at first light. Slowly, relent-lessly, the two ships, who in the halcyon days before war came had traded together in these same waters as equals, were drawing together for a rendezvous that could have only one ending.

Dawn broke on the 28th with a suddenness characteristic to the low latitudes, moving from complete darkness to half-light in a matter of minutes. The weather was fine and clear, the wind light and variable, presaging another warm and sultry day to come. The *Clan Buchanan* was 600 miles south-west of Minikoi Island, the northern marker of the Eight Degree Channel, and steering a course of 067 degrees to pass 10 miles south of the island. Her patent log was registering a speed of 15 knots.

Chief Officer Stanley Davidson, who had the watch on the bridge, had just finished his morning star sights and was about to work out the ship's position when a flurry of shells dropped out of the sky and burst all around the ship. Stopped in his tracks as he made for the wheelhouse, Davidson saw gun flashes on the starboard quarter at a distance he estimated to be 3 to 4 miles. As he ran into the wheelhouse to sound the alarm more shells screamed overhead and sent up tall spouts of water near the bow.

There was little need for Davidson to sound the alarm bells, for on this fine tropical morning there were few in the crew of the *Clan Buchanan* who were not already up and about. Captain Davenport-Jones was on the bridge within seconds of the first shells falling. Outwardly calm, but raging inside at the gross unfairness of being caught by the enemy so close to journey's end, he issued orders to dump all code books and secret papers over-board and to clear away the lifeboats. Briefly, he was tempted to make a fight of it with his 4.7, but it was already too late. At that precise moment the gun, blasted from its mounting by a well-aimed shell from the *Pinguin*, went spinning in the air and crashed down on the engine-room skylight. Davenport-Jones thanked God he had not yet sent men to man the gun.

The shells were coming thick and fast, bursting on board and filling the air with flying shrapnel. And through all the mayhem Second Radio Officer Walter Clarke remained at his key, hammering out an urgent SOS. When the raider's signal lamp flashed the message, 'CEASE USING YOUR WIRELESS OR WE WILL CONTINUE SHELLING YOU', Davenport-Jones knew it was time for a decision to be made. His officers were standing firm, but the Lascars were panicking, having already abandoned the engine-room. At that moment a shell hit the bridge and, realizing that only deaths could follow, he ordered Clarke to cease transmitting and destroy his equipment. He then rang the engines to stop. Chief Officer Davidson describes what happened next:

'The raider ceased shelling us about 0525, after ten minutes continuous firing, and sent her motor boat alongside our ship with a boarding party, consisting of Commander Waring [Warning] and six heavily-armed ratings, who came on board and took charge of the bridge. They demanded the secret papers, which had

159

already been dumped and were not forthcoming. By this time the Captain had ordered the boats into the water. No.1 boat had been damaged too badly to be lowered, but the other lifeboats were lowered and the crew were standing by the ship in three lifeboats. In the meantime, fire had broken out in the after part of our ship. I called out to the 2nd Engineer, who was in one of the boats, to come back to the ship, and with the help of the 3rd Officer, who came down from the bridge, and the German sailors, we put out the fire.

'When I returned to the bridge I found the German officers in the Captain's room asking him questions. Upon the 2nd Wireless Operator being asked who gave him permission to wreck his machine, the Captain replied, "I did".

We were ordered to take as much clothing as we possibly could from the ship and proceed to the raider in our lifeboats. The Captain was taken away in the motor boat by the German officers. Another boat came over from the raider and proceeded to systematically loot the ship of foodstuffs, wines, tobacco, wireless sets and all papers found in the Captain's and my rooms.

'On arrival on board the German raider the 25 European crew were immediately conducted to the prison cell, No.2 hatch, tween deck, on the port side of the vessel. They then took our names, rating, money and every article we had in our pockets and made us open our parcels of clothing, from which they took various items, such as knives, papers, cigarettes and liquors. After taking our names, etc., they told us to make ourselves at home in the cell. The cell had 24 bunks and a hammock was supplied for the 25th member of our crew. At the head of the bunks there was a table capable of seating twelve people. The room was about 30 feet long by 15 feet wide and about 9 feet high. To the right of the doorway there was a WC, 2 washbasins and 2 showers. The room was fitted with air-cooling device but there were no portholes and no lining to the ship's side. There was no room to walk about after we had our meals.

'Our crew of Lascars (96 men) were placed in a cell on No.3 tween deck.

'About 0700, immediately after our names had been taken by the German Captain, I heard two distinct heavy explosions, and the Captain remarked that that must be our ship.'

The *Clan Buchanan* was sunk by scuttling charges at 0700 and the *Pinguin* then continued on her way. Krüder was still determined to find his tanker and, in order to do so, was prepared to go deep into the Arabian Sea if necessary. This would be taking a huge risk, for although the *Clan Buchanan*'s SOS had not been answered by any radio station ashore or afloat, there was always the possibility that it had been heard. The Royal Navy had bases all around him, at Aden, Karachi, Bombay, Colombo and Mombasa, and the hunt for the *Pinguin* might already be in progress. However, Krüder had not yet lost confidence in his ability to outwit the enemy. Looking ahead, he now contacted Berlin, requesting that the *Alstertor* meet him south of Diego Garcia on 8 May, where he planned to offload his prisoners onto the supply ship. He also ordered the *Adjutant* to make her way towards the rendezvous point.

Krüder would have planned otherwise had he known that the *Clan Buchanan*'s call for help had in fact been heard by two shore radio stations, Aden and Colombo. The signal was weak and garbled, but the gist of the message was plain enough. Ships of the East Indies Station were already on the alert and when the news of the attack reached the C-in-C East Indies Station (Colombo), Vice-Admiral R. Leatham, he ordered HMNZS *Leander* out from Colombo, while a formidable force consisting of the heavy cruiser *Cornwall*, the light cruiser *Hawkins*, and the aircraft carrier *Eagle* sailed from Mombasa and raced north. Suddenly the Indian Ocean had become a very dangerous place for the *Pinguin*.

Oblivious to the net closing around him, Krüder steamed into the Arabian Sea and almost to the entrance to the Gulf of Oman searching for the one prize that eluded him. But, even with the Heinkel airborne every day, he sighted no ships of any consequence. By 4 May he at last became concerned that he was lingering too long close to the lion's den and turned south again. The *Pinguin* crossed the approaches to the Gulf of Aden, but even here, once one of the world's busiest shipping crossroads, she found nothing of interest. Continuing south, she passed the lonely island of Socotra and shaped a course for the Mozambique Channel. Still nothing.

At long last, on 6 May, after more than three weeks of painstaking search, Krüder found his tanker. Two mastheads were sighted at first, then a tall, thin funnel and, as the rest of the

161

ship lifted above the horizon, the familiar outline of an oil tanker, funnel aft, bridge amidships, became clear. She was the 3663-ton *British Emperor*, one of the British Tanker Company's oldest and smallest ships. Under the command of Captain A.I. Henderson, with a crew of nine British officers and thirty-six Lascar ratings, the *British Emperor* was in ballast from Durban, bound for Abadan at the head of the Persian Gulf.

A jubilant Krüder gave chase, shadowing the tanker on a parallel course, using the *Pinguin*'s low profile to keep out of sight below the horizon. At dawn on the 7th he closed the range and opened fire with a full salvo from his port guns. On this rare occasion, perhaps because they were too eager, the *Pinguin*'s gunners were less than accurate. The shells that were meant to carry away the *British Emperor*'s aerials missed their target and fell over her. The surprise was lost and the tanker's radio burst into life, sending over and over again the terse message, 'QQQQ de (from) BRITISH EMPEROR 0830N 5625E'.

The *Pinguin*'s guns opened up again, this time deliberately bracketing the fleeing tanker, for Krüder desperately wanted this ship intact. The raider's signal lamp urgently flashed the order to stop and surrender, but the *British Emperor*, black smoke pouring from her tall funnel, continued to run for her life, with 32-year-old Radio Officer John Thomas at his key pounding out the QQQQ message.

Despite her advanced age – she was built in 1916 – the *British Emperor* had a good turn of speed, and, reluctantly, Krüder conceded that she must be stopped by force. He ordered his gunners to shoot to sink and the next salvo burst on board the tanker, setting her on fire and smashing her steering gear. She began to circle out of control and some of her crew could be seen jumping overboard. She finally drifted to a halt and her radio fell silent.

It did not end there, for while the *Pinguin*'s boats were along-side the *British Emperor* taking off her crew, her radio was heard transmitting again. Radio Officer Thomas was back at the key and broadcasting his ship's plight to the world. Krüder could not open fire again while his boats were alongside the tanker and it took some time to clear them. Then the *Pinguin*'s guns opened up again, pounding their target mercilessly. Only when the *British*

162

Emperor's bridge was destroyed and her accommodation on fire did Thomas cease transmitting.

The burning tanker was now sending up a huge pall of smoke, which must have been visible for many miles over the horizon, and the raider's wireless office was reporting other ships relaying Thomas' QQQQ signal. Krüder, who had now given up all hope of saving the ship, was anxious to sink her and quit the scene as soon as possible. It was plain that his guns would take a long time to finish the *British Emperor* off so, reluctantly, he was obliged to torpedo her. With the tanker dead in the water, this should have been a simple operation, but this was not a good day for Krüder. The first torpedo ran amok, circled back and almost put paid to the *Pinguin* herself, the second missed completely, and only the third scored a hit on the burning tanker. Even then, she went down with agonizing slowness. This small, 26-year-old ship had sold herself dearly.

It was quite obvious to Ernst Krüder that his failure to stop the *Clan Buchanan* and the *British Emperor* transmitting might lead to his downfall and that it was time to abandon the search for a tanker. Accordingly, he set course to the south-east to keep his appointment with the *Alstertor* to off-load the 236 prisoners he now had on board. He was not to know that he was about to keep an appointment with another ship in another place.

Chapter Fourteen

Five hundred miles to the south of the *Pinguin* HMS *Cornwall* had just crossed the Equator on passage from Aden to refuel at the Seychelles. The *Cornwall*, a County-class, 8-inch gun cruiser of 9850 tons, was slow-steaming at 12 knots, a speed that did nothing to take the residual heat out of the ship. Below decks the air was hot and clammy, and in the engine-room, although only four of the cruiser's eight boilers were in use and her extractor fans were running at full capacity, the temperature was already over 100°F.

With half an hour to go to dawn, Captain P.C.W. Manwaring was on the bridge savouring the light breeze made by the ship's passage through the water. It promised to be another flawless day; the sea was oily-calm, with a low SW'ly swell, the sky clear and the visibility maximum, marred only by a cluster of rain squalls on the horizon to the north-west.

As he sipped at a cup of hot, strong tea, Manwaring was handed a signal form with the *British Emperor*'s QQQQ message. Minutes later, orders were received from the C-in-C East Indies Station to steam northward at all speed to intercept the German raider. *Cornwall* was best placed, but Colombo had also ordered the heavy cruiser *Liverpool* and the light cruisers *Glasgow* and *Leander* to join the chase. Meanwhile, the armed merchant cruiser HMS *Hector* was directed to cover any other merchant ships in the area. For the second time in a week Krüder had stirred up a hornet's nest in the Indian Ocean.

Manwaring, armed with a D/F bearing of the *British Emperor*'s last message taken by an astute wireless operator, flashed up his remaining boilers, reversed course and increased speed to 25 knots. The *Cornwall* was capable of 32 knots, but was running low on fuel, and, with the possibility of a long search in mind, Manwaring was loath to waste his oil. At sunrise he flew off his two Walrus reconnaissance aircraft to search ahead and astern of the ship. The cumbersome amphibious biplanes were museum pieces even in the 1940s, but their stability and a flying speed so low that they almost hovered put them in the front rank of ship-borne reconnaissance planes.

The aircraft returned before dark, having covered countless square miles of ocean with no sighting of the enemy raider. However, the *Cornwall* had steamed some 300 miles to the north-ward since morning and, in the event that the raider was on a southerly course, Manwaring considered he should by now be close to the enemy. Having stopped to hoist his aircraft aboard, he began to search to the east and west at a reduced speed of 13 knots, unwilling to go further north in case the raider slipped past during the night. The sky was cloudless and there was a bright moon, giving excellent visibility.

Manwaring's caution was justified, but his lookouts were not sufficiently alert. The *Pinguin* was on a SE'ly course, making 15 knots, when at 0300 on the 8th, with the moon low in the west, Oberleutnant Levit saw a dark shadow on the horizon to port. Using his binoculars, he could make out the silhouette of a ship. She was no freighter or tanker, but had the sleek lines of a warship and, as such, she could only be British. Levit called Krüder to the bridge.

Krüder quickly confirmed the Watch Officer's suspicions and at once altered course away from the stranger, calling on the engine-room to give him all possible speed. Vibrating heavily to the increased power of her engines, the *Pinguin* slipped back into the night. The other ship maintained her course and speed, giving no sign that she had seen the raider.

Dawn came on the 8th with the *Pinguin* on a SW'ly course and still slicing her way through the calm seas at the maximum speed her 1,800 horse power engines could produce. Krüder, who had not left the bridge, was becoming concerned at the extra fuel being burned at this forced speed, but the need to put distance between himself and the stranger of the night was paramount.

However, the rising sun revealed the sea to be empty all around, fully justifying the *Pinguin*'s headlong flight. Then his heart sank. As the sun came up, a black speck appeared on the horizon ahead, moving slowly from port to starboard. Krüder snatched up his binoculars and focused on the distant object, hoping against hope it was nothing more than a sea bird winging its way towards the Maldives. He was disappointed. The powerful Zeiss glasses revealed a small flying boat, which this far from land could only be a spotter plane from a British warship – the stranger of the night. Now there was nowhere for the *Pinguin* to hide, yet Krüder remained calm. Over 328 days and 59,000 miles the raider had led a charmed life. If Nemesis was now at hand, so be it.

At sunrise aboard the *Cornwall* Captain Manwaring was still unaware of his quarry's position and at first light had catapulted off both his aircraft, one to search north and the other to go south, The Walrus allocated the northern sector was piloted by Lieutenant Wilfrid Waller, with Lieutenant Paul Wormell observing and navigating. At 0707, on the westward leg of their search pattern and some 65 miles to the west of *Cornwall*, they sighted a merchant ship steaming to the south-west. She might be a British ship going about her lawful business, probably heading for the Mozambique Channel and the Cape, but her sleek lines and the curl of her bow wave convinced them she was something else – probably the ship they were looking for.

Aware that the Walrus must have been seen by the unidentified ship, Waller flew off in the opposite direction to the *Cornwall* until he was out of sight. He then banked and headed back for the cruiser, keeping radio silence as instructed by Manwaring. The Walrus landed on the water alongside the *Cornwall* at 0800. Informed of the sighting, Manwaring was convinced the raider was within his grasp, but, unwilling to use his radio to recall the other plane, he lay hove to awaiting its return. It was 0930 before both aircraft were hoisted aboard and *Cornwall* was under way again and heading for the reported position of the suspect ship at 20 knots.

At 1015 the second Walrus, piloted by Lieutenant Frank Fox, with Lieutenant-Commander Geoffrey Grove observing, was catapulted off with orders to take a closer look at the other ship and report back. Once aloft, and with an unlimited horizon in the clear air, Fox had little difficulty in locating his quarry. He descended low over the water and circled the ship, keeping a respectful distance while he and Grove examined her.

Fox had no cause to worry for the safety of his aircraft; no flak came the way of the slow-flying Walrus. Krüder had decided to bluff it out to the end. He kept most of his men below, leaving only a few around the decks, all of whom were dressed as would be expected of merchant seamen in these latitudes – threadbare shirts and ragged shorts, with the odd bare chest. On the bridge Krüder and his officers were also in nondescript dress – not a sign of a uniform anywhere, as might be expected of a Norwegian merchantman. The *Pinguin* was flying the Norwegian ensign at the main and her adopted name, *Tamerlane*, was prominently displayed on either side of the bridge.

Fox brought the Walrus in closer and began to circle while Grove used the Aldis lamp, flashing: 'WHAT SHIP? WHERE BOUND? WHAT CARGO?

And now Krüder made a fundamental mistake that was eventually to lead to his downfall. Like most naval officers, he was of the opinion that merchant seamen were largely incapable of signalling coherently by lamp and decided to put on an act to deceive the Walrus. He told his men on deck to hoist the *Tamerlane*'s signal letter flags in response to the challenge and to do it slowly and awkwardly, as would be expected of a bunch of inept merchant seamen. He forgot that in taking the name of one of Wilhelmsen's ships he was assuming the mantle of a crack cargo liner, in which uniform would be worn on the bridge and signalling, lamp or otherwise, would be top line. The act was overdone and Fox was suspicious. He flew directly over the raider, examined her closely and then flew away.

Back aboard the *Cornwall*, Fox reported to Manwaring on the sighting of what appeared to be a Norwegian merchant ship heading south-west at around 15 knots. When checked in the book, the signal letter hoist proved to be that of Wilhelmsen's *Tamerlane*, and her silhouette in Talbot Booth's 'Merchant Ships' matched what Fox and Grove had seen. But the *Tamerlane* was not on Manwaring's list of merchant ships known to be in the area and, having listened to Fox's suspicions, he decided to investigate without delay.

Manwaring rang for full speed and the *Cornwall* worked up to 26 knots, then 29 knots. He delayed catapulting off the second Walrus for as long as possible, so that it would not run out of fuel while the chase was on. The plane went off at 1345, piloted by Lieutenant Waller, with Lieutenant Wormell observing and Leading Aircraftman Neil Gregory manning the Walrus's single Lewis gun. Manwaring estimated the other ship would be within 32 miles, assuming she had maintained her course and speed. This proved to be correct, for the *Pinguin* was sighted by the Walrus as soon as it gained height.

Seeing the enemy aircraft return and begin to circle his ship again, Krüder was tempted to shoot it down, which he could have done without much effort. He resisted the temptation, knowing that whatever ship was below the horizon she must by now be fully aware of his position. Shooting down the plane would destroy any chance remaining of continuing his bluff, which he was determined to do. In any case, it proved too late to do anything else. A few minutes after the Walrus appeared overhead the *Pinguin*'s lookouts sighted a thin column of smoke astern. This soon became two columns, and then three, and Krüder knew he had a British heavy cruiser on his tail. This was confirmed when two slim masts and three funnels lifted above the horizon. The day of reckoning for the *Pinguin* was very near and Krüder sent his men to their action stations, warning them to keep out of sight and not to reveal their guns. He was still hoping to gain the advantage of surprise.

Bearing down on the stranger, Manwaring approached with extreme care. Not that he suspected a trap, but only a few days earlier, while on patrol, he had encountered a British merchantman which had refused to stop when challenged. He had been on the point of opening fire, and would have sunk one of his own ships, had she not identified herself in transmitting an RRRR message. It had been a near thing and he did not wish to make the same mistake again.

Manwaring's doubts were compounded when the other ship began transmitting a raider report, identifying herself as the Norwegian ship *Tamerlane* being attacked by a German warship. In the opinion of *Cornwall*'s wireless office, the transmitter being used was of British make.

For the first time since the search for the raider began Manwaring now broke radio silence. He instructed Lieutenant Waller, who was still circling the other ship, to inform her by lamp that the ship approaching was a British warship, and that she should heave to. The message was passed, but Krüder's only reply was to present his stern to the *Cornwall*, a perhaps typical reaction of a suspicious merchantman.

At 1656, having closed the range to 19,000 yards, Manwaring, still wary, made the signal by lamp, 'HEAVE TO OR I FIRE'. This was repeated three times slowly, and then backed up by one round of 8-inch fired over and to the left of the fleeing ship.

The shot across the bows was no more than Krüder was expecting, but he carried on with the charade. His plan was to entice the British warship to within range of his guns, and then to turn and give battle, hoping to disable the cruiser with his first broadside, or to torpedo her. As things were, it seemed that Manwaring was falling into Krüder's trap, for the *Cornwall* continued to close the gap.

Manwaring, meanwhile, plagued by the memory of his earlier encounter with an unidentified merchantman, was loath to open fire in earnest. Also at the back of his mind was that if this ship was the enemy raider he was seeking, she would be likely to have British prisoners on board. If he sank the ship, innocent lives might be lost.

In order to help solve his dilemma, Manwaring had the second Walrus armed with two 250 lb bombs and readied for launching. Lieutenant Fox, who was to fly the aircraft, had orders to drop one of his bombs ahead of the Norwegian, and if she did not then stop, to drop the other bomb on her forecastle head. All the *Cornwall*'s guns, eight 8-inch and eight 4-inch, were manned and loaded, standing by to open fire on orders from the bridge.

Aboard the *Pinguin* the tension was rising visibly. Chief Officer Stanley Davidson of the *Clan Buchanan* describes how the prisoners were faring:

'After we had been five days on the raider, our Captain was told that in the event of an air or surface raid all prisoners would be brought up to the main deck and placed in an alleyway where they would have a chance of escape.

'At 1000 on the 8th of May, prior to returning to our cell after exercise on deck, our Captain was again told about the prisoners being brought up to the main deck. On this day we gathered from the amount of activity around the decks that something unusual was happening. At lunch-time this became more obvious, as our famous soup had no salt in it, also the prison guard outside our cell was dressed in his best and had his lifebelt and gas mask handy. No exercise was allowed that afternoon and during the course of the afternoon various alarms were sounded throughout the ship and we heard the Germans running to their action stations.'

At 1710, the *Cornwall*'s signal lamp again flashed the order, 'HEAVE TO OR I FIRE'. Another round of 8-inch dropped close ahead of the *Pinguin*. The range was now down to 12,000 yards, and Manwaring at last became concerned that he was too close to the stranger, yet he felt compelled to go still closer to correctly identify his quarry.

On the bridge of the *Pinguin* Krüder realized the game would soon be up, but held his fire and willed the enemy cruiser to come closer. Manwaring obliged, continuing to overtake with all his guns trained, but silent. At 1714, with the range down to 8000 yards, Ernst Krüder gave the order for the *Pinguin* to drop her disguise.

The Norwegian ensign was lowered and the red, black and gold swastika of the German Kriegsmarine run up in its place. At this, the raider bared her teeth. Her shutters were raised to reveal the muzzles of her 5.9s, ranges and bearings were called down from the bridge, breeches clanged shut and, as Krüder brought his ship around to port to present her broadside, he gave the order to open fire.

With five of her big guns firing simultaneously, the *Pinguin* staggered and her port side was engulfed in a cloud of smoke and flame. The smoke was blown away and a cheer went up from her decks as tall spouts of water erupted all around the enemy cruiser. It was a brave gesture, but one that should have brought swift retribution on the German ship had not a chain of disasters chosen this moment to strike HMS *Cornwall*.

It was as *Cornwall* was swinging to port under full helm to give her guns a clear field of fire that a small fuse in the electrical circuit controlling the training of the cruiser's gun turrets worked loose.

The circuit went dead and the big guns stayed where they were, pointing out to sea. Captain Manwaring summed up his embarrassing predicament: 'I had the annoying experience of being at effective gun range of an enemy ship and with His Majesty's Ship under my command under rapid and fairly accurate fire, frequently being straddled and the main armament pointing anywhere but at the enemy.'

Manwaring took the only action open to him, hauling off to port to get out of range of the enemy's guns until repairs were affected to his turret training circuit. The situation was compounded by a complete breakdown of telephone communications between the bridge and the guns, followed by the line to the catapult going dead. It was now that Manwaring desperately needed the bombed-up Walrus in the air, but when an officer, sent aft from the bridge, reached the catapult he found that the Walrus had been damaged by a shell splinter and was unable to take off. Manwaring was rapidly losing control of the situation.

And in the midst of all this confusion, the *Pinguin* scored her first direct hit. The 5.9 shell struck forward, just above the waterline, and in way of the cruiser's flour store. A flour store is not usually regarded as a vital spot in a warship, but in the *Cornwall*'s case the store contained some important electrical wiring. The bags of flour served to deaden the explosion, but shell splinters severed the wiring between the lower steering position and the steering motors, and also put the engine-room telegraph out of action. More splinters penetrated the lower steering position, slightly wounding three men, and a fire was started in the Marines' messdeck. With her steering gone, the *Cornwall* veered out of control, but it took only minutes to change over to the after steering position and she was soon back on course.

Three minutes later the *Pinguin*'s gunners registered a second hit, this time in the Chief Petty Officers' pantry. Another small fire was started, but this was soon put out and the residual damage was minimal.

By this time, only seven minutes after power to the turrets had been lost – seven minutes that might easily have ended in disaster for the *Cornwall* – her guns were back in action and hurling shells at the raider. With the Walrus aloft spotting, she was soon straddling the *Pinguin*. German sources claimed that at this point

Krüder fired a salvo of torpedoes which might have sent the *Cornwall* to the bottom, had not the Walrus seen the tracks and radioed a warning. It was said that one torpedo passed under the cruiser's stern, missing her by only a few yards. In his report of the action, Manwaring says that no torpedoes or their tracks were seen, either by the Walrus or by those on board *Cornwall*.

The *Cornwall*'s guns had not yet scored a hit on the *Pinguin* and she continued to run away at full speed, but Manwaring had wisely opened the range and the raider's shells were all falling short. Krüder realized that he was wasting his ammunition and it could only be a matter of time before the enemy cruiser landed a full broadside on the *Pinguin*. When one of *Cornwall*'s shells carried away his foremast and rigging, the German captain decided it would be pointless to carry on this one-sided fight any longer. Reluctantly, he gave orders for his guns to cease fire and for the ship to be scuttled and abandoned.

Krüder's orders came too late. After a disastrous start, Manwaring's gunners had at last settled in and a salvo of four 8-inch shells slammed into the *Pinguin*. One burst on the fore-deck, the second demolished her bridge, the third penetrated the engine-room and exploded with devastating effect. The fourth shell delivered the *coup de grâce*. This burst in *Pinguin*'s No.5 hold, where the 130 mines she was to lay off the Indian coast were stowed. The raider was blown apart by the subsequent explosion.

Captain Manwaring witnessed the end of his opponent from the bridge of the *Cornwall*:

'I was on the point of closing in again on the enemy to about 13,000 yards, being well before her beam, when at 1725 she blew up on being straddled abaft the funnel by a broadside of which probably about three shells hit.

'The whole ship disappeared in a thick white cloud which also rose vertically at least 2000 feet and hung as a cloud for many minutes afterwards. No noise of the explosion was heard.

'A few seconds after the explosion the bows of the enemy ship, from the bridge forward, began appearing out of the explosion still going ahead, and as two bright flashes, taken for gunfire, were seen, two more salvoes were fired. However, when it was seen that the rest of the ship had disappeared, firing was stopped and this part of the ship lost its way and slowly sank backwards.'

Chief Officer Stanley Davidson witnessed the end of the *Pinguin* from the other side:

'At approximately 1710 the Germans fired a salvo of shells, including the gun immediately over our heads. The firing continued for about 8 minutes, when our lights were extinguished and a terrific blast shook the ship, throwing us from one side of the cell to the other.

'When I picked myself up, I found that I was beside the prison door, which was open. (I later discovered that a minute before the blast a German had opened the door of the cell.) We walked through this door and proceeded up the first flight of stairs without the slightest sign of panic amongst us. When we arrived at the top of the ladder a German sentry pushed me back and told me to wait. He shut the door and just then a shell struck the ship and we could hear splinters falling. Shortly afterwards he opened the door again and called to his friends at the nearby gun. As he received no answer, he walked away and we immediately followed him.

'On gaining the shelter deck where the guns were, I went to the ship's side to ascertain what was happening, and found that the after end of the ship had been completely blown away and the ship was sinking rapidly by the stern. By this time the majority of my comrades were on deck and the Captain was standing in the centre of them smoking his pipe. I shouted to him that the ship was sinking rapidly and that it was every man for himself and to jump quickly. In acknowledgement he waved his hand. Just then the ship lurched violently to starboard, and I and a few other men jumped overboard from the port side. On reaching the water I turned on my back and swam away from the ship. By this time the raider's bow was vertical in the air, and she sank almost immediately. As she was sinking I noticed that the ship's bottom was very clean, as if she had just come out of dry dock.'

Davidson later told Manwaring that the bright flashes seen on the *Pinguin*'s foredeck were in fact two of the *Cornwall*'s shells striking home. They destroyed the two 5.9s on the forecastle head, killed their crews and, unfortunately, they also resulted in the death of Captain Davenport-Jones, who was hit by flying debris.

Obersteuermann Ernst Neumeister, *Pinguin*'s chief quarter-master, was one of the few men to survive when the raider's bridge was hit. He had just moved from the port to the starboard side when the shell struck and was knocked unconscious. When he came to again, he saw the port side of the bridge, where Krüder and his officers had been standing, was no longer there. By the time Neumeister reached the boat deck the *Pinguin* was so far over on her side that the top of the funnel was awash. As he jumped overboard, the wrecked bridge was disappearing under water.

Davidson and Neumeister ended up clinging to the same liferaft while they awaited rescue. Their wait was a long one, for, although the action was over, the *Cornwall* was again in trouble.

Having watched the enemy ship disappear beneath the waves, Manwaring turned his attention, firstly to recovering the Walrus still in the air, after which he intended pick up survivors visible in the mess of floating debris left by the *Pinguin*. He instructed Lieutenant Waller to land and then passed the word to the engine-room by messenger – the telegraphs were still out of action – to slow down to 12 knots prior to stopping. Nothing happened and the cruiser raced on at 25 knots towards the aircraft, which was now on the water.

Commander (E) Robert Blaxland, the *Cornwall*'s chief engineer, had a crisis on his hands brought about by the lucky hit scored by the *Pinguin*'s gunners on the cruiser's flour store. In the course of the violent manoeuvring during the action the broached compartment had been flooded to sufficient depth to short-circuit the ring main fed by No.1 dynamo. The dynamo ground to a halt, resulting in the engine and boiler spaces being plunged into darkness. In the confusion that followed, steam valves were shut in error and the cruiser's two other dynamos slowed down. All the extractor fans stopped and within minutes the temperature below had soared to 200°F. This was heat beyond human endurance and Blaxland was forced to evacuate both engine-room and boiler-room. In spite of this, several officers and ratings were overcome by the appalling heat. One of them, Lieutenant (E) George Winslade, subsequently died of heat exhaustion.

While confusion reigned in her engine-room, the *Cornwall* charged on, unstoppable. Manwaring had to leave his aircraft on the water and could do no more than throw out a Carley float as he sped past the *Pinguin* survivors. The cruiser swept around in a wide circle until her runaway engines were eventually brought under control and stopped. She drifted to a halt in the midst of the *Pinguin*'s wreckage, and there she lay, disabled, until well into the night.

Before darkness fell *Cornwall*'s boats picked up a total of eighty-four survivors, sixty of the *Pinguin*'s crew and twenty-four of her prisoners. Of the 401 Germans aboard the raider, only three officers, Dr Werner Hasselmann, one of her two surgeons, Dr Ulrich Roll, the meteorologist, Leutnant Oskar Boettcher, a prize officer, and fifty-seven petty officers and ratings survived. As to the 238 prisoners she carried, Second Officer Wilfred Wright, of the *British Emperor*, and Chief Officer Stanley Davidson, seven other officers and fifteen Lascar seamen of the *Clan Buchanan*, were the only ones to be picked up. Second Officer Wright, who had been badly wounded, died three days later and was buried in the Seychelles. Apart from the tragic death of Lieutenant Winslade, the *Cornwall* suffered only four men slightly injured.

The action which ended with the sinking of the *Pinguin* lasted just twenty-nine minutes. It was a furious gunfight in which the German raider's guns fired 200 rounds and HMS *Cornwall* replied with 186 rounds from her 8-inch and 4-inch guns. Despite the catalogue of disasters that befell the British cruiser, the day was a considerable success for Captain Manwaring. Armed merchant service raiders sailing under disguise have always been difficult to deal with and the *Pinguin* was no exception. From start to finish of the chase Manwaring had been worried by the possibility that he might be about to open fire on an innocent, but incredibly stubborn, friendly merchantman. In the end the matter was decided for him by Krüder firing the first shots, but when Manwaring learned he had been responsible for the deaths of so many British and Indian seamen his distress was great.

Kapitän-zur-See Ernst-Felix Krüder, who died on the bridge of the *Pinguin*, received due recognition from his Führer in the form of the posthumous award of the Oak Leaves to his Knight's Cross. The success his ship had achieved as a commerce raider was without equal in the two World Wars. The *Pinguin*, ex-*Kandelfels*, had donned the trappings of war and returned to wreak havoc in the Indian Ocean amongst the very ships with which she had once shared these waters in a common calling. With her guns, torpedoes and mines, she had deprived the Allies of nearly 200,000 tons of priceless shipping, even reaching down into Antarctica to ply her adopted trade. And yet, throughout the 328 days at sea and 59,188 miles steamed, Krüder had acted towards his enemies with commendable humanity, saving life wherever possible, sometimes putting his own ship in danger to do so. For this he should be remembered

HMS *Cornwall* reached Port Victoria, in the Seychelle Islands, on 11 May, where her survivors were landed and her damage temporarily repaired. She remained in the Indian Ocean and on 5 April 1942, sailing in company with HMS *Dorsetshire*, she met a powerful Japanese force in the Bay of Bengal, consisting of three battleships and five aircraft carriers, accompanied by cruisers and destroyers. The two British cruisers, sailing without air protection, were attacked by waves of Japanese carrier-borne aircraft and sunk before they could come to grips with the enemy ships. Captain Manwaring survived, but 198 of his officers and men went down with the *Cornwall*.

The ex-whaler *Adjutant* arrived at the rendezvous with the supply ship *Alstertor* on 8 May and there her commander, Leutnant Hemmer, listened in to Krüder's last message to the German Naval Command, 'After sinking 136,550 gross register tons and obtaining excellent mine results am now engaged with British heavy cruiser *Cornwall*'. After that there was silence and Hemmer knew he had lost his mother ship. The *Adjutant* was then ordered to join the *Komet*, another German ex-merchantman raider operating in the Indian Ocean. She met up with the *Komet* on 21 May and acted as her scout until 1 July. By this time the whaler's engines, pushed to the limit of their endurance and without proper maintenance for so long, could run no more. She was abandoned and scuttled. Leutnant Hemmer and his crew returned home in the *Komet*, which successfully broke through to Bordeaux, arriving on 31 November 1941.

Chapter Fifteen

The final chapter in the saga of the slow convoy from Freetown, SLS 64, was closed when, on 1 March 1941, a salt-stained ship's lifeboat came ashore on the Lizard peninsula.

Twenty-three days earlier, at dusk on 6 February, the 5237-ton *Gairsoppa*, staggering under a heavy load of pig iron from India, had been forced to drop out of SLS 64 in order to conserve her rapidly dwindling supply of coal. From then on her future was in jeopardy, for, weather apart, she was entering one of the most dangerous stretches of water in the world, where the U-boat and Focke-Wulf held sway. With 1,700 miles to go to the Western Approaches, steaming at a reduced speed of 5 knots and with not even the protection of an unescorted convoy around her, the British India ship faced the prospect of treading the thin line between survival and extinction for another two weeks.

On the morning of the 15th the *Gairsoppa* was 315 miles north-west of Cape Finisterre and steaming into the teeth of yet another howling gale. The enemy had not yet shown himself, nor was anyone on board aware that the convoy they had left had been savaged by the *Admiral Hipper*. In spite of the battering she was taking at the hands of the weather, the consensus of opinion was that the sturdy old ship would reach home safely. This optimistic view was not, however, shared by Captain Gerald Hyland. His engineers were already working on the far corners of the coal bunkers and, prevented from entering the English Channel or Irish Sea by the mine barriers, he was committed to taking the long road around the north of Ireland into the North Channel. His only comfort was that, if at any time his coal was in danger

177

of running out completely, he would have the option of entering a neutral port on the west coast of Ireland.

The *Gairsoppa* finally met up with the enemy on the morning of the 16th when she was crossing the western approaches to the Channel. Struggling to make headway against the heavy seas, she was sighted by a patrolling Focke-Wulf which, keeping its distance, circled the ship for an hour before flying away without attempting to attack. When darkness closed in and the enemy plane had not returned, the relief felt aboard the British ship was great. It was, however, misplaced.

While the Focke-Wulf circled out of reach of the *Gairsoppa*'s guns, as dictated by the new spirit of cooperation between the Luftwaffe and the Kriegsmarine, it had been homing in a nearby U-boat. *U-101*, commanded by Kapitän-Leutnant Ernst Mengersen, was on her way back to base after a long and not particularly fruitful Atlantic patrol. In three months she had sunk only four ships, totalling 22,500 tons, the last, sunk only two days earlier after a long, barren interval, being the Newcastle-registered *Holystone*. Now, the Focke-Wulf had delivered into her hands a heavily-laden British merchantman making such slow progress that she resembled a stationary target. Mengersen submerged and moved in on his prey.

At 2030 Mengersen's torpedo struck the *Gairsoppa* in way of her No.2 cargo hold, ripping open her hull and bringing her fore-mast crashing down. Her reserve buoyancy was lost and, weighed down by her heavy cargo, she began to sink by the head at once. Captain Hyland gave the order to abandon ship.

Lowering a ship's lifeboat is a difficult operation in the best of circumstances; in the case of the *Gairsoppa*, conditions could hardly have been worse. It was a black, storm-swept night, the ship was on fire from end to end and, with her main engine still going ahead at full speed, she was driving under bow-first. And, to make matters worse, *U-101* had surfaced and was firing on the ship with a machine gun. What on earth can have been Mengersen's motive for this heartless action is hard to imagine.

The *Gairsoppa* was equipped with four lifeboats, but, in the rush to abandon, three of these were smashed against the ship's side by the heavy seas. Only one boat survived to reach the water and it had lost its rudder. In command of the boat was Second

Officer R.H. Ayres, who had with him eight Europeans and twenty-five Lascar seamen. Out of a total crew of eighty-five they were the only ones to get away. With a makeshift rudder rigged, Ayres hoisted sail and cleared away from the ship's side, narrowly avoiding being dragged under as she went down.

Before leaving the ship, Radio Officer Robert Hampshire made a gallant attempt to send an SOS, but the torpedo had brought down both the *Gairsoppa*'s main and emergency aerials, and his transmission did not reach beyond the radio-room. Hampshire was fortunate enough to find a place in Ayres' boat and was able to acquaint the Second Officer with the hopelessness of their situation. The outside world knew nothing of the loss of the *Gairsoppa* and, until such time as she was considered long overdue, no search would be made for survivors. Only one course lay open to Ayres and that was a long and arduous sail to the north, hoping to make a landfall on the south coast of Ireland.

The gale, shifting between west and north-west, raged for nine days without let-up. Ayres fought to maintain a northerly course, but with the tiny cockleshell of a boat sliding crazily from crest to trough of the waves, his compass would not settle. And there was no help from the sun and stars, which were hidden through-out behind a heavy overcast.

The fresh water ran out on the third day and, with the boat being regularly swamped by the bitterly cold sea, men soon began to die. By the twelfth day only Ayres, Hampshire, Gunner Norman Thomas and four Lascars were still alive. Ayres' feet were badly frostbitten and they were all very weak, past caring whether the cruel grey sea took them or not. And so they slipped away one by one, until on the morning of 1 March only Ayres, Hampshire and Thomas still lived and their hours were numbered. Then their fortunes changed. Held with its bows pointing roughly north, but carried to the east by the inflowing Gulf Stream, the boat had crabbed its way into the English Channel and at daylight on the 2nd the rocky promontory of Lizard Point was sighted. Ayres tried to rally his two remaining companions to row for the shore, but they were too far gone. The boat was flung onto the rocks at the foot of the Lizard and all three men were thrown into the boiling surf. Only Ayres survived. Some hours later four evacuee children out gathering driftwood saw him lying on the rocks unconscious and alerted the Coastguard. Ayres was carried ashore, the only survivor of the *Gairsoppa*'s crew of eighty-five. The bodies of Radio Officer Robert Hampshire and Gunner Norman Thomas came ashore later and were buried in the graveyard of the ancient church of St. Winwallow, within sound of the waves that break on the Lizard. There they lie to this day.

The exact location of the *Gairsoppa*'s last resting place is not known, only that she went down some 300 miles south-west of Galway. One day in the future the underwater probes of the salvage hunters will seek her out. Meanwhile, she languishes 1,500 fathoms deep, with her fortune in silver bars increasing in value as each day goes by.

Having dealt with the fire discovered in her cargo when twenty-four hours out of Freetown with SLS 64, the *Nailsea Lass* was under way again by noon on 31 January. By this time, however, the 23-year-old Liverpool tramp was nearly 60 miles astern of the convoy and resigned to completing the voyage on her own, for there was no way she could hope to close the gap with the other ships. On 2 February, near the Cape Verde Islands, she exchanged signals with a British cruiser and met an armed boarding vessel to the west of Biscay on the 16th, both meetings serving to remind her that she was not entirely alone. The weather, too, had been kind and she was making a steady 6 knots, albeit a frighteningly low speed given the dangers that abounded in these waters, but then this was all her much-abused engine could manage.

That night the Atlantic showed its winter face, whipping up a stiff NW'ly gale that soon had the *Nailsea Lass* struggling to maintain steerage way. She continued to inch her way to the north, but it was not until 23 February that she reached the Western Approaches. Then, as if to welcome her into home waters, the weather relented. The wind dropped and the skies cleared. By next morning the *Nailsea Lass* was making good a NNE'ly course at 6 knots in light variable winds, with clear visibility and only a slight swell. Captain Thomas Bradford, like Captain Hyland of the *Gairsoppa* before him, intended to hug the west coast of Ireland as he made for the North Channel. Unfortunately, time was also running out for the *Nailsea Lass*.

U-48, commanded by Kapitän-Leutnant Herbert Schultze, was

idling on the surface 60 miles south-west of the Fastnet Rock when, at 1930 on the 24th, the *Nailsea Lass* was sighted heading slowly northwards. Schultze, one of Dönitz's up and coming aces, already had 95,000 tons of Allied shipping to his credit. He submerged to move in on yet another easy victim.

Second Officer Ernest Knight, then off watch and about to turn in, was forced to change his plans:

'At 1945 on the 24th February, in position 60 miles SW from the Fastnet, there was a heavy shock, the ship heeled over, and a second later a loud explosion. I was in my room at the time, the Chief Officer being on watch. I learned later from the lookout man that there was no flame, but a jet of water was thrown up which came down on the bridge. The torpedo struck the port side of the ship abreast of the foremast, between No.1 and 2 holds about 60 feet from the bow. The ship vibrated, then took a gradual list to port which steadily increased. No wireless message was sent out as the valves were broken by the explosion.

'I heard the Captain give orders to take to the boats, so I collected my lifejacket, went on the lower bridge and put the confidential books and papers over the side in a weighted bag. The ship had now started to go down by the bow. We got away in two boats and as we pulled clear the ship sank, about a quarter an hour after she was torpedoed, at 2000. The crew were all safe at this time, although their quarters were forward.

'When the ship had disappeared the submarine broke surface near the port lifeboat, in charge of the Chief Officer. We heard the Germans asking the name of our ship, who was in charge of that boat, then they ordered it alongside and took off the Chief Officer. The submarine steamed over to us and a German, who I think was the Commander, as he was speaking from the conning tower, asked us if anyone was injured. We said no, and he replied, "We are not all bad Nazis, and I hope the war will soon finish". There was a group of Germans standing around on deck, talking amongst themselves in English, but with a German accent: they had no proper naval uniforms. The Commander then told the Captain to come aboard, after which the U-boat immediately steamed off on the surface.'

In taking Captain Tom Bradford and Chief Officer Alfred Hodder prisoner, Herbert Schultze was following orders from

Admiral Dönitz, whose policy it was to remove from circulation as many senior Allied merchant ship officers as possible. Having done so, Schultze handed over two cartons of cigarettes to the boats and gave them a course to steer for the nearest land.

When the U-boat, her rattling diesels indicating they were sorely in need of maintenance, had disappeared into the night, Second Officer Ernest Knight, now the senior surviving officer, brought the two lifeboats together to discuss their plight. It was then discovered that the compass of the second boat, now in the charge of 19-year-old Third Officer Denis Gouge, had been smashed by the exploding torpedo. It was therefore imperative that the boats kept together and it was agreed that Knight would lead, while Gouge followed closely in his wake. The wind was too light for the heavy lifeboat sails to be effective, but, as the south coast of Ireland was little more than 60 miles away, they set off rowing with a will.

The two boats stayed together until midnight, but then the weather suddenly changed. The wind came away from the east, and was soon blowing gale force. Sails were hoisted, but from then on Knight and Gouge were each involved in their separate struggles to avoid being blown westwards into the wastes of the North Atlantic. They soon lost sight of each other.

Knight decided to carry on alone, hoping that if they reached the land to send help for the other boat. Land, probably Mizen Head, 12 miles to the west of the Fastnet, was sighted at 1500 on the 25th, but, with darkness fast coming on, Knight decided to heave to for the night. A sea anchor was streamed and the survivors settled down to wait for the dawn. Their ordeal was a cold and miserable one, with the boat rolling and pitching crazily, being constantly swamped by the seas and lashed by icy rain squalls.

In the first grey light of dawn on the 26th it was found that one man had died of exposure during the night and that the land was no longer in sight. The wind was still strong from the east – in an area where usually south-west to westerly winds prevailed – a bitter blow to Knight, for he realized the boat was being carried out to sea. In desperation, he hoisted sail again and, tacking as close to the wind as possible, he fought to make headway to the north. But ships' lifeboats, heavy and cumbersome craft, are built to sail before the wind. Progress to the north was minimal.

When the wind at last relented, and backed to the south, land was again sighted. This proved to be Great Blasket Island, which lies off the south-west coast of Ireland. Knight brought the boat in through the narrow Blasket Sound and into Dingle Bay, making a landing near the village of Ballyoughtraugh. Third Officer Denis Gouge, meanwhile, had been waging a similar battle with the elements, but at a greater cost. Four of his men died of exposure before, late on the 26th, he brought his boat into the Kenmare River, on the other side of the Dingle peninsula, and came ashore near Caherdaniel.

It was late on the afternoon of 12 February when Captain Ivor Price led the demoralized remnants of SLS 64 away from the scene of its annihilation by the *Admiral Hipper*. With the *Margot* were three British ships, *Volturno*, *Clunepark* and *Blairatholl*, and the Greek-flag *Anna Marazaki* and *Polyktor*. The *Blairatholl* had on board eighty-six survivors from the *Warlaby*, *Shrewsbury*, *Oswestry Grange* and *Westbury*, while the *Polyktor* had picked up twenty-one from the lifeboats of the *Perseus*. Some of the ships were damaged, some had lost their boats, all were desperately in need of a safe haven in which to recover from the devastating ordeal they had suffered on that day. The convoy was then 200 miles east of the Azores and 345 miles north-west of Madeira. After some consultation with the other masters, Price decided to set course for Funchal, Madeira. This meant doubling back, but Funchal was likely to have the best repair facilities.

The six-ship convoy reached Funchal on the morning of the 14th and was directed to an anchorage off the port. After anchoring, Price contacted the British Consul and arrangements were made for the necessary repairs to be put in hand. The Portuguese authorities, neutral but very pro-British, were most cooperative and seemed quite unconcerned as to how long the ships remained in their waters. Madeira, the garden island of the Atlantic, with its warm, benign climate, offered the crews of the ships a temporary escape from the war and they were prepared to make full use of this. Their new-found good fortune was, however, short-lived. Next morning Madeira was hit by a freak hurricane and once gain they found themselves fighting for their lives.

Captain Ivor Price and Chief Officer D.J. Morris were both ashore when it began to blow and the sea in the anchorage rose so quickly that they were unable to get a boat to take them back to the *Margot*. In the absence of the two senior men, Second Officer A.M. Davies took command of the ship. With the wind blowing directly on shore, and increasing in force by the minute, he decided to weigh anchor and put to sea.

The *Margot*'s anchor cable was by this time bar tight and vibrating under enormous load. Even with the engines going ahead, the strain on the windlass was immense as it strove to bring the anchor home. Link by link, the cable was dragged up through the hawsepipe, while the wind howled and seas broke over the forecastle head, threatening to sweep the anchor party over the side. Then there was a loud bang and the windlass gypsy shattered under the strain. The brake was hurriedly applied and the chain prevented from running out, but a close inspection of the windlass revealed that, without major repairs, it would never work again.

The other ships in the anchorage had already put to sea and the *Margot* was left to fight her battle alone. Davies decided the only thing to do was to let the cable run right out and then let go the chain locker end. In all the best seamanship manuals this is presented as a comparatively simple operation, involving knocking out the pin securing the last link of the cable to the after bulkhead of the locker. In reality this pin is usually solid with rust and the cable must be cut free. This was so in the case of the *Margot* and, given the parsimonious attitude of the British shipowner of the day, she had no cutting or burning gear on board. The only tool available was a hacksaw. And so, with the ship rolling and pitching jerkily to her anchor, with seas breaking over her decks, the attempt to cut her free began. Radio Officer John Cave was a witness to the drama:

'I shall never forget the few days of that terrifying storm. Not one of us would admit to any fear at the time, but the violent, unusual motions of the ship, at the mercy of the huge waves and the fearful strain the bow was taking as it tried to break away from the restraining chain and respond to the sea, together with the constant screaming of the wind through the rigging, were terrible. Each one

184

of us must have had his own thoughts on how much longer the "spec job" hull could sustain such a battering. The thought of the ship foundering at any moment brought out a herd instinct, and many of us slept together on the saloon deck, although no one would admit to suggesting it.

'Working in relays, under appalling conditions in the chain locker, the engineers took almost two days to cut through a cable link. The vessel responded immediately. Her head came round into the wind, and the incessant heavy pitching, rolling and pounding ceased to a great extent.'

Three days later, when the storm had finally blown itself out, the *Margot* returned to Funchal, having by then been given up for lost. With her windlass broken, she was unable to anchor, but, after steaming up and down outside the port for several hours, a berth was found for her alongside the mole in Funchal. An inspection then revealed that the damage to the ship was far worse than had at first been thought. Much of the damage could be repaired, but the seas had swept away all her remaining boats and life-rafts. These the Portuguese could not replace. After consulting with the Consul, Price called his crew together and offered them the choice of either staying in Funchal for weeks, or even months, until replacement lifeboats were found, or sailing for home under escort as soon as essential repairs were completed. John Cave remembers:

'The decision was not an easy one. The local Portuguese inhabitants and the evacuees from Gibraltar were going out of their way to give us all a good time. Few barmen would charge us for cigarettes and there always seemed to be someone at your elbow to offer a drink. Understandably, not one of us was inclined to leave this paradise for a while and we began to appreciate the agonies Fletcher Christian must have sustained. However, patriotism prevailed, and within a few days we had all volunteered to go home with a strong escort, but without lifeboats or life-saving equipment lost during the hurricane.'

On the morning of 25 February the *Margot*, dressed overall, with the town band playing her out and the local inhabitants cheering on the quay, broke away from her berth and put to sea. Outside the port she was joined by the *Blairatholl* and *Volturno*, and the three ships steamed out to join their escort of three British destroyers waiting beyond the 3-mile limit.

To the men of these merchant ships, who had in the past faced so many dangers alone, a destroyer apiece seemed too good to be true – and so it was. When daylight came next day the three destroyers were nowhere to be seen and once again the *Margot*, *Blairatholl* and *Volturno* were left to face the enemy alone. A rather cheap trick had been played on them, but they carried on nevertheless, and, given good luck and persistent poor visibility, they all reached home unharmed.

An interesting sequel to the *Margot*'s voyage was provided by D.G. Stanley, who served in another of Kaye, Son & Co's vessels, the *Marton*, as third officer:

'Following an accident on board, I was working in Kaye's office in London when the *Margot* returned to the UK after the encounter with the *Admiral Hipper*. Captain Price was summoned to the office to account for his actions. As I recall, his initial report was that when the convoy encountered the German raider, he set off all the smoke canisters on board, and with the entire crew abandoned ship. He claimed that by this action the enemy would assume the ship had been hit, and was finished, and would cease their attack. This ruse was apparently successful. After the raider had disappeared, Captain Price and his crew returned to the ship and resumed the voyage. This action, however, was not approved by Sydney Kaye and his fellow directors. They took the view that in abandoning the ship he had laid open the possibility of others boarding the vessel, which could have been lost in a heavy salvage claim, and by his thoughtless action Captain Price was dismissed from the Company.'

The directors of Kaye, Son & Company appeared to have missed the point that, in the mêlée that followed the savaging of SLS 64, no other ship's captain, however avaricious, was likely to be remotely concerned with the prospect of boarding an abandoned ship with salvage in mind. Ivor Price was a first-class seaman and a shrewd Welshman to boot; his quick thinking undoubtedly saved his ship and her crew. And he did more, as the Ministry of Defence was quick to recognize. The following is an extract from the *London Gazette* dated 11 June 1941:

Award of the George Medal

Captain Ivor Llewellyn Price, Master.

The ship was attacked by a surface raider, the Master turned away and burnt smoke floats. Owing to the strong wind these did not wholly screen the ship but gave better cover to three other ships which escaped. Captain Price fired on the enemy when his guns bore and the raider directed his full attention to the ship, firing as he closed. The raider subsequently made off. Captain Price gathered together the ships remaining and after searching for and picking up survivors, proceeded to port.

When Ivor Price was in London on 23 October 1941 to receive his George Medal from the King at Buckingham Palace, the *Margot*'s owners were so embarrassed that temporarily office-bound Third Officer Stanley was instructed to entertain Price to lunch – anything to keep him away from the office. Captain Price's comments on his cavalier treatment by his owners are not on record.

Bombed and machine-gunned by a Focke-Wulf, Glen & Company's short-sea trader *Varna* continued to limp along in the wake of HG 53. Being so far astern of the other ships probably saved her when *U-37* attacked the convoy for the second time on 10 February, but there was no escaping from her old enemy, the sea. Next day what was described by Captain Saul as 'a moderate gale' blew up, and the badly damaged ship began to take in water at an alarming rate. Soundings taken showed seven feet of water in the main hold and it was necessary to list the ship to port by jettisoning deck cargo, bringing the hole in the starboard side of the hull above water. Only then could the pumps contain the rising water.

The gale blew itself out on the morning of the 12th and for the next three days the weather held fair. This allowed the *Varna*'s main hold to be pumped dry and temporary repairs were effected by caulking the strained plates and plugging over one hundred rivet holes. Coal was shifted in the bunkers to reduce the list and every effort was made to make the ship as seaworthy as possible.

While the weather was fair the *Varna* was just able to keep the tail end of convoy in sight and Captain Saul dared to hope that the battle had been won. Then, on the 15th, the situation changed dramatically when the *Varna* ran into the hurricane-force winds that had come so near to putting an end to the *Margot* off Funchal. All but hove to in mountainous seas, she dropped further and further astern until the convoy was lost from sight. Soon after dark she was struck by a violent squall from the north-west and took a heavy list to starboard, from which she did not recover. There was water in her main hold again and, although the pumps ran continuously, they failed to keep it in check. At 2200 the engine-room reported to Saul that water was pouring into the stokehold from the reserve bunker. He took swift action, ordering the watertight door between the bunker and stokehold to be closed and altering course to put the wind and sea on the port bow. He then set his crew to jettisoning more deck cargo to decrease the starboard list.

By 0030 on the 16th the *Varna* had been brought upright again and given a list to port, but seas were now breaking clean over her decks, indicating she was sinking lower in the water. At 0230 the bulwarks on the port side of the foredeck collapsed and the remainder of the cargo of pit props broke adrift, carrying away winches and derricks, and smashing hatch coamings. Half an hour later the *Varna* was down by the head with much of her foredeck awash and it was clear to Captain Saul that his ship was in danger of sinking. On this black, stormy night he feared for his crew.

Miracles do happen at sea and now it was the *Varna*'s turn. A few minutes after 0300 a ship was seen overtaking on the starboard side. Saul fired distress rockets and signalled the other ship to stand by him. She was another straggler from HG 53, the *Empire Fern*. Her master, Captain Valler, agreed to stand by the *Varna* until daylight, when her crew would take to the boats.

At first light, at around 0700, it was evident that the *Varna* had not long to go and Saul gave the order to abandon ship. As he did, a sea broke over the boat deck, carrying away the starboard lifeboat with only one man aboard. The port boat was launched with a full complement and others, including Captain Saul, got away on a liferaft. Moments after they cleared the *Varna* she rolled over to starboard and slipped beneath the waves to her last

188

resting place. Saul and his men were picked up by the *Empire Fern*, which then searched for the missing man. He was found clinging to the upturned boat and, with a magnificent display of seamanship in heavy weather, Valler manoeuvred his ship close enough for a rope to be thrown. The lonely survivor was hauled aboard, cold and wet, but little the worse for wear.

The two ships to receive the heaviest damage from the *Hipper*'s shells, Ropner's 4860-ton *Ainderby* and the 4934-ton Glasgow tramp *Lornaston*, reached Ponta Delgada, the principal port of St. Michael's in the Azores, on 13 February. There they lay for almost four months while they were patched up for the voyage home. This long respite from the war at sea was an idyllic interlude for the crews of the two ships, for, as with the ships sheltering off Funchal, the local Portuguese made them more than welcome. The only shadow that hung over them was the daily appearance of the German Consul on his balcony overlooking the harbour, telescope in hand. It was common knowledge ashore that he was reporting the sailing of all ships to Berlin, and through there to U-boats waiting off the Azores.

At last, in early June, both being declared seaworthy, the *Ainderby* and *Lornaston* sailed north from Ponta Delgada. The *Lornaston* reached her destination, but the *Ainderby*, bound for Glasgow, did not. Her luck finally ran out at 1030 on 10 June, when some 200 miles west of Ireland, and so close to home, she ran across the track of *U-554*. A torpedo struck the *Ainderby* forward of the bridge and she broke in two, the forward part of the ship sinking immediately. With it went twenty-one of the *Ainderby*'s crew. The survivors were picked up by a British destroyer next day.

Chapter Sixteen

Returning from her foray against Convoy SLS 64, the *Admiral Hipper* arrived in Brest on 14 February, joining the battle-cruisers *Scharnhorst* and *Gneisenau*, which were already making use of the extensive facilities of the French port. Inevitably, this concentration of German capital ships drew the attention of RAF Bomber Command and over the following weeks the port was subjected to almost continuous attack by high-level bombers. In one heavy raid on 24 February fifteen bombs fell within 200 yards of the *Hipper*, but otherwise she bore a charmed life and when, after five weeks in port, her refit was complete, she was undamaged. On 15 March she ventured out into the Atlantic again and, having refuelled at a rendezvous off south-east Greenland, Kapitän Meisel took her through the Denmark Strait under the cover of bad weather on the 23rd. She reached Kiel on the 28th and began a major refit.

While the *Hipper* languished in Kiel Hitler's dream of world domination moved on towards fruition. In June 1941 he turned on the Soviet Union – in his opinion the true enemy of the German Reich – with the launch of Operation 'Barbarossa'. At 0400 on 22 June 120 divisions of German infantry and armour, supported by nearly 3000 aircraft, advanced into Russia on a front running from the Baltic in the north to the Black Sea in the south. This was an outrageously ambitious undertaking, but Hitler, like another famous dictator before him, confidently predicted he would be in Moscow before the next winter came. To his peril, he ignored the reality of 12 million Soviet men and women under

190

arms, with many tens of millions more ready to lay down their lives for their homeland.

The Russians contested every inch of their soil with their blood, but the superior German armies rolled relentlessly eastwards, until by the spring of 1942 the front line was within 70 miles of Moscow. The cost of this unremitting offensive, as might be expected, was prohibitive, the Germans suffering over a million killed and missing, with another half a million wiped out by the severity of the Russian winter and disease. But Hitler, having come this far, had no thoughts of halting to consolidate his gains. He planned to make a dash for the oilfields of the Caucasus and from there to drive on into Iran and the Persian Gulf, where lay enough oil to serve the German war machine indefinitely.

While the Russians had manpower in plenty, they lacked sufficient tanks, guns and aircraft to stem the German advance. For some time Britain and America had been attempting to help their eastern ally, ships loaded with arms and equipment braving the long, hazardous route through Arctic waters to Murmansk and Archangel. Now the need to increase the convoys was urgent, but the US Navy was fully committed to fighting the Japanese in the Pacific and the Royal Nay was only just holding its own against the U-boats in the North Atlantic. Convoy escorts were in short supply and ships loaded for Russia had begun to pile up in British ports.

Coincidentally, Hitler had developed an obsession that the Allies intended to invade Norway at an early date and he ordered Admiral Raeder to move large units of the German surface fleet into Norwegian waters to counteract this threat. The *Admiral Hipper* had by then at last completed her refit and on 22 March 1942, now under the command of Kapitän-zur-See Hans Hartmann, she sailed from Kiel for Trondheim in northern Norway. There she joined the 42,900-ton battleship *Tirpitz* and the pocket-battleships *Lützow* and *Admiral Scheer*. Ringed by anti-torpedo nets and hidden from the air by the steep mountains that drop sheer to the deep waters of Trondheim Fjord, the big ships awaited the call to action. When it came, it was from an unexpected quarter.

In early summer, in the face of strident and increasing demands

191

from the Russians for more arms, in spite of the dangers posed by almost continuous daylight in the Arctic, it was decided to try to clear the backlog of loaded ships by forcing through a convoy. PQ 17, the largest single shipment of military supplies ever attempted to Russia, was proposed for the end of June. It was to be made up of thirty-five merchant ships, twenty-two of which would be American-flag, carrying some 200,000 tons of cargo. With them would be two British fleet tankers, whose role it would be to refuel the convoy's escorts, and three rescue ships. The latter, ex-British North Sea ferries specially adapted for rescue work and with medical facilities on board, were a sad, but very necessary, adjunct to such a high-risk convoy.

It was agreed in London and Washington that for PQ 17 to get through to Russia it would need to be heavily defended and to this end no fewer than sixty-two Allied warships were allocated. PQ 17's close escort would consist of an all-British force of six destroyers, four corvettes, two submarines, three minesweepers, two anti-aircraft ships and four anti-submarine trawlers. Within call would be an Anglo-American force comprising the heavy cruisers HMS *London*, HMS *Norfolk*, USS *Wichita* and USS *Tuscaloosa*, accompanied by the destroyers HMS *Somali*, USS *Wainwright* and USS *Rowan*. Hovering out of sight over the horizon would be a covering force of two battleships, HMS *Duke of York* and USS *Washington*, the aircraft carrier HMS *Victorious*, the heavy cruisers HMS *Nigeria* and HMS *Cumberland*, twelve British destroyers and the top-rate American destroyers *Mayrant* and *Rhind*. Scouting ahead would be the British submarines *Sahib*, *Seawolf*, *Sturgeon*, *Tribune*, *Trident*, *Unrivalled*, *Unshaken* and *Ursula*, the Free French submarine *Minerve* and six Soviet submarines. Rear-Admiral Sir Louis Hamilton, RN was to command the close escort and cruiser force, while command of the distant covering force was in the hands of the Commander-in-Chief Home Fleet, Admiral Sir John Tovey, RN. The political importance of PQ 17 may be judged by the unprecedented protection it was to be afforded.

The primary reason for this huge array of escorts was undoubtedly the known presence of the German capital ships in Arctic waters. The *Tirpitz*, *Lützow*, *Admiral Scheer* and *Admiral Hipper*, lurking in Trondheim less than twenty-four hours fast

192

steaming from the North Cape, mounted between them eight 15-inch, twelve 11-inch, thirty-six 8-inch and forty 4.1-inch guns. It was a frightening array of big guns, capable of wiping out PQ 17 and her combined escort force if properly used. However, Adolf Hitler, traumatized by the humiliating loss of his super-battleship *Bismarck* in May 1941, only a few weeks after she had first put to sea, was reluctant to allow these ships to be used unless the odds were heavily in their favour. When German Naval Intelligence received word of the intention to sail PQ 17, Admiral Raeder saw the opportunity to use the big ships at Trondheim to great advantage. He proposed Operation 'Rosselsprung' (Knight's Move), which would be a combined attack on the convoy by the surface ships, the U-boats and aircraft based near the North Cape. After a great deal of persuasion, Hitler finally gave permission for 'Rosselsprung' to go ahead, capital ships included.

PQ-17 sailed from Hvalfjord on the west coast of Iceland on 27 June, routed north about through the Denmark Strait, south of Jan Mayen Island, north of Bear Island, and then south-east to the White Sea and Archangel. The 2000-mile voyage, to be made at a speed of 8 knots in almost continuous daylight and passing close to the northern ice pack, the enemy apart, was fraught with many dangers. This was made evident soon after sailing when three merchantmen ran ashore in fog and two were forced to return to Iceland.

To give early warning of the approach of PQ 17, a pack of six U-boats, codenamed 'Eiseteufel' (Ice Devils), had been stationed across the northern end of the Denmark Strait, but their presence proved to be of no avail. With the advantage of poor visibility, the convoy slipped through the U-boat net unseen on the 29th. It was not until the early hours of 1 July, when PQ 17 was some 50 miles east of Jan Mayen Island, that contact was made. The ships were first sighted by *U-456*, commanded by Kapitän-leutnant Max-Martin Teichert. She was soon joined by *U-408* (Kapitänleutnant Reinhard von Hymmen) and *U-255* (Kapitän-leutnant Reinhart Reche), and the three boats settled down to shadowing the convoy, reporting its position at regular intervals.

Operation 'Rosselsprung' began in earnest on 2 July when other U-boats moved in and Heinkel 115 torpedo bombers took off from their bases in north Norway. Later that day the *Tirpitz* and the *Hipper* sailed from Trondheim, accompanied by a flotilla of six destroyers, and steamed north for Altenfjord. Admiral Otto Schniewind, Chief of Staff to Admiral Raeder and in command of the surface ships, flew his flag in the *Hipper*. Schniewind's orders were to attack and sink or disperse PQ 17's escort with the *Tirpitz* and *Hipper*, while the *Lützow* and the *Scheer*, following in their wake, descended on the undefended merchant ships and blew them out of the water. It was a bold plan, but it went wrong from the start.

The *Tirpitz* and *Hipper*, with their escorting destroyers, reached Altenfjord, 80 miles from the North Cape, next day, but disaster struck the other half of Schniewind's force. Steaming at high speed in poor visibility and using notoriously inaccurate Norwegian charts, the *Lützow* and three of the six escorting destroyers piled up on rocks and were so badly damaged they were ordered back to Trondheim. At midday on the 4th the *Scheer* and the three remaining destroyers joined the other ships in Altenfjord. Hidden behind the string of islands that fronts the deep fjord, Schniewind's somewhat depleted, but still formidable, force was now only a few hours steaming from the Russian convoy routes.

In the early hours of that morning PQ 17 passed north of Bear Island in thick fog. The closely guarded convoy had already beaten off attacks by torpedo bombers and U-boats without loss, and was hurrying eastwards, taking advantage of the poor visibility. As luck would have it, the fog suddenly lifted at around 0200 and, being then full daylight, within minutes a lone Blohm & Voss flying boat had appeared overhead. Her sighting report brought in a swarm of Heinkel 115s, Focke-Wulf 190s and Junkers 88s, all eager to attack the convoy with bombs, torpedoes and machine guns. The fierce barrage put up by the merchantmen and their close escort held the planes at bay for a while, but eventually some broke through, and four ships were hit and damaged. Two of these were later sunk by U-boats, which had again appeared on the scene, and another was sunk by the escort.

That night PQ 17 was on a south-easterly course with only 700 miles to go to Soviet waters, where it was expected the convoy would come under the protection of Russian fighter aircraft. To the men in the ships, although they had already lost five of their number since sailing, the prospects for a safe arrival in port seemed good. London, on the other hand, was taking a very much more pessimistic view. The First Sea Lord, Admiral Sir Dudley Pound, had received word from the Norwegian Resistance of the movement of the German capital ships to Altenfjord, and from this he rightly deduced that an attack on PQ 17 by surface vessels was imminent. It was Pound's opinion that Schniewind's big guns were in a position to reach the convoy before Sir John Tovey's battleships arrived on the scene. In which case, not only the convoy, but its close escort and the covering cruiser force were in danger of annihilation. This was not a risk Pound was prepared to take and that evening he gave orders for Rear-Admiral Hamilton's cruiser force to withdraw to the west and the convoy to scatter. In the confusion that followed, the destroyers of PQ 17's close escort also withdrew and the fleeing merchant ships were left to fend for themselves.

The cruel irony of this bizarre situation was that the order for the convoy to scatter need never have been given. When the *Tirpitz*, *Scheer* and *Hipper*, escorted by seven destroyers and two motor torpedo boats, sailed from Altenfjord at 1100 on the 5th Admiral Schniewind was aware that he might find himself up against a powerful Allied force, including two battleships and an aircraft carrier, and he was uneasy. His concern was increased when, on reaching the open sea, the fleet was sighted by a Russian submarine and, an hour later, by a Catalina of Coastal Command. The element of surprise had gone and at 2200 that day Schniewind signalled that his destroyers were running short of fuel and he turned the task force around and returned to Altenfjord. Later reports claimed that Admiral Raeder, fearful of losing one or more of his big ships to the Albacore torpedo bombers of HMS *Victorious* – and thus incurring the wrath of the Führer – had ordered Schniewind to return to port.

The withdrawal of the German surface fleet did nothing to save PQ 17. Without escort and scattered to the four winds, the unfortunate merchantmen were picked off one by one by the U-boats and aircraft eagerly pursuing them. Of the thirty-eight ships that originally sailed from Iceland only eleven reached

Archangel, delivering just 70,000 tons of the 200,000 tons of war supplies loaded. It was some consolation that, largely due to the calm seas prevailing, only 153 men died in the ships. On the German side only five aircraft were shot down and two U-boats damaged, the latter victims of the over-enthusiasm of their own aircraft. By far the greatest damage was suffered by the Royal Navy, which as a result of a wrong decision made ashore, lost a great deal of credibility as a fighting force. For the *Admiral Hipper* PQ 17 was just another in a continuing series of opportunities lost.

After the massacre of PQ 17 it was decided to suspend convoys to Russia during the long hours of summer daylight. A trickle of fast merchantmen sailed unescorted, but it was not until mid-September that another attempt was made to force a full convoy through. PQ 18 was well defended, but was heavily attacked by aircraft and U-boats off Bear Island, thirteen out of thirty-nine ships being lost. A week later QP 14, a convoy of empty ships homeward bound, was also heavily attacked. Four merchant ships, a minesweeper and a destroyer were lost. The convoys were again suspended.

In the meantime, despite the failure of his big ships to come to grips with PQ 17, Admiral Raeder was laying plans for another surface attack on the convoys when they resumed, presumably with the coming of winter darkness. Operation 'Regenbogen' (Rainbow) was to involve the pocket-battleship *Lützow*, the light cruiser *Köln* and, once again, the *Admiral Hipper*. These ships, anchored in Altenfjord under the command of Kontor-Admiral Oskar Kummetz, were brought to immediate readiness on 17 November when it was learned that QP 15, more empty ships returning home, had sailed from Archangel. At the last moment lack of air support, due to the almost continuous darkness, caused Raeder to cancel the operation. Once again he showed himself unwilling to risk his big ships. The U-boats, operating alone, sank only two ships of QP 15.

Encouraged by the lack of determined opposition, the Admiralty sailed Convoy JW 51A (Russian convoy numbers had been changed to confuse German Intelligence) for Archangel on 15 December. Made up of fifteen heavily loaded merchantmen and a fleet tanker, JW 51A was escorted by seven destroyers and five smaller craft, with the light cruisers HMS *Sheffield* and *Jamaica* and two more destroyers providing distant cover. Making a fast passage in fine weather, the convoy was not sighted by the enemy and arrived in the Kola Inlet on the 25th, a welcome Christmas present for all concerned.

The other half of JW 51, fourteen British and American ships carrying nearly 100,000 tons of tanks, aircraft, vehicles, fuel oil, aviation spirit and stores, had sailed from Loch Ewe, on the west coast of Scotland, on 22 December. JW 51B was escorted by six destroyers of the 7th Flotilla, *Onslow*, *Orwell*, *Oribi*, *Obedient*, *Obdurate* and *Achates*, the corvettes *Hyderabad* and *Rhododendron*, the minesweeper *Bramble* and the trawlers *Northern Gem* and *Vizalma*. Captain Robert St. Vincent Sherbrooke commanded the escort in HMS *Onslow*.

The voyage was without incident until late on the 27th when, to the south-east of Jan Mayen Island, JW 51B ran into a severe gale. Very soon, battered by heavy seas and blinded by sleet and snow, the orderly convoy degenerated into a ragged collection of ships fighting to stay afloat and on course. Some of the merchant ships, their deck cargoes of aircraft breaking adrift, were forced to heave to. During the night HMS *Oribi*, the US merchantman *Chester Valley*, the *Bramble* and the *Vizalma* lost contact with the convoy and failed to rejoin.

The gale slowly subsided and by noon on the 30th the convoy was 50 miles south of Bear Island and, to the best of Sherbrooke's knowledge, still undetected by the enemy. This agreeable situation was soon to change. The improvement in the weather brought with it clear skies and excellent visibility, a blessing to Karl-Heinz Herbschleb in *U-354*, who had been patiently patrolling back and forth across the convoy route for some days. Herbschleb attacked, but was driven off by Sherbrooke's destroyers. He retired to a safe distance and called for help.

U-354's sighting report was received by Narvik and was passed to Altenfjord. That night, with Kontor-Admiral Kummetz flying his flag in the heavy cruiser, the *Lützow* and *Hipper*, screened by the destroyers *Richard Beitzen*, *Friedrich Eckholdt*, *Theodor Riedel*, *Z-29*, *Z-30* and *Z-31*, put to sea and raced northwards to intercept JW 51B. The destroyers alone, each of around 2,500 tons and mounting five 5.9-inch guns, were a powerful strike force, more than a match for Sherbrooke's 1500-tonners and their antiquated 4-inch and 4.7s.

New Year's Eve, 31 December 1942, came in crisp and clear and full of hope. With a light NW'ly wind and smooth sea, JW 51B was making 9 knots on an easterly course. Sherbrooke's remaining small ships, the corvettes *Hyderabad* and *Rhododendron* and the trawler *Northern Gem*, were scouting ahead of the convoy, *Achates* was bringing up the rear, while the other destroyers guarded the flanks. Being then only 300 miles to the west of Murmansk, Sherbrooke was expecting his depleted escort force to be reinforced by Russian warships at some time during the day. All the indications were that JW 51B would repeat the success of its other half.

Unknown to Sherbrooke, *U-354* was still with him, and she had been joined by *U-626*. The shadowing submarines were reporting the convoy's position every two hours to Kummetz, who was coming from the south at all speed. The Admiral planned to approach the convoy from astern, split his force and attack from both flanks. The *Hipper*, *Friedrich Eckholdt*, *Richard Beitzen* and *Z-29* were to come in first from the port side, while the *Lützow*, *Theodor Riedel*, *Z-30* and *Z-31* attacked from starboard. The assumption was that the British escorts would be drawn off by the *Hipper* and her destroyers, leaving the field open for the *Lützow* to destroy the undefended convoy with her big guns.

At around 0830, with a visibility of 10 miles, marred only occasionally by passing snow squalls, *Hyderabad* sighted two unidentified destroyers to the south. The corvette assumed these to be the vanguard of the expected Russian reinforcements and did not report the sighting to Sherbrooke. A few minutes later, *Obdurate*, stationed to starboard of the convoy, signalled *Onslow* by lamp that she had two strange destroyers in sight to the south-west. Sherbrooke ordered her to investigate. She reversed course, ran back and found three destroyers crossing astern of the convoy. A challenge by lamp was answered by the strangers with a barrage of shells.

Seeing the gun flashes, Sherbrooke ordered *Achates*, *Hyderabad*, *Rhododendron* and *Northern Gem* to cover the convoy and then called for *Orwell* and *Obedient* to join him. As the three destroyers, steaming in line abreast at 20 knots, moved to meet the enemy, so the *Hipper* suddenly appeared out of a snow squall 8 miles to the north-west. Sherbrooke recognized the German heavy cruiser at once and radioed a sighting report to the Admiralty. He then raced ahead, opening fire on the *Hipper* at 9000 yards. *Obedient* joined him, while *Obdurate*, on Sherbrooke's orders, made smoke to cover the convoy.

Three times the *Hipper* tried to get at the convoy, but each time *Onslow* and *Obedient*, heeling under full helm as they weaved in and out of the shells falling all around them, drove her off, answering the cruiser's 8-inch guns with their 4.7s. The destroyers' smaller guns had little effect on the *Hipper*, but so ferocious was their assault that Kummetz feared this was the prelude to a torpedo attack, the one thing he could not afford to risk.

But the might of the *Hipper*'s big guns prevailed. *Achates*, having joined the fray, was caught by a full salvo of 8-inch shells and suffered severe damage. She dropped out of the fight, her speed down to 15 knots. Sherbrooke's *Onslow* was next to be hit, an 8-inch shell bursting against the top of her funnel and raking her bridge with a hail of jagged steel splinters. Captain Sherbrooke was blinded in one eye, but stayed at his post. Another salvo landed, smashing two of the destroyer's 4.7s and killing both guns' crews. The forward Fire and Repair party was wiped out, all communications were cut, fire raged and scalding hot steam spewed out of severed pipes. The *Onslow* was grievously hurt, but she was not yet out of the fight. Her remaining guns continued to fire.

Then, despite the odds heavily in his favour, Kummetz decided he had had enough. He ordered the *Hipper* up to full speed and, with the three destroyers in company, made off to the north-east, leaving the convoy to the *Lützow*, then closing on JW 51B from the south. At 1036 Kummetz chanced upon and took his revenge on the *Bramble*, which was still searching for the convoy. The little minesweeper fought back gallantly with her single 4-inch, but was soon crippled by the *Hipper*'s secondary armament. The *Friedrich Eckholdt* finished her off. There were no survivors.

Aboard *Onslow* the wounded Sherbrooke had at last been persuaded to go below and the next senior officer, Lieutenant-Commander David Kinloch, in the *Obedient*, took command of the escort. Kinloch was not aware of the approach of the *Lützow* and left only *Rhododendron* to the south, keeping his destroyers between the *Hipper* and the convoy ready to fend off another attack. In consequence, when the *Lützow* came up on the convoy, only the corvette, armed with one 4-inch and a 2-pounder, stood between the merchant ships and the 11-inch gun pocket battleship and her supporting destroyers. Then, just when the *Rhododendron*'s crew were preparing to sell their lives dearly, the *Lützow*, with the destroyers following in line astern, crossed ahead of the convoy without opening fire, hauled around to the west and disappeared in the gloom. In the light of the fact that the convoy was at the mercy of the *Lützow*'s guns, this was an extraordinary failure to take advantage of the situation. The pocket-battleship's commander, Kapitän Stänge, blamed the onset of total darkness and lack of visibility due to smoke and snow squalls for his decision not to attack.

Kummetz, unaware that Stänge had deserted him, now brought the *Hipper* and her destroyers back for a second attack, breaking through the snow squalls to the north at 1100. Kinloch immediately turned *Obedient* to meet the challenge and, followed by *Achates*, *Orwell* and *Obdurate*, all making smoke to cover the convoy, charged at the enemy. The four British destroyers, their bow waves creaming and guns spitting defiance, made a brave sight, but in no way were they a match for the *Hipper* and her oversize destroyers.

HMS *Achates* was first to be hit. Having successfully dodged several of the *Hipper*'s salvoes, the destroyer's commander, Commander A.H.T Johns, miscalculated and ran straight into a broadside of 8-inch shells. One shell scored a direct hit on *Achates'* bridge, killing Commander Johns and all his staff, severing all communications and smashing the main steering transmission. With the ship steaming in circles at 28 knots, it fell to *Achates'* first lieutenant, 24-year-old Lieutenant Loftus Peyton-Jones, to take command. Peyton-Jones ordered the engine-room to make smoke and, with the emergency steering gear connected, attempted to escape to the south-east. It was a vain effort, for by this time the *Hipper*'s gunners had got the range and soon reduced the fleeing destroyer to a burning hulk. The *Achates* capsized and sank, leaving only eighty-one survivors to be picked up by the *Northern Gem*.

Only three British destroyers, *Obedient, Orwell* and *Obdurate*, now stood between Kummetz and the merchantmen of JW 51B. The destroyers bravely exchanged shell for shell with the German ships, but it could only be a matter of time before the overwhelming superiority of the enemy's guns prevailed. Then, like the vengeance of the gods, a double salvo of twenty-four 6-inch shells fell from the skies and exploded all around the *Hipper*.

When Captain Sherbrooke sent his first enemy sighting the light cruisers *Sheffield* and *Jamaica*, with two destroyers, were only 30 miles to the north of the convoy and returning to the west, after delivering JW 51A to Archangel. Due to overcast weather, the British cruisers had been without sights since leaving the Kola Inlet and, when Sherbrooke's message came through, were unsure of their exact position. It took them some time to locate JW 51B, but, when they did arrive on the scene, their intervention was swift and effective. Kummetz was caught completely by surprise, all his attention being focused on wiping out the convoy's destroyer escort. The *Hipper* was hit repeatedly by salvoes fired by the British cruisers. Her starboard boiler-room was wrecked and, as she hauled round to the west with her destroyers frantically making smoke to cover her escape, she was on fire in several places. Her situation took another turn for the worse when the *Friedrich Eckholdt* was blown apart by the concentrated fire of *Sheffield* and *Jamaica*. Kummetz, believing the whole of the British Home Fleet must be attacking, ordered all his ships to break off the engagement and make a run for Altenfjord at all possible speed. *Sheffield* and *Jamaica* followed in pursuit, but the faster German ships soon left them astern.

Having survived an attack by a vastly superior foe, JW 51B reached port without loss, delivering to the Russians another 100,000 tons of desperately needed war materials. The cost to the Royal Navy of its brilliant defence of the convoy was heavy, the *Achates* and *Bramble* being lost with a total of 193 men. But Captain Robert Sherbrooke's gallant action – for which he was awarded the Victoria Cross – went far beyond saving JW 51B. The *Hipper*'s mauling at the hands of the British light cruisers was such that she was never fully operational again. Furthermore, when Hitler heard of the humiliating defeat suffered by Konter-Admiral Kummetz's powerful force, he ordered all German capital ships to be withdrawn and scrapped.

The *Hipper* completed temporary repairs in Norway at the end of January 1943 and sailed for Wilhelmshaven, where she was paid off on 28 February. As a result of Hitler's edict to scrap the big ships, permanent repairs were cancelled and the cruiser was towed to Pilau in East Prussia and there laid up. A change of policy in late 1943 resulted in limited repairs being put in hand and the *Hipper* was recommissioned at the end of April 1944, but not for active service. By this time the fortunes of the Third Reich were on the wane. Operation 'Overlord', in which Britain and America would land two million men in Normandy, was only six weeks away, while in the East Russian divisions were advancing on the borders of Poland. The *Hipper* was relegated to the Training Squadron.

In January 1945 the *Hipper* was at Gotenhaven, anchored behind the Hela Peninsula, near the spot where the *Pinguin* had embarked on her memorable career in June 1940. But this was the beginning of the end for the *Hipper*; the Russians were at the gates of Warsaw, and British and American tanks were racing through Holland and Belgium to the German border. Warsaw fell on the 17th and the Russians, outnumbering the tired German armies by three to one, swept through East Prussia and were outside Königsberg by the end of the month. Gotenhaven lay only 60 miles away on the other shore of the Gulf of Danzig. It was time for the *Hipper* to run again, and this she did with her decks crowded with 1,500 German refugees fleeing before the advancing Russian hordes bent on vengeance. She returned to Kiel, and there, painted in black and brick-red to resemble a dockside building, she awaited her fate. Her camouflage did not save her; in the mass air attacks on Kiel by the RAF in the closing days of the war she was hit repeatedly, and finally damaged beyond repair in Bomber Command's last raid over Germany on 3 May 1945. As a result, she suffered the final ignominy of being towed out to sea and scuttled in the Heinhendorfer Bucht.

It was a sad but perhaps fitting end for a ship that aspired to such greatness, but succeeded only in bringing disrepute on the German Navy. For all her sophistication, her speed, her big guns, the *Admiral Hipper*, in an active career spanning over three years, sank only 69,000 tons of Allied shipping, less than some of

202

Dönitz's U-boats sank in one good patrol. It cannot be said, however, that all the blame for such a lamentable performance rested with the ship or her crew. Throughout her undistinguished life, the *Hipper* was blighted by Adolf Hitler's reluctance to risk his capital ships in battle with anything but a markedly inferior opponent.

Postcript

The ex-Norwegian tanker *Storstad* – briefly the auxiliary minelayer *Passat* – parted company with her mother ship *Pinguin* in the South Indian Ocean on 10 December 1940. She then set course to the west and north, embarking on a voyage few on board would ever forget.

Manned by her original Norwegian crew, persuaded to stay by threats of reprisals against their families at home, the *Storstad* was under the command of Leutnant Helmut Hanefeld. Backed by a German prize crew of only twenty men, Hanefeld was expected to control 524 prisoners of war, some 300 of which were British, belligerent and notoriously enterprising. Segregation was Hanefeld's first line of defence. He confined the captured ships' captains to cabins below the bridge, where they could be closely watched, the eight women from the Port Line ships were in the tanker's hospital, while the 200 Lascar seamen, who presented a low security risk, were housed aft in the mine compartment. As for the others, the potentially dangerous group, they were accommodated forward and completely cut off from the rest of the ship. Captain Brian St. John Smith, then an 18-year-old apprentice plucked from the *Port Wellington*, was among them:

'We were all up forward, about seventy or eighty officers in the fo'c'sle and the sailors and firemen down in the forward hold. The bridge front was sheer from the deck right up to the bridge. There was a Spandau machine-gun mounted on each corner of the bridge. If we had tried anything I don't think many of us would have got to the bridge. The ladders from the deck had been removed and the opening blanked off with tight-fitting hatchboards. There was no chance of getting through.

'We were never allowed aft. Several ideas were floated. There were two mad Australians up forward, and they were all for storming the bridge. There would have been terrible carnage. The only time we might have done it was on Christmas Eve 1940. We hit really bad weather about 500 miles south of the Cape of Good Hope. She shipped two really big seas on deck which stove in the hatchboards at the fore end of the bridge. But as the ladders had been removed it would have been impossible to reach the next deck. The foredeck was not a nice place to be on that night. Anyone trying to rush the bridge, if not mown down by the machine-guns, would probably have been washed overboard.'

As an additional precaution, Hanefeld had rigged all prison spaces forward with explosive charges capable of being detonated from the bridge, while his 20-man prize crew was armed at all times with rifles and grenades. And yet, the British, led by the intrepid Captain Thornton of the *British Commander* and Captain Dudley Crowther, passenger in the *Nowshera*, were constantly plotting to take over the ship. It was just as well for all concerned that Hanefeld always seemed to get wind of a plot in time to forestall it.

The 8999-ton *Storstad* was built to be manned by a crew of forty and, with a total complement of nearly 600 on board, her resources were stretched beyond all reasonable limits. As might be expected, it was the prisoners who suffered most. They were always hungry and thirsty – water was rationed to one cup per man per day in the final weeks of the voyage – their quarters were cramped and sanitary arrangements minimal. One single toilet served the 300 men in the forward hold, whose only beds were teased out strands of old mooring rope laid on the bare steel deck. Weather permitting, they were brought up on deck under guard, twelve at a time, for ten minutes each day for fresh air, and, if they so desired, to wash under a salt-water hose. The rest of the time they were battened down in the hold in the musty darkness, to sleep, to talk, to wait on the next inadequate meal to be lowered to them. It was a thoroughly miserable existence, made all the more intolerable by the knowledge that they were sailing into captivity.

On 6 January 1941 the *Storstad* reached the waiting area 'Andalusien', which lay in mid-Atlantic halfway between St Helena and Tristan da Cunha. There she found the *Admiral Scheer*, the commerce raider *Thor*, the supply tanker *Nordmark* and the *Scheer*'s prize, the British refrigerated ship *Duquesa*. Hanefeld transferred the 6,500 tons of diesel remaining in the *Storstad*'s cargo tanks to the *Nordmark* and in return received several hundred cases of eggs and corned beef from the *Duquesa*'s cargo. Thereafter, the prisoners' diet was supplemented by five eggs a day and the occasional slice of Libby's corned beef. For men who were by now severely malnourished, this was undreamed-of luxury.

Having spent two days at 'Andalusien', the *Storstad* set out on her long voyage north to the Bay of Biscay. Steering a lonely course in mid-Atlantic, she escaped detection, crossing the Equator on 16 January. As she moved north, the warm, sultry weather slowly gave way to rough seas and falling temperatures, bringing further discomfort to the prisoners in their dark, squalid quarters. These men remained supremely optimistic that the Royal Navy would rescue them, but throughout the whole of her 5000-mile voyage north the *Storstad* was sighted only once by the enemy, and then not until she had entered the Bay of Biscay. A patrolling Sunderland of RAF Coastal Command flew low over her, challenged by lamp, and then circled menacingly. Hanefeld adopted a simple subterfuge, spreading a large Turkish flag out on deck and deliberately garbling the reply to the lamp challenge. Accepting that she had stumbled on a particularly stupid foreign tramp, the Sunderland eventually gave up in disgust and flew away.

The *Storstad* entered the Gironde estuary on the morning of 4 February, thus ending – for the prisoners at least – a harrowing voyage that had lasted fifty-eight long days. And for these men and women the ordeal was only just beginning. Captain Thornton:

'At Bordeaux we were placed in a transitory prison camp, where the general conditions were bad and the food vile; the women were also brought to this camp, and although they were provided with a separate hut, no proper sanitary arrangements were provided for

206

them. After remaining for about eight days in this camp, the women were transferred to another camp nearby, subsequently travelling to Germany with us after three weeks. We were subsequently transferred to a large military prison called Stalag XB, about 32 miles from Bremen. A portion of this camp was reserved by the German Navy for their own prisoners. We eventually lost contact with the women, but they were allowed to write to us, and it appears they had experienced a terrible journey from Bremen to Lake Constance, taking a month to reach their new camp. I was very sorry to hear that the youngest member of their party subsequently died from an internal haemorrhage. She was not a strong woman, and I should imagine this terrible experience hastened her death.'

At Stalag XB, situated near the village of Sandbostel on the windswept North German moors, the *Pinguin*'s prisoners again found themselves on a starvation diet and were forced to work long hours in the fields. But, by and large, their treatment by their captors was generally good. The same could not be said for those they had left at home. John Stevenson, son of Second Engineer Stevenson of the *Port Brisbane*, has unhappy memories of those days:

'The ship was sunk on 21st November 1940; mother received a telegram to that effect from the War Office in late November, followed by a letter of confirmation from Port Line with the same news, but also advising that my father's wages would cease to be paid from the day of the sinking of the vessel.

'Nothing further was heard, other than one lifeboat containing some twenty-five members of the crew under the command of Mr Dingle had been found by an R.A.N. warship, but my father was not among those rescued.

'In May 1941 father was "presumed dead lost at sea", and my mother was awarded a widow's pension of around £3 per week, with 7s 10d for myself and 3s 10d per week for my brother. Up to then we had been relying on savings and support from my father's family, who were Newhaven fisherfolk and a very close community.

'In August of the same year a postcard was received from my father, via the Swiss Red Cross, to the effect that he had been landed at Bordeaux, and was now a prisoner of war of the Third Reich.

'I was nine, and vividly remember my mother being almost inconsolable a few weeks later, when she received an OHMS letter to the effect that as she was no longer a widow, would she please refund the fourteen weeks' pension paid to her. Failure to do so carried a penalty of a fine or possible imprisonment.

'My father returned from Germany, complete with demob suit, on 24 May 1945, and signed on on 16 July in Glasgow as chief engineer of the *Port Chambly* for a voyage to India. A total leave of forty-seven days after five years!

'Incidentally, he was eventually paid 50 percent of the salary he would have earned in the five years he was a POW. The covering letter, if it could be called that, stated, "this is a goodwill payment" on behalf of the shipowners and not the Government, who were completely disinterested. My parents had taken their case to the local Labour MP, but eventually gave up and accepted the 50 percent offered.'

Such was the lot of the British merchant seaman in the Second World War. But perhaps the cruelest blow of all was dealt to Robert Deus, a survivor of the *Domingo de Larrinaga*. On the night of 4 May 1941, his first wedding anniversary, Deus lay awake in Stalag XB reflecting on the chance meeting in the South Atlantic that had snatched him from the woman he had married and his unborn child. Mercifully, he was not aware that, as he lay in his comfortless bunk, his home town of Liverpool was suffering one of its heaviest air raids of the war. On that night Liverpool was laid waste; 10,000 houses were destroyed and 3,812 people killed, among them Robert Deus' bride of twelve months. His girl child lived, but he would not see her for another four years.

Bibliography

Behrens, C.B.A., *Merchant Shipping and the Demands of War*, HMSO 1955

Bekker, Cajus, *The German Navy 1938–1945*, Hamlyn 1974

Blair, Clay, *Hitler's U-boat War: The Hunters 1939–1942*, Weidenfeld & Nicolson 1997

Blake, George, *The Ben Line: The Story of a Merchant Fleet at War*, Thomas Nelson 1946

Brennecke, H.J., *Ghost Cruiser HK 33*, William Kimber 1954

Brice, Martin, *Axis Blockade Runners of World War II*

Churchill W.S., *The Second World War Vols I–VI*, Cassell 1950

Dreyer, Grondahl, *Handelsflåten I Krig 1939–1945*

Falls, Cyril, *The Second World War*, Methuen 1948

Graves, Philip, *The Sixth Quarter*, Hutchinson

Gray, Edwyn, *Hitler's Battleships*, Leo Cooper 1992

Haldane, R.A., *The Hidden War*, Robert Hale 1978

Hampshire, A. Cecil, *The Blockaders*

Hinsley, F.H., *British Intelligence in the Second World War*, HMSO 1979

Hinsley, F.H. and Stripp, Alan, *Code Breakers*, Oxford University Press 1993

HMSO, *British Vessels Lost at Sea 1939–45*, Patrick Stephens 1984

Hocking, Charles, *Dictionary of Disasters at Sea During the Age of Steam 1824–1962*, Lloyd's Register of Shipping

Hough, Richard, *The Longest Battle: The War at Sea 1939–45*, Weidenfeld & Nicolson 1986

Kaplan, Philip and Currie, Jack, *Convoy: Merchant Sailors at War 1939–1945*, Aurum Press 1998

Keegan, John, *The Second World War*, Century Hutchinson 1989

Langmaid, Captain K., *The Sea Raiders*, Jarrolds 1963

Lloyd's, *Lloyd's War Losses: The Second World War Vol I*, Lloyd's of London Press 1989

Lund, Paul and Ludlam, Harry, *Atlantic Jeopardy*, Foulsham 1990

Martiensen, Anthony, *Hitler and His Admirals*, Secker & Warburg 1948

Masters, David, *Epics of Salvage*, Cassell 1953

Masters, David, *In Peril on the Sea*, The Cresset Press 1960

McCart, Neil, *Atlantic Liners of the Cunard Line*, Patrick Stephens 1990

Middlebrook, Martin, *Convoy*, William Morrow 1976

Middlemiss, Norman L., *The British Tankers*, Shield Publications 1995

M.O.D (Navy), *German Naval History: The U-boat War in the Atlantic 1939–1945*, HMSO 1989

Montgomery, Michael, *Who Sank the Sydney?*, Leo Cooper 1983

Morrison, John & Annie, *Lewis & Harris Seamen 1939–1945*

Muggenthaler, August Karl, *German Raiders of World War II*, Robert Hale 1978

Peillard, Léonce, *Sink the Tripitz*, Jonathan Cape 1968

Poolman, Kenneth, *Armed Merchant Cruisers: Their Epic Story*, Leo Cooper 1985

Poolman, Kenneth, *Periscope Depth*, William Kimber 1981

Robertson, R.B., *Of Whales and Men*, Macmillan 1958

Rohwer, Jürgen, *Axis Submarine Successes 1939–1945*, Patrick Stephens 1983

Roskill, S.W., *The War at Sea Vol I*, HMSO 1954

Saunders, H. St George, *Valiant Voyaging*, Faber & Faber

Schmalenbach, Paul, *German Raiders: A History of Auxiliary Cruisers of the German Navy 1895–1945*, Paul Schmalenbach

Slader, John, *The Fourth Service: Merchantmen at War 1939–1945*, Robert Hale 1994

Smith, Gordon, *The War at Sea: Royal and Dominion Navy Actions in World War II*, Ian Allan 1989

Tarrant, V.E., *The Last Year of the Kriegsmarine May 1944–May 1945*, Arms & Armour 1994
Terraine, John, *Business in Great Waters: The U-boat Wars 1916–1945*, Leo Cooper 1989
Thomas, David A., *The Atlantic Star 1939–45*, W.H. Allen 1990
Whitley, M.J., *Cruisers of World War II*, Arms & Armour 1995
Woodward, David, *The Secret Raiders*, William Kimber 1955
Young, George, *Farewell to the Tramps*, Midgley 1982
Young, John M., *Britain's Sea War: A Diary of Ship Losses 1939–1945*, Patrick Stephens 1989

OTHER SOURCES

B.P. Shipping
Ben Line Group
Bundesarchiv Militärarchiv, Freiburg
Flower Class Corvette Association
Imperial War Museum
Merseyside Maritime Museum
Nautical Magazine
Navy News
P & O Steam Navigation Company
Public Record Office
Sea Breezes
Shipping Today and Yesterday
Ships Monthly
The Times
The Wirral Globe

Index

212

213

214

215